Praise for *There Was a Time for Everything*

T0339138

"Judith Friedland's intelligent and generous memoir, which speaks back to both patriarchy and medical hegemony in health care, invites the reader to contemplate the immense changes in the conditions of possibility for Canadian women (especially from the upper-middle class) over the past eighty years. It also allows a broader audience a taste of the wisdom and kindness that has made Professor Friedland such a beloved mentor to so many in health care."

Dr Ayelet Kuper, *Wilson Centre and Department of Medicine, University of Toronto*

"Judith Friedland's wonderfully emotive memoir illustrates the old saying 'keep calm and carry on.' A very worthwhile read for occupational therapists and anyone interested in little-known stories of feminism-in-action."

Elizabeth (Liz) Townsend, *Professor Emerita, Dalhousie University*

"I was absorbed in this book from cover to cover. I smiled, laughed, nodded my head in strong agreement, and shed a few tears. It is beautiful, moving, and authentic. I'm not an old woman but also not a young woman and I strongly connected with the content."

Mary Forhan, *Associate Professor and Chair of the Department of Occupational Science and Occupational Therapy, Temerty Faculty of Medicine, University of Toronto*

There Was a Time for Everything

Everything

A Memoir

JUDITH FRIEDLAND

UNIVERSITY OF TORONTO PRESS
Toronto Buffalo London

ISBN 978-1-4875-4695-3 (paper)
ISBN 978-1-4875-4696-0 (EPUB)
ISBN 978-1-4875-4697-7 (PDF)

Library and Archives Canada Cataloguing in Publication

Title: There was a time for everything : a memoir / Judith Friedland.
Names: Friedland, Judith, 1939– author.
Description: Includes index.
Identifiers: Canadiana (print) 20220407711 | Canadiana (ebook)
20220407819 | ISBN 9781487546953 (cloth) | ISBN 9781487546960 (EPUB) |
ISBN 9781487546977 (PDF)
Subjects: LCSH: Friedland, Judith, 1939– | LCSH: Women college
teachers – Ontario – Toronto – Biography. | LCSH: Jewish women –
Ontario – Toronto – Biography. | LCGFT: Autobiographies.
Classification: LCC LB2332.34.C3 F75 2023 | DDC 378.1/2092 – dc23

We wish to acknowledge the land on which the University of Toronto
Press operates. This land is the traditional territory of the Wendat, the
Anishnaabeg, the Haudenosaunee, the Métis, and the Mississaugas of the
Credit First Nation.

University of Toronto Press acknowledges the financial support of
the Government of Canada, the Canada Council for the Arts, and the
Ontario Arts Council, an agency of the Government of Ontario, for its
publishing activities.

 Canada Council
for the Arts
Conseil des Arts
du Canada

 ONTARIO ARTS COUNCIL
CONSEIL DES ARTS DE L'ONTARIO
an Ontario government agency
un organisme du gouvernement de l'Ontario

Funded by the
Government
of Canada
Financé par le
gouvernement
du Canada

Contents

Acknowledgments   vii

Prelude   ix

Growing Up

1   Tillie: A Mother's Life and Early Death   5
2   Mike: A Father's Enduring Presence   13
3   The Jolofsky Family: Keeping the Sabbath and More   23
4   Childhood and Adolescence: My Mid-Century Toronto   33
5   Daughter, Stepdaughter, Sister: Relationships Reconfigured   48

Growing Together

6   Student/Wife/Worker: My Roles Begin to Multiply   61
7   New Roles: Motherhood and Living My Husband's Life   76
8   Multitasker: Full-Time Mother, Part-Time Worker,
      Grad Student, and Dean's Wife   92
9   Variations on a Theme: Different Environments,
      Same Situations   104

Still Growing

10   Academia: Tiptoeing into a New Life   119
11   Difficult Times: Family Troubles and Work Troubles   130
12   Big Fish, Little Pond: Director, Division of
      Occupational Therapy   142

Contents

13 Little Fish, Big Pond: Chair, Department of Occupational
      Therapy   157
14 Post-Chair and Retirement: Not Ready to Stop   169
15 From Some Darkness into Light: When the Margins
      Aren't Clear   185
16 Last Chapter   196

Notes   209

Index   229

Acknowledgments

I had a lot of help, inadvertently, when it came to remembering my past. I had things that had been my mother's, a scrapbook from my teenage years, and letters we had written home when my husband and I were travelling or living abroad that my mother-in-law had kept. My brother, Barry, had transcribed an interview he did with our father, and my cousin Carol had compiled a booklet of reminiscences of our grandparents. And there was a treasure trove of photos I could call on that awakened my memories. As for "seeing" my place in the past, the now-vast literature on feminism helped as I reflected on my upbringing, education, early marriage, and working life. Feminism infused much of what I wrote in the memoir almost without my awareness – at least in the beginning. Less tangible but also important to me were casual comments from women, old and young, who, upon learning about my book, said they could identify with it. That was validating. My thanks, then, to everyone who unknowingly helped me remember.

Many people knowingly helped with this book. Two graduate students and one undergraduate student worked as my research assistants – dredging up materials on specific issues, checking references and endnotes, and importantly, showing me where they thought more context was needed so that younger readers – like themselves – would understand what I was trying to convey. A special thanks to Lauren Stacey, who was with me at the start and periodically throughout the entire project. She was extremely helpful, sharing her knowledge of feminism and using her already strong research skills to search the literature. And thanks also to Allison Bonnell, who was there in the middle, and Gobika Sithamparanathan, who helped at the end, each contributing to the whole.

I had readers who read everything, at one stage or another, cover to cover, including Mark Abley, Jane Errington, Nancy Friedland, Sharon

Friefeld, Christina Gallucci, Bonnie Kirsh, Barry Pless, and Carol Sures. There were also specialist readers who checked content in particular chapters, including Professor Udi Avitzur, Naomi Davids-Brumer, Charles Erlichman, Stephen Erlichman, Jenny Friedland, Tom Fried- land, Rabbi Frydman-Kohl, Harry Glicksman, Rayna Jolley, Linda Off- man, Mari Silverman, Joyce Spiegel, and Holly Stitt. And then there were friends and family members who provided support – sometimes by just not asking too many questions about my progress, like Gil- lian Diamond, Elizabeth Peter, and Liz Smythe, while others, like Lisa Herschorn, Kyo Maclear, and Miriam Shuchman, provided important information at just the right time.

My husband, Marty, was a cover-to-cover reader, a content special- ist, and an overall in-house supporter. He read umpteen drafts and revisions of the manuscript and was patient and helpful throughout. His own experiences with publishing helped immensely – even when I argued that his experiences publishing, or in his work-life generally, were not mine. Fortunately, he concurred with everything I wrote about our courtship and now long married life.

It has been a joy to work with UTP. My thanks to Barbara Tessman, who copy-edited the manuscript with great care. I am grateful to Chris- tine Robertson, associate managing editor, for answering my questions without delay and for reassuring me, from time to time, that all was well. Thanks also to Stephanie Mazza, product marketing specialist, for presenting the book to the public with such skill. Finally, my most sincere thanks to Len Husband, my editor. At a time when there was so much uncertainty about everything during the COVID-19 pandemic and when memoirs seemed to be popping up everywhere, he saw my story as a worthy addition and a good fit for UTP. That was a most wel- come vote of confidence. I am so grateful that he took on the project and so skillfully saw it through.

Prelude

I tell my story through the lens of an older woman who is a mother of three, a grandmother of eight, an occupational therapist by training, an academic, the wife of a prominent academic, and Jewish. What complicated my life growing up in Toronto in the 1940s and '50s is the fact that my mother died just after I turned ten.

My story begins where my mother's story ends. I write about her and the bits I know about my life before she died. I write about her death, how we managed, and how she remains a presence in our lives. And I write about the rest of my life.

In the years that followed my mother's death, my father took on the task of parenting my brother and me. My mother's large family stayed close, as did my parents' friends. Jewish family life made for another layer of protection from my disrupted sense of belonging. I learned to pick up and move on, not in an unfeeling way, but simply as a way of coping. Over time, I must have learned that there was a way to persevere, to fashion darkness and create light.[1]

When I was a child and an adolescent, my school life and my social life were happy; I felt loved and cared for at home, and I developed a good sense of self. Toward the end of my teenage years, I, like most young women in my time and place, had put getting married at the top of my to-do list. I not only managed to achieve that goal, but I did so early and well. I was engaged by the time I entered the University of Toronto and married a year later, in 1958, at the tender age of nineteen. I continued with my course in physical and occupational therapy and my husband finished his program in law. After graduating in 1960, we moved to Cambridge, England, for a year for my husband to do graduate work. I worked as an occupational therapist in a psychiatric hospital in Cambridge, and then in Toronto, before starting a family.

I thoroughly enjoyed being a mother, raising three children, and creating a home. I found it meaningful and fulfilling. I knew about the feminist movement at the time but did not identify with it. I felt my mothering role was important, and my husband reinforced that feeling. I doubt that I noticed that my husband's career determined the direction of my life: the sabbaticals "we" took, the house moves we made, the social life we led. I knew that in every marriage, two individuals blend their lives in some measure. The times being what they were when I married, it was natural that I blended my life into my husband's. Besides, it was a good life – rich, loving, and adventurous in its way.

None of the women I knew in my upper-middle-class world in the '60s and early '70s followed their own path. We went to university and typically had a profession – usually teaching. If we had ambitions beyond marriage and family, we must have hidden them, as they were never discussed. Having coveted the role of wife and mother, I never thought about my future and if I might take on a role some day that was just for me. I never even thought about going back to work.

But like the seventeenth-century women in Natalie Zemon Davis's *Women on the Margins*, while I may have been living on the margins, I was learning a lot from my experiences as a wife and mother.[2] The man that I married became prominent in the field of law and in academia, and that meant additional social roles for me as "wife of." The volunteer work I did with our local Home and School Association made me hone my organizational skills and build my confidence. My husband took over my homemaking and mothering roles for a few hours each week so that I could continue my formal education, one course a year, until there was a BA to add to my diploma in physical and occupational therapy.

Once my children are in school all day, and after thirteen years at home, my actions suggest I'm striving for something more. I add the roles of part-time graduate student, part-time (paid) worker, and eventually full-time worker. And then, everything begins to shift. I start to become another me – or maybe just a grown-up version of an earlier me. I become an occupational therapist again, I complete an MA, and I have a separate identity. The balance within my marriage also shifts a little. Perhaps not so coincidentally, it is now the mid-1970s and feminism is evolving too.

Then, out of the blue, I am invited to teach at the University of Toronto. In 1982, some twenty-two years after my first graduation (there were to be three more), I become a member of its faculty.

While it was exciting to have a job at the university, I quickly became aware of my second-class status. True, I was a member of the prestigious

Faculty of Medicine, but I was there as a member of a health profession that was not composed of physicians. Pay equity – or should I say the lack thereof – was a good example of how women like myself were valued within the university at that time. Our ability to be heard was a great concern then even as it (astoundingly) is now, albeit to a lesser extent. Nonetheless, I had embarked on a career. I was forty-three years old and on a trajectory that was my own. It was not always smooth sailing. The skills associated with perseverance, learned early on in life, were called on more than once. I received tenure, led my department, and became a full professor.

As my worker role grew and I took on new responsibilities, my life became more complex. With my family always coming first, and academia being so demanding, there were times when it was hard to juggle. There was stress, for sure, but, overall, the timing for me was right. My children were older, and my husband was supportive. There was little role conflict for me. I enjoyed the challenge of my expanded roles. I seemed to flourish.

I understand that what worked for me might not be desirable or, indeed, possible for others. I know that, to a large extent, my social position and the culture that surrounded me as a child and later as an adult, gave me the chance to shape my life in this way. I don't offer any solutions to women who willingly take on so many roles, other than perhaps to not see it as a problem but rather as just another way to live. Giving up roles, or forgoing certain roles, can also be problematic. I did not want to give up any of my mothering roles. Indeed, among the many studies that speak of the challenges of juggling roles, some suggest "multiple roles in general are beneficial."[3] One needs a certain degree of stamina and, I believe, a clear sense of what matters most. Maybe going from the job of wife and mother to that of a career woman is just another path to self-actualization. Maybe a linear path isn't always the best.

My story is not in the tradition of the great man – or woman. I have not made an important discovery, led a major company, or become famous for some reason. My story is a way of illustrating women's lives, of exploring how our varying perspectives and ways of living contribute to the larger picture of who we are.

I expect my story to resonate with older women, but also with some younger women who see themselves in my story, despite the times seeming to be so different. Academics may be interested in my atypical journey, as will those interested in the socio-cultural lives of girls and women growing up in Toronto in the 1940s and '50s, and the influences of family and religion. I hope men will also take an interest in my story, as it raises the issue, however obliquely, of dealing with gender equity within relationships as well as in the workplace.

I hope that, in the end, I will have made a case for how people in general, but women in particular, *can* have it all. Just maybe not all at the highest level, and definitely not all at once.

THERE WAS A TIME FOR EVERYTHING

Growing Up

1 Tillie: A Mother's Life and Early Death

I have few memories of the time before my mother's death. Old black-and-white photographs trick me into thinking that she looks familiar, but I cannot conjure up a real person – someone whose hand I held, whose scent I knew, whose voice I recognized. Tillie died just after I turned ten. She was diagnosed with leukemia at age thirty-five. My parents sent my brother and me off to an aunt's house nearby while they absorbed the news received in a doctor's office earlier that day. We were told nothing. My mother died three years later, in 1949.

I have bits of memories of the treatments my mother received. I remember accompanying her to what was then the Private Patients' Pavilion of the Toronto General Hospital – a huge and imposing building, lacking in warmth, focused solely on the tasks at hand. I don't know why I was there with her that day. It was all rather matter-of-fact. My dad would have driven us to the hospital, and I guess I amused myself somehow while my mother lay on a cold, hard plinth having cobalt radiation.

My mother's physician, Dr Vera Peters, was soon to become a renowned radiation oncologist.[1] More important for us, her relationship with our family was unusually warm, extending far beyond the doctor-patient interaction expected then and even now. We visited each other's homes and shared meals, and our friendship continued for some time after my mother's death. Vera and my mother were similar in some ways: about the same age and height, and each was one of seven children. But Vera grew up on a farm outside of Toronto and eventually went to medical school, while my mother grew up in a poor area of downtown Toronto, finished high school, and worked as a stenographer until she married. Tillie was outgoing and something of a beauty; Vera's quiet brilliance shone through her short brown bob, glasses, and engaging smile. The two connected, despite their differences. And I connected with Vera. Her embrace of my mother included me.[2]

Following the cobalt treatments, my mother came home and lay quietly on the sofa in our living room, not in pain so much as with a certain languor. I don't picture her taking to her bed, the one that she shared with my father until near the end, when they changed their double bed for twin beds to accommodate the sleepless nights each had for different reasons. After my mother died, my father abandoned his bed and took to sleeping in hers.

Tillie Jolofsky Pless was born on October 1st, 1910, at home, on 6 Bulwer Street in Toronto, the fifth daughter and second youngest of seven children. Bulwer was just barely outside the west boundary of "the Ward," the section of Toronto bounded by University Avenue, Yonge Street, College, and Queen, and home to new immigrants and the poor. My grandparents could as easily have been inside the Ward's boundaries, having fled Poland and its pogroms in 1906, with three young children, little money, few skills, and no English. By all accounts and remaining photographs, Tillie was a beautiful child and woman, happy and full of life, although her parents may have found the idea of a sixth child within eight years problematic.[3]

Tillie met my dad, Mike, at the Silver Slipper, a dance hall in Toronto. Mike was good-looking and personable and must have impressed my mother such that she agreed to dance with him, ditching the man who had brought her – something that was just not done. Tillie married Mike on June 16th, 1931, at 5 p.m. at Beth Hamidrash Hagadol, usually known as McCaul Street Synagogue. She was twenty, and he was twenty-eight. A wedding notice in the *Canadian Jewish Review* reports that my mother wore a gown of "embroidered Swiss organdy, and a veil of Brussels net arranged in cap effect and caught with tiny clusters of orange blossoms." Her wedding picture shows that delicate veil framing her lovely face, the orange blossoms tucked just under the veil, lying against her light brown hair. She has the slightest hint of a smile on her face and looks serene, as if to say, "there that's done."

Her wedding photo showed a very different face than the one I was to see the last time I was with

Tillie, 1931

her. She was in the hospital, lying on her left side in her bed, the tubes draining fluid from her lungs, trailing out from her back. I vividly remember her holding my hands in hers, her long, thin fingers, their manicured nails painted with bright red polish, clasping mine. She was still wearing her rings, her silver wedding band encrusted all around with tiny diamonds, and the canary diamond cocktail ring my dad had only recently given her. I could not describe her face as serene. Rather, it was almost expressionless.

We were alone in the room, my father purposely giving us this time on our own. Her voice was quiet, gentle, and calm. We spoke of everyday things – as if it was just an ordinary conversation. I don't believe that either of us cried. I was not thinking that I would never see her again. She would come back home, and life would continue as before. There was talk of a new spring coat for me. Or was I wearing the coat to show her? I don't know. But I did have a new coat that year, grey and white, glen check. My mother must have chosen it for me – or so I have wished to believe.

She died in the early hours of Thursday, April 7th, 1949. I awoke that day at my normal time, expecting to go to school. But I heard another man's voice in the house, and that must have alerted me that something was different. One of my dad's good friends (Percy Reitapple) had come home with him from the hospital after Tillie died, not wanting to leave him alone. Percy had an unusual voice, low and raspy; it would not have frightened me to hear it in our house at any other time, but it was strange to have him there so early in the morning.

My father came into my room and slumped down on the side of my bed. His eyes were red and so tired looking. In a voice that was soft and hesitant, he told me my mother had died. My heart galloped as I heard his words and took in the enormity of what he was saying. We held each other tight until our crying began to subside. I remember nothing of the rest of the day.

My father's emotions were depleted. To complicate matters, my mother's large family was of little comfort. Thinking my mother would know the end was near if they all visited in that last week, and wanting to protect her from that knowledge, my father had tried to keep them away. Mike was an only child and, with his own parents dead and his wife's relatives now bearing a grudge, there was no family to support him. Fortunately, the circle of friends that he and Tillie had developed over the eighteen years of their married life remained close: staunch friends and allies then, and for years to come.

The funeral was held the day after Tillie died, in keeping with the Jewish custom of burying their dead quickly, thereby allowing the person's soul, thought to be in limbo while the person is dead but not yet buried, to return quickly to God.

I was not allowed to attend the funeral. My maternal grandmother would have seen to that. She was a kind, clever, and loving woman, but her superstitious beliefs were strong: young children simply were not to attend a funeral for fear of tempting the "evil eye." My cousin Vicki, who was then fourteen, looked after me and two of my cousins at my grandparents' house that afternoon. I don't know that I wanted to attend the funeral or that I even understood what a funeral was. My brother attended the funeral, but he has no memory of it.

I was allowed to be at the *shiva* – the seven-day period of mourning that follows the burial – where friends and extended family visit the family of the deceased. The shiva was at my grandparents' home and, as dictated by orthodox practice, there were low wooden boxes for the immediate mourners to sit on.[4] The living room, normally a place for animated conversation, was quiet and still. People spoke in hushed tones. The piano sat silent.

During the nights of the shiva, I stayed with a family who lived just a few blocks away from us. Betty and Joe Hillman were dear friends of my parents. Betty, a strikingly beautiful blonde woman, warm and outgoing, was devoted to Tillie, bringing her flowers and poems, during the last period of her illness. Staying with the Hillman's comforted me. Betty and Joe were loving and lively, and their children, two girls (to be joined by a boy several years later), were on either side of my age. I hardly knew the girls and had never slept over at their place before; nonetheless, I felt protected in that home. Away from the heart-wrenching mourning at the shiva each day, life here was normal. Indeed, we listened to the hockey game huddled around the radio, and for the first time in my life, I heard Foster Hewitt shouting, "He shoots. He scores!!"

One evening, I went with the two Hillman girls to the drugstore at the top of their street, on Eglinton Avenue. It was a small store with a dispensing area and a few rows of personal-care products like shampoo and soap. My family had been customers there for some time, and the pharmacist knew that my mother was sick. But on that night, he did not know that she had died, and he innocently asked me how she was. I was too taken aback by the question to answer truthfully, and instead I just looked down and muttered, "Fine." Then I quickly exited the store, my eyes welling up with tears and my cheeks burning hot.

It was the first of many awkward encounters I was to have when someone inquired about my mother, naturally enough assuming that I had a mother. Aside from the upset it caused me, I always felt sorry for the person who asked, knowing how embarrassed they would be.

"How could you know?" was always my reply to their apology.

When the Jewish festival of Passover started five days after my mother's burial, the shiva stopped, in keeping with the custom of a religious holiday taking precedence. But how to celebrate Passover, a relatively cheerful holiday, as Jewish holidays go? In normal times, our

Passover *Seder* at my maternal grandparents' home, 1946

extended family of over twenty people gathered at my grandparents' home for two *Seders*, the festive dinners that start the holiday. We sat at the dining room table, which was extended for the occasion by several bridge tables partway into the living room to accommodate everyone.

In normal times, my grandfather led the Seder from his seat at the head of the table, specially dressed in a long white cotton robe, tied at the waist with a thin white sash. He read, in Hebrew, from the *Haggadah*, the prayer book that recounts the Exodus of the Jews from slavery in Egypt, their sojourn in the desert, and their return to the land of Canaan (Israel). He would explain the various symbolic foods, in a good-natured and cheerful tone. My grandmother sat beside him, except when she was running back and forth to the kitchen to oversee this feast with its many courses of traditional foods. The rest of the family, not quite so devout, participated in the readings or chatted quietly among themselves. Children, like me, were known to play under the table when we got bored. Some of the men and older boys snuck away briefly to listen to the hockey game because the Stanley Cup playoffs always occurred at that time of year. It was a long, but happy, night.

Passover 1949 was very different. The Seder proceeded with great solemnity. An older cousin remembers my grandfather crying throughout as he tried to lead the service, his youngest daughter having been buried just days before. I, however, have no memories of that Passover.

Awkwardness around any activity that involved mothers began when I returned to school. Making Christmas presents and cards for Valentine's Day was forever an issue, but Mother's Day headed the list. Do I pretend I have a mother and make something anyway? Do I just sit and do nothing? I see myself, working away at a drawing that would never be given to anyone, my cheeks, again, burning hot, my glance averted from my classmates and my teacher. In high school, mother-daughter teas and dinners, popular at the time, were especially awkward and unpleasant. I believe that these social activities set me on a path of feeling that I didn't quite fit in.

Within a few months of my mother's death, the attic over our garage became the place for her belongings, as they were gradually moved out from the house and before they were distributed elsewhere. My aunts and older cousins, and some of my mother's friends, came to look over her effects, choosing a sweater here, a dress there. I doubt I was present while they made their decisions, sensing it would have been uncomfortable for me, and for them. But I did wander in on my own from time to time to look at her things, holding up items of clothing, pressing them against my body, trying to recapture my mother in some way. I was drawn to a large, red leather shoulder bag with a gold-coloured clasp. It was soft and smooth to touch and looked almost new. At age ten, it was not something I could use, but I did covet it and always wondered what became of it.

Ultimately, many of my mother's effects did come to me. Some valuable items were left by design, such as that canary diamond ring my father bought for her toward the end – not that he could have afforded it any better then than in earlier years. A locket, engraved with the name "Tillie," taken by one of my mother's sisters initially, came back to me eventually and I gave it on to my first-born granddaughter, who has my mother's name. I kept other less valuable jewellery, left behind after others had picked the pieces over, and wear some of it from time to time as it comes back into fashion. Indeed, I have a habit of wearing some item of my mother's – perhaps a bracelet or a necklace – on special occasions, and I say to myself, "I'll take Tillie with me to the wedding," or whatever the event is.

I still have a bottle of my mother's cologne, Tigress by Fabergé. It was almost empty, but I diluted what remained with water so it would last. I also still have some scarves and belts, most of which I have never worn but cannot part with. When we sold our house eight years after Tillie died, my brother and I divvied up all the household items, including a set of good dinnerware. I use these Dresden-style plates at Passover each year. They are decorated with colourful flowers and are not at all what I would normally have, but they are perfect

Dresden-style china used at Passover

for the holiday and they remind me of my mother's passing at that time of year, so long ago.

My parents had, by all accounts, a very loving, albeit somewhat tempestuous, relationship. There were certainly raised voices in my house, and tempers could be short. I learned early on that that was how my parents aired their differences, that it generally led to a new level of understanding, and that calm soon returned. My maternal grandparents were also known to "fight." And most in my own family have followed suit. We air our grievances – better out than in – and within a fairly short time, we have "made up." Looking at a photo of my parents in Florida, just two months before my mother

Mike and Tillie, Florida, 1949

died, I see a couple with a strong marriage putting on a brave face for what lay ahead. My mother looks healthy in her two-piece bathing suit, slender but not too thin, tanned and smart looking. My dad looks preoccupied and has a distant look in his eyes.

My parents were never away on a holiday by themselves until that trip in January 1949. My mother's sister, Sarah, who did not have children of her own, stayed with my brother and me while my parents were away. Tillie wrote to us regularly as they drove south. In her first letter, written from Harrisburg, Pennsylvania, she starts with "here we are safe and sound," a phrase my whole family uses today when we are travelling and reach our destination. She describes their difficulty finding a hotel room in the state capital with the legislature in session, and then proudly adds, "Daddy said he was a member [of the legislature] so here we are." My father, always a good problem solver, was not going to let something like no rooms spoil their holiday.

Within a month of their return from Florida, my mother was in the hospital with pneumonia, a disease her weakened immune system could not fight. When she entered the hospital, my father gave her a get-well card and signed it for all of us – including our dog. Rather than the card representing the belief that she would indeed get better, it was likely another ploy of my dad's to have her think a get-well card meant there was still time.

My father put up a "double stone" when Tillie died, leaving room for him to join her, as he did, forty-eight years later. At the bottom of the stone are the words, "To be remembered is not to die." By that definition, my mother has not died. My son Tom, my niece Tamara, and my first-born granddaughter, Tillie, are all named for her. Her pictures are everywhere in my home. I still have many of her belongings. She has a strong presence in my life. And yet I do not see her in my mind's eye.

The literature on the early loss of a parent discusses the effects of the trauma and considers what helps life to go on. John Bowlby, the child psychiatrist whose work set the stage for research in this area, would have said it was those early years of attachment, *before* my mother died, along with the love and support of significant adults after her death, that facilitated my being able to cope.[5] Although I don't have explicit memories to exemplify that early attachment to my mother, my comings and goings as a child suggest I felt safe and secure.

There's a photo of my parents, my brother, and me, with one of my aunts, at a beach somewhere. I was confused when I first came upon the photo much later in life; I didn't see the little girl at the bottom left in the photo, who is me. The woman I *thought* was me was my mother – sitting beside me, and in front of my dad. I was shocked to feel myself so inherently, so physically, connected to my mother.

Clockwise: Mike, Aunt Sarah, Barry, Tillie, and me

Following Tillie's death, my dad became father and mother to my brother and me. Over time we settled into a new normal. There were difficulties, of course, but we three had a close and loving relationship. Housekeepers kept things working at home, and extended family, my parents' friends, my own friends, and teachers all played a part. I learned to cope with adversity. My resilience training began early on.[6] I learned to persevere.

2 Mike: A Father's Enduring Presence

I believe that I was able to cope with the early death of my mother because of the kind of person my father was and the role he played after she died. His strong character and engaging personality were responsible for the safe, caring, and interesting environment that surrounded my brother and me.

A handsome man, not tall but strong and trim, well-dressed but not dapper, always young -looking for his age, sporting an on-again-off-again moustache, Michael Abraham Pless was born in 1903 in Rokiskis – a *shtetl* (a small town or village, with a large Jewish population) about eighty kilometres east of Dvinsk, or Daugavpils as it is now called. At the time, Rokiskis was in Latvia (and considered part of Russia), but since 1915 it has been part of Lithuania. It was an old market town where, in 1897, by some estimates, Jews made up 75 per cent of its total population.[1]

Just a few months after my father was born, his father left Rokiskis for America to seek a better life and safety from the ever-present threat of pogroms. He went first to New York, where he had a brother, but, not liking the city, he then moved on to Brantford, Ontario, which he had heard good things about while on the boat. My grandmother joined him nine years later with my father in tow. Such a long separation was not uncommon; it took time for the husband to find work and save enough money to bring

Mike at eighty-seven

his family over, and it took time for the family to make their way. It was a wise decision to leave Rokiskis. While my grandmother's two brothers and two of her three sisters emigrated safely to South Africa, the sister who remained in Rokiskis perished in the Holocaust.[2]

My husband and I visited Rokiskis in 2015. Many houses that were once part of the *shtetl* are still standing, so it was easy to get the feel of the place. I could picture a six- or seven-year-old Mike (or Avrahm Mottel, as he would have been called) running around, playing games, shouting to his friends. When I stood in the town square, in front of

Russian silver vodka cups, Rokiskis Regional Museum

the big Catholic church, I could see my grandfather selling his scrap metal wares at the weekly market and my great-grandfather who brought his horses there to trade. Rokiskis looked like it had been a happy enough place for its Jewish population until trouble came – which it invariably did.

Visiting the Rokiskis Regional Museum, I stopped short at a display of household items: a copper samovar, a brass mortar and pestle, and a set of Russian silver vodka cups – all identical to items that my grandmother brought with her to Canada. My brother has the samovar and the mortar and pestle, and I have the silver cups. We used the cups (*bucharoles*) for the sacramental wine we drank at our Sabbath dinners when I was growing up, and I continued that tradition when I married. As our family grew to include our children's partners and our grandchildren, we kept pace by buying more silver cups, finding *bucharoles* in antique shops around the world wherever Jews had settled after fleeing Europe.

In 1911, Mike and his mother left Rokiskis for London, en route to

Mike with his mother, around 1911

Canada. However, their trip was interrupted by a lengthy stay in London when my grandmother fell and broke her leg. The leg developed gangrene, which led to its amputation and a lengthy hospitalization. For much of that time, my father, who was then about eight years old, says he "lived on the streets." He recounts stories of hitching rides on the back of double-decker busses and eating from market stalls, where he found he could pilfer fruit at will. He claims he managed just fine; going wherever he wanted, touring London by his "special method," and not attending school at all. But he also reports that there was a family in Whitechapel, then the centre of London's Jewish community, who kept an eye on him, so it's hard to know how much of his story about being on his own is true. Mike had a knack for telling a good story, leaving the listener to decide where the embellishments began and ended. Either way, he had managed while my grandmother was hospitalized – an early sign of his ability to cope with whatever life had in store.

My father and grandmother finally left England on September 26th, 1912 aboard the SS *Scotian*. After three weeks at sea, in steerage, they landed in Quebec, and from there, they travelled by train to Brantford, Ontario, where my grandfather had settled.

My grandfather is listed in the 1921 census as a pedlar, and on his death certificate as a junk dealer. I don't know how a distinction was made between the two trades, as both refer to the practice of collecting scrap materials, separating them into their parts, and selling the valuable copper and steel. After selling the metals, my grandfather took his commission and gave the rest of the money to the original owner of the scrap.

The family lived in rented rooms, and their lodgings included a stable for the horse that pulled my grandfather's wagon. There couldn't have been much money to spare, and, with the ever-present undertones of anti-Semitism in small-town Canada, the family did not have much of a sense of belonging in Brantford.[3] Mike seems to have had a good life, nonetheless. Even the landlady liked him, leaving him $100 when she died.

My husband and I visited Brantford and looked for the landmarks my dad referred to in the stories he told. We saw Brantford Collegiate Institute (BCI), where he played on the school rugby team, and imagined hearing what he claimed was the BCI chant: "BCI, BCI, rah-rah-rah, BCI, BCI, sis-boom-bah; hit 'im in the *kishkes*, hit 'im in the jaw, BCI, BCI, rah-rah-rah." While Jewish people in small towns such as Brantford were more integrated into society than they were in larger cities, I doubt his largely Christian team mates would have chanted his version, with the Yiddish word *kishkes* (guts)!

Mike's favourite BCI rugby story starts with him having gained pos-
session of the ball – which is fair enough. It continues, however, with
his teammates throwing *him* – clutching the ball – *through* the goalposts
(not just over the goal line but over the crossbar) and scoring the winning goal. He never wavered in telling the tale, naming players we
could contact who could vouch for its truth – which, of course, we
never did.

Having spent almost two years in England, Mike spoke English well
by the time he arrived in Brantford but was otherwise not prepared for
school. Placed in a classroom according to his age – which was nine –
he could not keep up and was put back a few times until he ended up
in Grade 1. Although he gradually caught up, his poor performance
found him at the bottom of his class in Grade 8. He explained that he
"had the mind for it [education], but not the motivation." Motivation
came later that year – in the middle of the First World War – in an emotional encounter with his teacher, who berated Mike over his poor performance: "You are a nuisance here. If *you* pass, there isn't a kid in the
Dominion of Canada who will not pass! Do the war effort a favour –
go to work on a farm and don't take up a useless seat [in school]."[4]
More than half a century later, he still remembered how that speech got
him "flaming mad" and was just the motivation he needed. He passed
fifteenth that year, bumping up his standing by 50 per cent over the
previous year. "Apparently," he said, "I needed the stimulation of an
emergency type of condition to bring out perseverance on my part."
And, indeed, he was exceptionally able in emergencies – never panick-
ing, always a confident problem-solver, and always persevering.

Mike left Brantford for Detroit right after high school taking whatever
jobs he could find and worrying about how to do the job afterwards,
even when it meant teaching himself to drive. Each job lasted for a few
weeks or months. If he requested time off to go home to celebrate the
Jewish High Holidays, and his employer refused, he quit the job, more
on principle than as a reflection of any deep religious beliefs.

When he eventually settled in Toronto, he found work as a travelling
salesman. He sold fabrics, then dresses, and finally ladies' coats, which
he continued to do for the rest of his life – except for one foray into the
building business. In 1932, he and his friend Percy Reitapple – the man
with the gravelly voice who had come home with Mike the night my
mother died – borrowed money, built small bungalows, and, when they
sold the houses and cleared a profit, paid back their loans. However,
by 1935, in the depths of the Depression, the profits were too slim to
clear their debts. They declared bankruptcy, and Mike went back to

selling ladies' coats. Years later, when we'd see the houses he had built on Duplex Avenue near Eglinton, we mused about what might have been had he been able to stay in the building business.

Work as a salesman of ladies' coats took Mike to southwestern Ontario for many weeks of "placing" in the spring and in the fall. As the manufacturer's representative – the middleman between the manufacturer and the retailer – he showed coat samples to shopkeepers, who then placed orders through him to the manufacturer. There were good placing seasons and bad ones, but, overall, he made a decent living.

The list of small towns Mike had to visit to make that decent living was long: he travelled throughout southwestern Ontario, from Windsor and Sarnia to Owen Sound and Orillia, and dozens of towns in between. He travelled those roads for close to sixty years, leaving home on Monday morning and returning on Friday night, when he was, in his words, "dog-tired."

Coat samples arrived just before each season began; spring coats arrived in the fall, winter coats in spring. He unboxed the coats and hung them up on a portable metal coat rack he had set up in his living room. He sorted through the coats, deciding which ones were more likely to sell and leaving the rest behind. He often asked me to model the coats to help him make his choices. When I tried on the coats, I'd often give my opinion – "I love this one! It's a great colour and feels warm and cozy" – but Mike was rarely impressed with my views, and I learned that what sells may not be the same as what one likes and that it might be necessary to sacrifice one's aesthetic values to make a living. As I put on each coat, Mike would settle it on my shoulders, lifting it up and pulling it forward, making the coat sit just so – something I continue to do instinctively. I learned the importance of trying on clothing, as my father taught me that you could not tell anything from how clothes looked on a hanger. And I hang everything back up after trying it on in a store, as that too was somehow expected: to treat the clothes, and the people selling them, with respect.

My Dad's work meant that he knew many people on Spadina Avenue, which was the heart of Toronto's *shmata* business, or "needle trade," as it was more genteelly known. That meant that I could get other clothes, not just coats, wholesale – a nice plus, for the most part, but there was a downside too. The selection in the showrooms on Spadina was never what it would be in a store and there were no fitting rooms. It was tricky to find a place among the racks of clothes where I could be out of sight to try on a dress, let alone find a mirror to see how I looked. Worst of all, I felt that I had to hurry because the owner of the showroom was doing us a favour. That always rankled me. Years later, I stayed away from so-called bargains, perhaps even going to the opposite extreme with my shopping.

Mike swimming in the lake at the cottage

There was a fullness to Mike's character and a determined way he went about his life. He loved the outdoors, appreciating the beauty of nature wherever he found it. He prided himself on being fit, not in a narcissistic way but for the sake of good health. He was a great swimmer with an idiosyncratic crawl stroke, his arms moving slowly and rhythmically, while his legs kept pace with an unorthodox, sideways scissors kick. People watched in awe as he swam for an hour or more without tiring even in his 80s. He swam at the "Y" (the Young Men's Hebrew Association), in the ocean on holiday, and in the lake at the cottage my husband and I bought in 1983. By the time we bought our cottage, Mike was seventy-nine. Entering the lake, where the water was typically on the cold side, he had a ritual. He walked in slowly from the shore and stopped when the water came up to his hips. Placing his hands just under his ribcage, he slapped his stomach with his hands, alternately and rhythmically, maybe a dozen times, Tarzan-style. Then lunging forward on one foot, arms up and over his ears, he dove into the depths. There was also a ritual after exiting the water. It started with getting out of his wet bathing suit immediately – no matter where he was. If he happened to be in public, he just covered himself with a towel and carefully wiggled out of the wet suit and somehow pulled a dry one on. His next priority was to have a drink – usually scotch. As he aged, he would often have a drink before *and* after swimming. Swimming was a passion to be pursued under all conditions. If he went into the lake on his own, we chastised him later, "Mike, please don't go into the water without someone watching you! What if something happened?" His answer, which we came to think made sense, especially as the years went by, was that he couldn't think of a better way to die.

For many years, Mike owned a canoe. In his younger days, he kept it in the Beaches area and paddled on Lake Ontario. Years later, he bought a tip-proof, pseudo-birch-bark aluminum canoe and took it on the Humber River. He had a long, wooden, double-bladed paddle – the kind used with a kayak only longer. Sometimes he had another person with him when he canoed, someone who had come to him, tacitly, for help. A canoe was a good place to talk, sitting behind one another allowed for minimal eye contact. Eventually, Mike brought that pseudo-birch-bark canoe and the paddle to our cottage, where he paddled himself and his wife May until he was eighty-nine.

Mike also walked. For years after Tillie died, he walked with the family dog at his side, before bed, to digest his food and clear his mind. He took my brother and me on hikes through leafy parks and hilly ravines on the outskirts of the city, and, in later years, he took his grandchildren on hikes in the ravine behind his apartment. They were probably just tame walks, but he heightened the sense of adventure by taking a rope along on those treks, suggesting they might be scaling steep cliffs and require such equipment.

Mike had indoor interests as well. He played cards under various circumstances. Especially in the years when he was on his own after Tillie died, he played lots of solitaire, sitting quietly at the dining room table for what seemed to me like hours on end. Before and after Tillie died, he played gin rummy and poker with "the gang," friends who gathered each Saturday night to play for penny stakes. They talked and kibitzed, ate and drank – and smoked – and remained staunch friends for decades.

Mike and his granddaughter Jenny

He taught his children and grandchildren to play chess and took great delight in the day when any of them could beat him. He was a patient teacher, unless he thought you weren't paying attention or weren't trying, and then he would become annoyed and dismissive. Maybe because he was normally a very gentle and loving man, we felt the sting when he got mad.

Mike was always reading something. He read the daily paper and always knew what was happening in the world. He had usually formed an opinion and was eager to engage in discussion. He was a regular at the library, going easily from what he called "junk" – his cowboy books and mysteries – to history, biography, and politics.

Music had been a part of Mike's life since he was a boy in Brantford. He had violin lessons for a time but when he didn't practise, and with no money to waste, it was soon agreed he should give it up. He had a lovely voice, often singing on his own when he thought no one heard. His repertoire included an assortment of old songs such as "Does Your Mother Know You're Out, Cecilia?" to "Show Me the Way to Go Home," and "It's a Long Way to Tipperary." Mike sang the blessing over the bread at our Sabbath dinners and became legendary for prolonging a note near the end of the blessing: "*hah . . . moytzie lechem min haoretz.*" Holding the "*hah*" has since become a tradition – and a contest within the family to see who can hold the note the longest.

When Mike first met Tillie at the Silver Slipper, he was already a good dancer, and as the years went on, he got even better. He could dance to anything, with anyone. He had a way of making his partners feel they were great dancers. He had great timing and rhythm; steps that others had to be taught came naturally to him. But he was not a show-off. He danced the way he lived, in an unassuming manner, without flourish, but with much skill and vitality.

Mike spoke with little evidence of his eastern European beginnings. On occasion, his "v's" would become "w's" – as in "eat your *wegetables*," but he otherwise had no accent. He used language in a manner that reflected his personality. It could include Yiddish expressions like *ach hoolaria* (to express frustration) or down-home expressions, like "when Hector was a pup," that seemed from a different era. It could also be somewhat cryptic, as when he referred to a swimming pool as a tank, or a bike as a wheel. His speech could be expansive and expressive, with weather on a summer day being "salubrious" and the water in the lake being "delectable." He used endearments like "honeybunch" and "sweetheart" liberally, reflecting his warm and loving nature.

Comfortable in small groups and certainly one on one, Mike was shy in larger gatherings, and never one to hold forth. He had a speech ready to give at my wedding, but when the time came, he simply could not deliver it. He started to speak and stopped. Tried again. Looked down at the words on the page he held in his hand but could not continue. Whether it was because he was too emotional seeing his daughter married, or simply too anxious in front of a crowd, we never knew. He always lamented the incident and seemed, at some level, not just embarrassed but ashamed.

Mike, or "Uncle Mike," as he was called by many, was especially popular with our friends. Several of my brother's friends looked on him as a second father and often turned to him for advice. As a good listener, he drew many to him. Remaining sharp until the day he died, he listened to others' problems throughout his life. However, he played this role in person better than on the telephone. I remember finding him asleep once while supposedly listening to a friend on the other end of the line. The friend seemed not to notice that he had stopped saying "uh-huh, uh-huh."

My Dad could usually sense when something was bothering me. His "Okay, what's up?" meant he suspected there was a problem, and he was usually right. I doubt I confided much of anything growing up; indeed, I was told that I seemed too self-sufficient, that I wouldn't "let people in." But in later years, when I was less defensive, I often came to him with problems – about the children or about work. As soon as I said I wanted his thoughts on something, he'd say, "Shoot." That was the signal for me to start talking. I don't remember him offering advice, although he may have laid out options. He mainly listened, and, of course, that was really what was needed.

Trying on coat samples for Mike

Mike moving samples from his van onto a rack

As Mike aged and had difficulty driving distances *and* selling his coats, he hired someone to drive his van. When the season was almost over, and he needed help for just a day here and there, other family members, including myself, had the chance to be his driver. I was thrilled to see this major part of his life first-hand. I drove the van into a smallish town and parked near the store where he had an appointment. We assembled the metal rack right there on the side-walk, hung the sample coats on it, and then wheeled the rack along the pavement into the store. Once there, I stood aside as my father interacted with the storekeeper.

After the initial greeting, I saw my fearless father transform him-self into a different person. While not servile or grovelling, he did become submissive and deferen-tial. I had imagined he would be more assertive as he gave his sales pitch, even gregarious, like the stereotypical salesmen in movies. Then it dawned on me that part of his success in life came from his ability to adapt his way of speaking and interacting to whomever he was with – at work and in life.

Mike managed what money he had well and was generous according to his own principles. He readily lent money to others in need, willing to take a chance on someone and giving that person a much-needed vote of confidence. His generosity did not extend, however, to the government when it collected taxes. Although he leaned left in his politics and supported the role of a centralized government helping those in need, he tried hard not to give the government more than what he thought was his share. He kept a record of his work-related expenses in little notebooks, detailing the costs: this much for gas and food, that much for hotels and parking; expenditures for liquor and chocolates for his customers. One such notebook from 1972 has each page stamped, rather ominously, with "DNR." It seems the Department of National Revenue (as the Canada Revenue Agency was called in those years) had reviewed those little notebooks. Mike was a willing taxpayer – but only to a point!

With Mike away from home so much of the week, and long-distance calls expensive, we developed a special relationship with the Bell Telephone Company. If he just wanted to "check-in" and see that I was ok, he called "collect" and asked for "Mr Tipping" (a derivation of the name of our dog, Tippy). The operator said, "I have a collect call for Mr. Tipping. Will you accept the charges?" If all was well and there was no need to speak, I refused to accept the charges, but, before hanging up, I'd try to add some other information, like, "No, he's just leaving for a movie."

My memories for the years immediately following my mother's death are of a general sense of well-being. When my father was home, he was an integral part of my life and our little family. When his work took him out of town – as it did for many weeks of the year – he was also "home," arranging with the housekeeper for our care, checking in by phone regularly, and appearing back on Friday nights in time for dinner. It wasn't ideal – but it worked. Mike was more than a survivor in the full life he lived. He didn't go looking for challenges, but when they came his way, he did his best to take them on. Silently and without any flourish, he set an example for my brother and me to follow.

3 The Jolofsky Family: Keeping the Sabbath and More

My maternal grandparents left their small town of Klobuck in Poland and arrived in Toronto in 1906 with three daughters, ages four, two, and one. Four more children would be born in the next six years as they built their new lives. My grandfather continued his work as a tinsmith, climbing onto rooftops to attach parts he made himself, until well into his 70s. My grandmother cooked and cleaned and sewed and did the laundry for the family of nine, in addition to taking in boarders and doing community work. Over time, the "Jolofsky Family," became well-known in Jewish circles in Toronto. Close with all their children and grandchildren, and active in their synagogue, my grandparents were a strong presence in all our lives. From them, I absorbed a Jewish way of living that felt protective. It stayed with me, even as I shed many of its layers as the years went on.

I walked with my grandmother to McCaul Street Synagogue on many occasions, my grandfather having left much earlier to perform his duties as *Gabbai* to assist in running the service. It was a short walk, from their home on Grange Avenue, across Beverley Street, and through Grange Park to McCaul Street, where we entered

Zaidie reading the newspaper to Bubie

the synagogue through its large, ornate doors. Immediately after entering, my grandmother and I made a sharp right turn to climb up a steep flight of narrow steps to the balcony. That's where the women sat. Although it was a Conservative *shul*, it held to many of the practices of the Orthodox tradition: no women were allowed to sit where the men sat.

My grandmother had a front-row, aisle seat in the middle section of the balcony. On regular Saturday mornings, most seats around her were empty, but during the High Holidays (Rosh Hashana and Yom Kippur), the balcony was full. My grandmother's row and more would be filled with her daughters, granddaughters, and friends. Although she did not read English, we believe she could read Hebrew – either that, or she had memorized every prayer and song, for she paid close attention throughout the service, followed along, and was not given to chit chat. While in the synagogue, she had a solemnity about her that stood in contrast to her everyday, cheerful, and talkative self.

Separated from the men and certainly not allowed to take an active role in the service, we could at least see and hear everything from the balcony at McCaul Street Synagogue. In comparison, many synagogues, especially in Europe and Israel, have a *mehitza*, a physical barrier of some sort, a mesh curtain or sometimes a screen of varying height and opacity, keeping the women out of sight of the men. The stated purpose of the screen is to prevent the men from being distracted from their prayers. However, in many cases, the screen also prevents the women from seeing or hearing most anything and greatly affects their ability to participate in the service. It's no wonder women are often thought to talk and not pay attention during services.

My grandparents – Bubie and Zaidie – followed the customs of their Orthodox beliefs. From the beginning of the Sabbath at sundown on Friday until sundown on Saturday, they did not turn on any electric lights or light their coal stove, keeping the Fourth Commandment, to "remember the Sabbath day, and keep it holy." My grandfather placed candles strategically throughout their semi-detached, narrow, three-storey house, and, just before sundown on Friday night, went around and carefully lit each one.

My grandmother prepared the food for Saturday on Friday, then left her oven at a low heat throughout the night and the following day to keep it warm. She lit candles to welcome the Sabbath at sundown on Friday and recited the traditional blessing. My grandfather then recited the *kiddush* over the sacramental wine and made a *moytzie* over the challah, the specially baked egg loaf. They marked the end of the Sabbath on Saturday night with the *Havdalah* ceremony that begins when three stars can be seen in the night sky, signifying nightfall, and indicating that the new week is beginning. That service includes three blessings: one over a full cup of wine, another over spices, and a third over a long, braided candle whose lit end is extinguished by dipping it in the wine that has purposely been allowed to overflow its cup. When I slept over at my grandparents' house on a Saturday night, I was the one to hold the candle and dip it in the wine. I watched the flame as it began to sputter and then sizzle as it went out. I felt close to my grandparents at these times, and very much a part of their world.

A light dairy dinner followed the ceremony and not long after, I went up to my grandparents' bedroom to get ready for bed. The room had twin beds separated by a night table and two dressers. I wondered why they had twin beds and learned only years later that it was to follow the Orthodox custom whereby the husband is not to have relations with his wife while she is menstruating (and considered "ritually impure"). I'm told that, at most other times of the month, the two slept together in one of those twin beds.

The bedroom was always cold, so I was glad to climb right into my grandmother's bed. I slipped under the white cotton comforter with its cut-out centre section exposing the rose-coloured satin that lay beneath. From there I watched my grandmother prepare for bed. She took out the pins holding her long salt-and-pepper hair in a bun and let it tumble down. Then she brushed her hair, which hung far down her back, using the brush from the silver-handled dresser set she had brought from Poland. Finally, she put on a long white nightgown and snuggled in beside me. Zaidie climbed into his bed a little later, wearing a white, long-sleeved nightshirt. Soon after, I could hear his rhythmic snoring. I was not afraid sleeping there with them. I felt safe.

Venturing up to the third floor in that house was a different story. Uncle Harry's bedroom was the problem. Harry fought in the Second World War, and, when he returned home, he "decorated" his room with wartime paraphernalia: guns and bayonets, a helmet, some knives and swords, and the like. I feared the room and always ran quickly past it.

Harry qualified as a dentist in 1930 and had a busy practice by the time war broke out. Before applying to the Faculty of Dentistry at the University of Toronto, Harry Meyer Jolofsky changed his surname to Jolley. It was understood that, with the quota on Jews in professional faculties at the time, a more anglicized name would increase his chance of acceptance. Never mind that he would have easily qualified had the process been fair and objective. Indeed, he demonstrated his ability by graduating at age twenty-one and was said at the time to be the youngest ever to do so.

He joined up in 1942 and served across Europe and North Africa with the Number 12 Canadian Light Field Ambulance. He did his dental work in a large ambulance-like vehicle, seemingly out of harm's way until one day, when German paratroopers were mounting a counterattack close by, shots hit his vehicle. Harry had been busy shaving, and with his face still covered in lather, he set out to investigate. Seeing two German soldiers, he pointed his gun, and shouted, "Hande Hoch!" (Hands up!), whereupon they surrendered. Fortunately, neither he nor the German soldiers knew that he had forgotten to take the safety off his gun.

The Canadian regiment fought with the fifty or so Germans who had appeared that day, and some of them, and some of our soldiers, were wounded. Harry then helped organize the stretcher-bearer parties. It was "in recognition of [these] gallant and distinguished services" that Harry was made a Member of the British Order (MBE) and mentioned in dispatches.[1] Soon thereafter, Captain H.M. Jolley became Major H.M. Jolley. Perhaps the most distinguished member of the Jolofsky family (and certainly its most dapper dresser), Harry was the president of the Council of the Royal College of Dental Surgeons of Ontario for two years, and the chief of dentistry at Mt. Sinai Hospital. He was also the first Canadian president of the Alpha Omega International Dental Fraternity.

Harry's dental practice continued to flourish after the war. His waiting room was always full, and he was always behind schedule. Although his patients (including me) were disgruntled by the wait, it didn't stop us from returning. Highly skilled as a dentist, he was also extremely deaf, and I was terrified that, when he turned away, he would not hear me choking on the many objects still sitting in my mouth. Harry's persona was gruff (though he was something of a softie inside), and he was not one with whom you could share your fears. He continued to practise until he was well into his 80s. I did not feel I could find a new dentist until he retired, for fear of hurting his feelings.

Harry was known as a "life-long bachelor," despite the fact that he had the same girlfriend from before he went off to war until he died in 2000. Charlotte (Charlie) was not Jewish and, for that reason, Harry believed they should not marry. A product of the tight-knit Jewish society of which his mother and father were long-standing and much-admired members, he could not dishonour his parents or risk having them disown him. Instead, Harry and Charlie "dated," in secret, for decades. When they went to a movie, they sat together but they did not walk in or out of the theatre together, lest they be seen.

After my grandparents died, Harry and Charlie "went public," and his siblings, friends, and colleagues all welcomed them as a couple.

Still, they did not marry. By then, they had established an arrangement that worked for them. They took trips together and went out at night together, including to Oakdale, the (Jewish) Golf and Country Club to which Harry belonged, but they each kept their own apartments and otherwise lived their separate lives.

Where Harry was gruff and hard to relate to, Uncle Joe, the baby of the Jolofsky family, was a kind and gentle man – and everyone's favourite. He studied drafting at Central Tech, hoping for a career in architecture but ended up in electronics sales. His real love, however, was the theatre. He had taken drama classes in his youth, while attending programs at the nearby University Settlement House, and that led to a life-long interest in theatre. Joe Jolley (he took the same anglicized surname his brother had taken) established his own amateur theatre company, Theatre 49. He was a well-respected director whose plays were reviewed by the critics of the day.[2] I once had a teensy part in his production of J.B. Priestley's *I Have Been Here Before*, which ran for three nights. I had a bad sore throat on opening night, and someone else had to say my lines off-stage as I mouthed the words, but just having an actor's make-up put on me was a thrill.

The Jolofsky girls, Emma, Sarah, Ida, Eva, and my mother, Tillie, were all smart, but none had the advantage of any postsecondary education. They took commercial courses in high school, which prepared them to be stenographers or telegraphers, not because of any special interest but because it was what was expected. The girls were also beautiful and accomplished. Sarah played the piano well enough to accompany silent films at local cinemas and she also sang; Ida served on hospital and community boards and was highly regarded; and Eva, who lived in the United States with her husband and daughter, kept close to her siblings and parents despite the distance and the many moves she made to accommodate her husband's work. Emma, the oldest of the siblings, lived the most upwardly mobile life, with an elegant home in Forest Hill, an upper-class area of Toronto. The

The Jolofsky family with Tillie front and centre

house was decorated in the style popular at the time with thick wall-to-wall broadloom, heavy drapery, and sturdy mahogany furniture. She and her husband travelled, and attended the theatre, ballet, symphony, and opera. I lived with Emma and Harry in my first year of university, after they had moved to a smaller, more modern, but equally lovely, home a little further north. Their more cultured way of life was different from what I knew growing up and it made an impression on me. I thought it worth emulating in many ways.

All the Jolofsky girls married and lived comfortably, except for Ida, whose husband fell on hard times and soon lost the substantial fortune he had when they first married. At one point, a few years after my mother's death, we thought our two families might buy a house to live in together. The move would have helped out Ida's family financially and would have given us a mother figure in the home. I adored my cousin Vicki and would have loved to live in the same house with her. I dearly wanted it to happen, but it did not.

Of the eight grandchildren – myself and my cousins – each boy went to university: one became an accountant, another an aeronautical engineer, the third an orthodontist, and the fourth, my brother, a pediatrician. Two of the four girls went to university; one did journalism and the other (me) became a physical and occupational therapist. Of the two cousins who did not go to university, one married at seventeen, had five children (and three husbands), and did a variety of clerical jobs when she was able to work outside the home, and the other, who trained initially as an X-ray technician, worked mainly in administrative jobs throughout her unmarried life. We girls were better educated than our mothers – but not as well educated as the boys. However, that was not something we ever thought about at the time.

About a year after the end of the Second World War, my grandparents received a phone call from the International Red Cross with devastating news. After a brief introduction, the caller explained that most of our relatives who had remained in Poland had died in the Holocaust. While I had no understanding of the events at the time, my older cousins remember my grandparents' anguished cries as they listened to the news. The few relatives that did survive the war were dispersed and were trying either to find a way back to their homes in Eastern Europe or to emigrate. My grandparents were determined to help. They located several relatives and helped bring them to Canada. I grew up knowing three of those families.

My grandmother's niece, Helen, who was known to us as Hinda, was born in a small farming village, Parzymiechy, near Czestochowa.[3] When the Germans invaded, she hid with her family in haystacks in their barn until bayonets, shoved into those haystacks, found them.

Hinda (middle) with Bubie and Zadie, possibly on her wedding day, 1951

They were then sent to a ghetto in Czestochowa. From there, Hinda was sent to a work camp in Klobuck, and finally on a forced march to Bergen-Belsen. When the British liberated the camp in April 1945, many prisoners, including Hinda, were gravely ill: 23,000 died within the first three months of liberation, 90 per cent of whom were Jewish.[4] Hinda remained at Bergen-Belsen to be treated for typhus, and when she was well enough to travel, the Red Cross sent her, along with 6,000 other survivors, to Sweden to recover more fully. My grandparents helped bring Hinda to Toronto in 1950. Once my grandparents had established communication with Hinda, the family, including me, wrote to her. I was eleven years old and Hinda was thirty-three but, by the time she arrived in Toronto, we had established a special bond. Hinda stayed with my grandparents until her boyfriend, Carl, whom she met and became engaged to in Sweden after the war, and who had spent his war years in a slave labour camp in Siberia, arrived a year later. They married in 1951, and together with their daughter Mari, they built a new life in Canada. Hinda did millinery work, and Carl established several successful bakeries in Toronto.

My grandparents also sponsored Guta (known to us as Gittel), my grandfather's niece, and her husband, Max Glicksman. They had started off the war living in the large ghetto in Czestochowa with some 39,000 Jews.[5] They married in 1940 and were separated many times when they were sent to work in different slave labour camps. Max was sent to Buchenwald, which was where he was liberated. Gittel was sent to Bergen-Belsen and, from there, she was sent on a forced, eight-day march to Dachau. Fortunately, Gittel never did get to Dachau. She managed to escape on the way and hide in a barn until she was liberated at the end of April 1945. Somehow, Gittel and Max found each other a few months later at a displaced persons' camp in Landsberg, Germany.

Max and Gittel arrived in Toronto in 1948 with their one-year-old daughter, Lenny. They stayed with my grandparents for about eight months and then moved out on their own. Two more children, Harry and Lisa, were born in Toronto. Max had been a tailor during the war, and my father found a job for him in a factory on Spadina Avenue soon after he arrived. Max and his brother, who had also survived the war and immigrated to Toronto, soon became successful manufacturers of men's wear and, later, property owners and developers. Max never forgot that Mike got him his first job and often mentioned how important that was to him. His gratitude for that first break may have been why he and Gittel decided to invite us, with our children and their children, to hear about their wartime experiences. After finishing our brunch, we sat together in their living room and listened to their stories: stories of forced labour, beatings, hunger, fear, disbelief, unimaginable loss, and ultimately, survival.

Madzia (known to us as Mattel), another of my grandfather's nieces and the first cousin of Gittel, was also brought to Toronto. She was sponsored in 1951 by my grandparents with help from Max and Gittel Glicksman, who had arrived three years earlier. Mattel had been taken from her home in Sosnowiec, Poland, to a concentration camp whose name remains uncertain but may have been Majdanek. She was the only member of her immediate family known to survive the camps. Upon being liberated, Mattel went to Brussels with a couple who had taken care of her in the camp. There, she met Aaron Erlichman, who would become her husband. He had moved to Belgium from Poland with his family as a young child and survived the war there because he was hidden by a Christian family. Aaron spoke French and Flemish, and Mattel spoke Polish; fortunately, they both spoke Yiddish. They immigrated to Canada with their first child, Charles, and arrived in Toronto in June 1951. They lived with my grandparents until they could find more permanent living arrangements. Aaron's first job was as a tailor on Spadina Avenue in the garment district. In 1958, he and Mattel rented a variety store at Bloor Street West and Manning Avenue. They lived above the store with Charles and their second son, Stephen, who was born in Canada. Those boys achieved what their parents could not. Charles became an oncologist, working first at the Princess Margaret Hospital in Toronto and then at the Mayo Clinic, where he was chair of the Department of Oncology from 2002 to 2012. Stephen, a lawyer with graduate degrees from Harvard and New York University, practised corporate law in New York and Toronto. He was the executive director of the Canadian Coalition for Good Governance from 2011 to 2018, and, in 2016, was noted as one of the "10 people around the world who have had the most impact on corporate governance."[6] The sons proudly celebrated their parents by having the laneway beside the variety store where all four had lived named Erlichman Lane, in their honour.[7]

I saw these relatives only at large family functions, but I always felt a deep connection to them, having first known about their plight in my childhood. I cannot comprehend what they endured during the war and how they survived, and I marvel at how their children managed, growing up with the after-effects of those experiences. My connections to these families made me more grateful for the secure life I lived and more sensitive to threats of anti-Semitism.

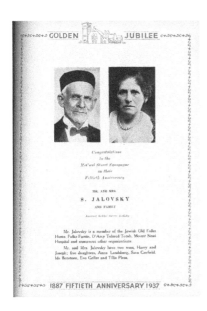

Bubie and Zadie in a program celebrating McCaul Street Synagogue's fiftieth anniversary, 1937

Helping relatives emigrate was one of many ways that my grandparents met what they saw as their duty to serve their community and give back. Despite their busy household and their meagre earnings, both of my grandparents were highly involved in their community. Alas, a program celebrating the fiftieth anniversary of their synagogue describes my grandfather's volunteer activities and none of my grandmother's.

The Jolofsky family's meeting place was "40 Grange," as we referred to my grandparents' home. The street was part of a larger Jewish enclave in downtown Toronto, where everyone knew each other. The kosher butcher shop was just a few doors away from my grandparents' house. The butcher, a large and jovial man, always greeted me with a big smile and then proceeded to pinch my cheeks, saying *"du bist a shayna maidele"* (you are a pretty little girl). The floor of his shop was covered with sawdust – presumably to cover the smell of dead animal parts, or perhaps to mix with any errant animal blood or fat so that no one would slip. I did not like going there with those smells and sights.

When McCaul Street Synagogue amalgamated with Goel Tzedec in 1955, the two congregations built an elegant new synagogue (Beth Tzedec) on Bathurst Street, three blocks south of Eglinton.[8] My grandparents soon followed and moved to a ground-floor apartment directly across the road from the new building. The move was an upheaval after all the years on 40 Grange. My grandfather especially missed Kensington Market, where he had previously done much of the grocery shopping. The market served the immigrant Jewish population then and continues to serve successive waves of immigrants today. There, my grandfather could speak Yiddish to the merchants and meet with friends. He could buy fruits and vegetables, or a live chicken or fish. (Disconcertingly, the live fish, usually a carp, would swim in the bathtub at home until my grandmother was ready to cook it.)

My paternal grandmother moved from Brantford to Toronto in 1935, just after her husband died. She lived in rooms on Baldwin Street before moving to Grange Avenue to live on the second floor of a house directly across the road from my maternal grandparents. It seemed odd that she lived on the second floor, given that she had an artificial leg, but those rooms would likely have been less expensive.

Bubie Pless must have been something of a trouper, staying behind with her son (my father) in Rokiskis while awaiting word from her husband as to when to leave for the new country. Then there was the trauma of having her leg amputated after she fell in London, followed by the trip to Canada, settling into Brantford, and adjusting to Canadian ways.

Bubie Pless was an observant Jew. While I don't remember her coming to *shul* with us, I picture her sitting at home with a prayer book on her knee, quietly praying on her own. She likely found it difficult to walk all the way to the synagogue, and then climb up the steps to the women's section, given that artificial limb. I also remember watching her wash her hands upon waking in the morning and reciting *modeh ani lefanecha*, the prayer that gives thanks for being alive for another day, and for having one's soul back from God, who was thought to have kept it through the night. I remember her as a gentle, soft-spoken, and kindly woman, with a pretty face and lovely soft skin. I liked to visit her and regretted not knowing her better. She had a stroke and I believe she stayed with us for a while after that.

Those years must have been especially hard for my father. Around the same time as his mother had her stroke, my brother was hospitalized with polio, and my mother was being treated for leukemia. The stress would have permeated the home in which I was living as a child. Although unaware of it at the time, these events likely prompted an interest in being a health care provider when I grew up. It would be one way to try to make the world a better place.

Bubie Pless holding me, about 1942

4 Childhood and Adolescence: My Mid-Century Toronto

My parents and brother were living with my grandparents at 40 Grange when I was born in 1939. I joined them there after my mother and I were discharged from Mt. Sinai Hospital some twelve days after my birth. Nothing was amiss – that was a typical stay for a delivery in hospital in those days. My dad paid $74.70 for Tillie's stay (and mine), which included $5.00 for use of the delivery room.[1]

We moved to the upper floor of a duplex at 15A Rusholme Drive when I was three. My only memory there is of our dog biting my grandfather, who was visiting. He had playfully hit me on the backside, and Tippy, ever my protector, bit him on the ankle. The bite was not serious and there were no hard feelings between man and dog; indeed, my grandfather seemed rather pleased that the dog was so protective of me. Outside the duplex was the ever-present, most delicious smell coming from the Neilson Chocolate factory just a block or so away. The aroma wafted through the air day and night.

When I was five, we moved "up north" to Glencedar Road, in an area known as Cedarvale, a middle- to upper-middle-class area of single detached homes, built mostly between 1920 and 1950. There were few mature trees and the street directly behind our house was mainly an open field. Ours was a nondescript, two-storey, three-bedroom

Me, about age two

home, clad in yellow brick, with a single-car driveway, an attached garage, and a good-sized backyard. It looked bigger than it was because it covered the width of the lot. Further south on our street, near the Cedarvale ravine, the houses were much larger and more elegant.

I remember a happy and loving household. I think my mother must have taught me the *Shema* – the prayer for bedtime – because she is explicitly mentioned in my version. The prayer asks God to keep one's soul safe through the night. I said, "*Shema Yisroel, Adonai Elohenu, Adonai Echad*" (Hear O Israel, the Lord our God, the Lord is one), and then I moved into a detailed list of family members to be blessed: "God bless Mommy and Daddy, two Bubbies and Zaidie [one grandfather had already died], Uncles and Aunties, Cousins and Friends. Make Barry and Judy, Tippy and my bicycle, good, strong, healthy boy and girl, dog and bike. Amen. Goodnight."

I think my mother was happy to have her own house, to decorate it, and make it a warm and welcoming place for her children and their friends, and for her and Mike's friends. When her friends met at our house to play mah-jong, I crouched down on the upper landing of the stairs and peered through the banister's rails, silently watching them in the living room below. I can still hear the tiles click-clacking and the women chatting – and I can almost smell the smoke from their cigarettes as it swirled up into the air. A group of women, taking a break from their day, laughing with one another, enjoying being together and away from their relatively isolated lives. Now and then the room went quiet, and I heard deep sighs as they shared something of their troubles, trouble with a child, or spouse, or an in-law, trouble with finances and illnesses.

A large weeping willow stood on the front grass near the road and acted as a playhouse for me when I was little. Its long green branches swooped down to make the walls of my house, whose floor was the grass beneath; cool to sit under in the summer, and still cozy in spring and fall. I was usually joined by a few dolls and sometimes our dog. Being close to the road, the willow sent its long, thirsty roots out in search of water that was there for the taking in the nearby sewer. I was heartbroken when the city Works Department cut the tree down and replaced it with an insipid little sapling of no play value whatsoever. Playing alone under that willow sounds melancholy, and maybe it was, but today when I see willow trees in the spring as their golden branches begin to turn green, or in the summer when they are in full leaf and offer their coolness, my heart skips a beat and reminds me of how much I enjoyed playing beneath that tree.

The flagstones on our front walk were perfect for hopscotch, once I scratched the numbers in with a stone. I skipped rope on the driveway and played ball against the side of the garage. I played games like "ordinary, moving, laughing, talking" or the alphabet one, "my name is Annie and I come from Alabama ...," among others. These alphabet people always came from American cities (or states), but I didn't think it odd that they weren't Canadian.

The backyard was a very good place to play. The flowers and bushes were low-maintenance and resistant to the impact of dogs, horseshoes, softballs, feet, and neglect. My dad usually planted marigolds, nicotiana (which we just called "nicotines"), and some petunias up against the back wall of the garage. Lilac bushes – a pale mauve one that always seemed on its last legs, and a more robust one with dark purple, tiny florets – bloomed on schedule in early spring. The fragrance of the lilacs was in the air for a week or more, drifting into the house through open doors and windows.

I attended John R. Wilcox Public School from Kindergarten through Grade 8. I don't remember being bullied, and although I myself was not always nice, I don't think I ever bullied anyone. When I arrived at school, I played in the girls' schoolyard, then entered the school through the door marked "GIRLS." Once in our classrooms, we girls were free to enjoy co-educational learning but, like the signs on the entrance doors, there were implicit pathways for us. As Adrienne Rich has pointed out, much of what we learned in school revolved around the accomplishments of men. We never thought about the not-so-covert message we were being given, "that men are the shapers and thinkers of the world." We didn't realize how "the content of education itself validates men even as it invalidates women."[2] We didn't see ourselves anywhere.

We began each morning by reciting the Lord's Prayer, and we sang hymns, as all Canadian school children did in the '40s. When we sang "Jesus Loves Me," I, and any Jewish classmates, never said the word "Jesus"; we just hummed at that point with our mouths firmly closed. Our actions show that we saw this situation as problematic, but we did not discuss it.

Children "got the strap" in my day and, although I was generally well behaved, I was afraid it would happen to me. My Grade 3 teacher was a tall, thin woman with tight grey curls and glasses, very upright in her stance. She seemed never to smile and was very strict. One day, she sent me out of the room – likely for talking – and told me to stand in the hall. I was certain I was done for. I know I prayed while I waited in the hall, "Please God, please don't let me get the strap." At the very least, I was sure I would get "the Ruler" – a twelve-inch wooden ruler smacked across the knuckles or maybe the palm. But it never happened.

As it turned out, I became something of a favourite – not a "goody-two-shoes," but a favourite, nonetheless. By Grade 8, the final year in my elementary school, I was being asked to do special chores, running errands around the school, and even answering the office phone sometimes. I was also asked to tutor a girl in Grade 2 who was having trouble with reading. As I saw her reading improve and realized I was partly responsible, it gave me a good feeling.

Life was good outside of class too. I was on the girls' softball team in Grade 8 and had several girlfriends and one boyfriend: he and I lived in the same area and walked home from school at the same time – but separately. On at least one occasion, he crashed into me, which I interpreted as a sign of affection. After school, I played on my own or with neighbourhood friends. With no television in our house in those early years, I also read – the Bobbsey Twins and Nancy Drew series, *Heidi*, *Little Women*, the usual girls' fare. And I took lessons: piano and ballet.

Harvey Silver, a musician who had his own Dixieland band and who taught piano in his spare time, came to our house to give lessons to my mother and to me. Harvey's method was to teach all the basics of classical piano but also to teach us how to use the chord notations in sheet music, which freed us up to play all kinds of popular songs. He was a gentle man, patient and soft-spoken. When he came for my lesson the first time after Tillie died, his eyes welled up, and his usually controlled stutter was apparent. He could hardly bear to look at me. I continued with the piano for several years – in part, perhaps, as a way to stay connected to my mother. Tillie had played "Till the End of Time," and I learned to play "Autumn Leaves" – both such mournful songs.

I started taking ballet lessons at the Boris Volkoff Studio a few years before my mother died. In an early lesson when I was probably seven or eight, the teacher told us to clap out a rhythm and then repeat it for our classmates to copy. I could make up a rhythm, but I couldn't repeat it for my classmates. I was upset when I came home and shared my worry with my mother, certain she would have a remedy. She told me to sing a song in my head, and clap in time with it. I mentally sang "God Save the King" – "duh tah duh tahh-duh tah; duh tah duh tahh-duh tah," etc. Not the most rhythmic tune but it worked.

I loved ballet. I loved the piano music that Margaret Clements played to accompany our pliés and relevés. I loved the makeup and costumes when we performed at the Eaton Auditorium. But I greatly feared Volkoff himself, dressed in his brown beret, baggy pants, and mustard-coloured shirt, circling the room, always stern and impatient, his presence even more ominous because of the stick he carried – a stick that was often aimed at one's protruding derrière.

I don't know who told the ballet school of my mother's death, but, when I returned to class after the shiva, my classmates gave me a framed reproduction of one of Degas's ballet paintings (*L'Étoile*) as a show of sympathy. I still have the picture, now battered and torn from years of bringing it along with me through life. I might have continued with ballet, but when I was about fourteen and dreaming of becoming a ballerina, there was a mysterious fire in the studio. It was several weeks until the place was cleaned up and we could return. But the still pungent smell of smoke and the sight of charred walls were too much for me and I quit.[3] I doubt I would have had the discipline to go on in any event, but stopping those lessons was not just a loss of a pastime – it was also the loss of another link with my mother.

My dad managed our family and our home for seven years after my mother died before remarrying. We had proper housekeepers at the start. "Aunty" Ettie, a pleasant older Jewish woman who was related to our next-door neighbour, was the first. She cooked familiar foods and kept house for us for a few years, but, despite the potential for her to relate well to us, we never felt close to her. Perhaps it was just too soon. Then Mrs Ellis

Backyard ballerina

My print of the Degas painting *L'Étoile*

arrived. I remember nothing of her background, but I see her still – a tall upright woman, with a kindly disposition, warm and caring. She was just what we needed at the time, and she became a favourite. When I was near the end of high school, and my brother had left for university, "business girls" lived in the small finished basement of our house. They cooked and did light housekeeping in return for their lodgings and keeping an eye on me.

I had no sense of growing up in privilege, in a house, in a good area of the city, with love and support and no want for (reasonable) material things. I did not know how fortunate I was. If anything, as I grew into my teen years with a typical teenager's perspective, I became aware of what living in Cedarvale was not: it was not Forest Hill. Forest Hill lay to the north and east of Cedarvale. It was a much more prosperous and, by many standards, desirable location. The Lower Village (south of Eglinton and east of Bathurst) boasted some of Toronto's most beautiful old homes, set on large lots on wide streets lined with decades-old trees, manicured lawns, and formal flower beds. The Upper Village (north of Eglinton) had a more mixed population and newer, less stately, but large homes. As a child, I was not aware of the affluence of my Forest Hill neighbours or the prestige of the area's schools, but I became acutely aware of both as I grew older.

In the summer, I went to sleep-over camp, in part to alleviate the need to have someone watch over me when school was out. Summer camp was common in the social environment in which I was raised. My brother went to Camp Northland – a boys' camp near Haliburton, and I

attended its partner camp for girls, B'nai Brith on Lake Couchiching, at Longford Mills, near Orillia. Both camps were run by the non-profit Jewish Camp Council. The Longford Mills camp had been built on the site of an Ojibwe settlement, which we were often told about, especially when we were on hikes and being shown specific areas.

My first year at B'nai Brith was in 1948, and I guess it felt quite normal, as my mother was still alive. The following year was different, as my mother had died just a few months before camp started. I have

My parents and a great uncle from South Africa (at left) visiting me at summer camp, 1948

since met women who were coun-
sellors at that camp who remember the time and the sadness and
disbelief it brought. They remembered my parents visiting me with
my great uncle from South Africa
that first summer and thinking
how well my mother looked –
dressed in a pretty dirndl skirt,
her white blouse fashionably tied
at the waist, wearing a smart summer necklace and earrings. It had
to be a sobering thought to know
that she died just eight months
later. My father looks distracted
in a photo from that visit, but not
to the degree seen in the one the
taken the following summer with
just the two of us.

I did not spend entire summers
at camp. I also went on small trips
around Lake Ontario, first with both
my parents, visiting with friends

My father visiting me at summer camp,
1949

and relatives here and there, and later, with my father. In 1952, when
I was thirteen, we visited with my aunt Sarah at the Gateway Hotel in
Gravenhurst. Sarah was something of a fixture at the Gateway, where she
spent many summers, on her own during the week and joined by her
husband, Ben, on the weekend. They were great ballroom dancers and
easily cleared the dance floor, cha-cha-ing and doing the tango. She was
always "up" during the summer, as flamboyant in her dress and speech as
she was on the dancefloor. Alas, her mood at other times of the year was
often very down – likely a result of a long-standing, undiagnosed bipolar
disorder. With no children of her own and a husband who was busy with
his dental practice (and with his dental nurse), Sarah's happiness seemed
to depend on those summer stays.

When we visited Sarah that summer of '52, she had a photo taken of
my dad and her and me. Mike is lying on the ground, Sarah is sitting
next to him, and I'm sitting on the far right at the front. Just behind
me, is the almost twenty-year-old waterfront director, Marty Friedland,
who, six years later, would become my husband. He just happened to
be in the photo. I took no notice of him, nor he of me. We learned about

From left: Mike, Aunt Sarah, Marty, and me at the Gateway Hotel, 1952

this prophetic meeting only when we saw the photo in Aunt Sarah's collection decades later.

I continued going to summer camp into my teenage years. At fourteen, I switched to Camp Kawagama, a co-ed, private Jewish camp near Dorset, just outside of Algonquin Park. Some of my high school friends were regulars at Kawagama, so it seemed like a good plan. My cabin mates had expensive clothing and sports gear, something that would not have had a place at my previous, agency-run, non-profit camp. Geraldine Sherman's later description of Kawagama in "The Girls of Summer," for the magazine *Toronto Life*, captures the polarized feelings that camp could engender: the need to belong, and the horrors of being left out.[4] I wasn't left out, but, as I was beginning to expect in life, neither did I quite fit in.

I experienced some of those same feelings when I first arrived at Vaughan Road Collegiate Institute for high school. My brother had graduated just months before I entered, and his presence lingered. He had been well-known for his roles in the Gilbert and Sullivan operettas the school put on; he was a great Mikado, and a fine major-general in *Penzance*, engaging and funny, albeit with a so-so voice. Everyone seemed to know him, and each new teacher asked me, "Are you Barry Pless's sister?" I didn't feel I quite belonged as a person in my own right.

There was a not-so-subtle division by gender for extra-curricular activities – and academic subjects – in high school. The boys played basketball and football while the girls cheered them on and did gymnastics. We participated in charity-oriented clubs while they joined the radio club. We were good at English and art, and the boys excelled in math and physics – or so it seemed.[5]

Gilbert and Sullivan operettas were left behind by my time; instead, we had *Brigadoon* one year and *Petty Harbour* – a Canadian musical – another. I had small roles in both, but more important at the time was the fact that rehearsals provided proximity to a boy on whom I had a crush. I don't think he and I interacted very much, but that was all right. High school, at least in my early years, seemed like a time for girls to be onlookers.

I adjusted to being "Barry's kid sister" and went out for different extracurricular activities. I became the treasurer of the Red Cross, the president of the Girls' Club and the "Simpson's Rep," which brought with it a Saturday-morning job at the department store of the same name in downtown Toronto. I was comfortable socially. I knew what to wear to be part of

Grade 13 class photo: with me second from left in the first row

the scene. I had my saddle shoes and socks, and my long skirts with a belt and a white blouse.

The proportion of Jewish students at Vaughan was large, and there was an awareness of our prescence. We tended to be high achievers and do well in sports, so there was a sense that the administration was happy to have us. I did not feel any open discrimination, and it was never a problem to be away from school for Jewish holidays. The student body was multi-ethnic and fairly close-knit, although we did not mix much outside of school.

My best friend, Joyce, and I laughed our way through many classes. We laughed at how one of the more-bosomy teachers seemed able to balance a book on her chest, and we laughed in every choir class we attended. The slightest incident could bring forth a knowing glance between us and a laugh that was hard to suppress. We talked a lot in class and did not always pay attention. In those days, we were expected to stand up beside our desks when the teacher called our name. One day, while Joyce and I were busy talking to each other, the teacher said something about having a "choice." Joyce stood up immediately, thinking her name had been called. And, of course, we laughed about that.

My grades in high school got progressively worse as the years went by and seemed to be negatively correlated with the amount of fun I was having. Several factors influenced my increasingly dismal performance: having fun with Joyce was one; becoming interested in boys was another. While, for the most part, we admired boys from afar, the time taken for that act of admiration added up. But there was also the issue of the learning environment. A tall, thin man with a full head of thick, silvery hair and a bright twinkle in his eye taught us trigonometry. He was probably a very nice man. He may even have been a good teacher, especially for those already good in math. You could see he loved the subject. But he quickly lost his temper with anyone who didn't understand straight off what he was trying to teach. From that class on, I had a strong antipathy to anything math related. Years later, when I studied statistics – a math skill that I desperately needed to learn or, at the very least, grasp the idea of – I was still affected. In contrast, our art teacher, a tiny woman (also with a fierce temper), instilled a love of art in me and made me feel I could do artistic work.

English was the subject I enjoyed the most, being lost in the stories and amazed at the analyses discussed in class. And I have always been grateful for having studied Latin, especially because it became so helpful for understanding medical terminology. I took zoology and have vivid memories of Joyce and me in the backyard on Glencedar, flashlights in hand, late at night, laughing as we dug up earthworms. We planned to cut the worms in half to observe each part regenerate into two separate worms – an act I now know to not be possible (except in certain species and then only if cut in a very precise manner). I doubt our marks in that subject reflected our in-depth, experiential learning.

From about Grade 11 on, I was "dating." To attend a dance or a party meant going with a date or, at the very least, with a group. No girl ever went alone. I, like my female peers, sat at home and waited for the phone to ring. As it got closer to Saturday night, it was difficult to decide whether to answer the phone if it rang. With no "call display," there was no way of knowing who was on the other end. Even if it were someone great calling to ask me out, that scenario could be outweighed by being seen to be available so late in the week. I was popular enough but not in the way that some girls were, with the phone ringing off the hook. It was such an awkward time.

High school, in my time and place, also meant fraternities and sororities. Delta Psi, one of four Jewish sororities in the city, invited me to join. I remember, and greatly regret, that when I became president of that sorority, I didn't try to change the process for joining. Sorority sisters put forward names and then voted to accept or "blackball" the nominees. I am embarrassed to now recall the whole phenomenon of a sorority and know in my heart that we did harm to girls who wanted to join but were left out. Some of them would have been, like me, from "the other side of the tracks" (as in *not* from Forest Hill), and therefore likely not as welcome. I never knew why I had been asked to join. Indeed, I always felt different from the other girls, living in Cedarvale, not having the wealth their families had, and, of course, not having a mother.

Meetings were held at each other's homes, but I don't remember holding any meetings at my house.

I like to think the sorority did some good – mainly in the way of raising money for charity. We held a tea in 1955 and raised $600 for the Canadian Cancer Society, a commendable act for teenagers then, even as it would be now. The idea of raising money for a good cause would have been instilled in us through the religious tenet of *Tzedaka* – of fostering justice or being righteous – as well as by the example set by the adults around us. In my grandmother's day, the concern was mainly to help the poor and the sick within their own community. By the late '40s and early '50s, fundraising was for the new state of Israel. The mothers of most of my sorority sisters belonged to Hadassah, a women's fundraising organization established in Canada in 1916.[6] I never knew my mother to be involved, but Marty's mother was a dedicated member. Jewish women and men soon also lent their support to more secular causes, particularly in the arts.

A note in my scrapbook

I started going to some university fraternity events when I was still in high school. My scrapbook tells me that the "boy" who would later become my husband was at one of those events. I was with a date at a dance put on by Sigma Alpha Mu ("Sammy"), the Jewish fraternity to which Marty belonged. I must have had a good look at him because the note in my scrapbook says, "Sammy Sweetheart Ball – Beautiful Affair. (Marty Friedland, sigh!)"

When it was time to start working in the summer, it seemed natural to find a job at a camp. Although too young at fifteen for jobs at a regular camp, I was hired as a junior counsellor at Boulderwood, a camp for underprivileged children. The camp, located in Gravenhurst, was run by Toronto's University Settlement House, founded in 1910 during the early years of the settlement house movement in North America. Like other settlement houses of the time, it addressed the needs of its neighbourhood's poor and immigrant populations, providing various health and social services, and educational programs such as English language classes, music lessons, and sewing classes. My mother and her brothers and sisters had all taken advantage of activities at the University Settlement House when they were growing up. Years later, the same settlement house was providing an opportunity for inner-city children to learn new skills in a safe camp environment while appreciating nature and making new friends. And it gave me my first summer job.

Sandy, a good friend of mine, also worked at Boulderwood that year. The program director at the camp, and in the city, was Bill Stern, a highly respected social worker. He had an easygoing manner in the midst of what often seemed to us like chaos. I learned a great deal that summer about how to work with children and how to handle groups. I watched in awe as one of the senior staff members never raised her voice above a gentle and calming tone, thus lowering the temperature of often out-of-hand situations, a lesson that I like to think stayed with me, at least in work situations, if not always in my personal life.

It was a difficult job, trying to keep some measure of control over the kids while also tending to their many unmet emotional needs. On our only day off, Sandy and I went to see my dad, who had rented a cottage nearby with some friends. I was not paying attention when I got out of his car, and I slammed the door on my own index finger. My nail had to be removed and the nail that grew in its place remains misshapen to this day. It's a reminder of the exhaustion from working so hard that summer – and the exhilaration from learning so much. It was the time when I first became aware of poverty and how social services helped families. At some level, I began to think about a job where I could feel I was promoting social justice in some way.[7]

The following summer, when I was finally the age to be taken as a counsellor in training – a CIT – I felt ready for more. Fortunately, I was a good swimmer and had earned various life-saving certificates during my summer at Camp Kawagama. Those qualifications were enough for me to secure an assistant swim instructor position at a new camp for young children. Camp Wahanowin was on the very site in Orillia where I had attended Camp B'nai Brith as a child, my old camp having recently relocated. My brother was the head counsellor at the camp, but that didn't affect my role, as I was responsible only to the swim director.

Relationships made at summer camp were unique. The living situation was intense, and relationships bloomed – and withered – at an accelerated pace. There was a lot to be learned, socially, in this hothouse environment. In the first year, I met up with a friend of my brother's whom I had dated a little in the city. He was just visiting the camp – ostensibly not to see me – but we did, nonetheless, have a romantic "encounter." The fact that he was drunk and several years older somehow made it all that much more romantic and dramatic, as far as I was concerned.

The following year, when I was a junior counsellor at the same camp, I had a few almost platonic, but physical, relationships with male staff. These summer "flings" provided an opportunity to learn to flirt and navigate a relationship. They never went beyond the limits of what was expected of a "good girl" in those days, almost a decade before the widespread use of the birth control pill. I was kept busy enough socially throughout Grade 12, and, by the winter of Grade 13 (then the final year of high school), I had a steady boyfriend.

The summer of 1957 marked a turning point in my young life. I was eighteen and considering a job as a swimming instructor at another private Jewish camp, White Pine. It was a new camp, having been established in Haliburton just the year before. Joe Kronick, a former social worker who owned and ran the camp, set high standards. He was highly respected in the camping world and much loved by all who knew him. Before signing my contract for the job, I wanted to know more about what my position would entail. Joe suggested I contact the person who was going to be the head of the waterfront: Marty Friedland. The name was certainly familiar – what with me having written that note in my scrapbook ("Marty Friedland, sigh") only two years earlier. So, sitting at the kitchen table in our house on Glencedar, I nervously dialled Marty's number, my heart pounding. I told him Joe had suggested I call to get some details about the job. I tried hard to sound nonchalant. I asked what the job would entail. I don't know what I expected to hear – maybe something about the hours, the types of classes we would give. He said, "Don't worry, it won't be too difficult." That was reassuring. But then he added, "You won't have to stand on your head and spit plug nickels or anything." I had no idea what that meant. Not then and not to this day. I've asked Marty what it meant, and he claims not to know either. This encounter was intriguing and sort of funny. I'm sure I giggled. It made me think there might be some fun ahead.

I accepted the position, notwithstanding the vague parameters for the job. I left my steady boyfriend at home in Toronto but took his picture with me and set it on a little wooden shelf beside my bed. We were in a good relationship, and I was not looking for anyone new. I looked forward to his visiting me on my day off. Then, the intensity of camp life came into play. I spent all day, each day, on the waterfront with Marty. We gave lessons to individuals and cabin groups, and twice a day we kept watch over a hundred or more kids in the water during general swims. We blew our whistles regularly and shouted, "Buddies up!" and then nervously counted the pairs of kids in each swimming area, making sure that all were accounted for. We spent time planning special waterfront activities and we conferred over the progress reports we wrote to the campers' parents. There were few conflicts and lots of laughs. He was a good boss. We got along well and started spending some time together in the evenings. Something was happening.

When the day came for my boyfriend to visit on my day off, I left camp with an uneasy feeling. He picked me up, and we drove off to a nearby resort to spend the day together. He drove me back to camp later in the evening and we said goodbye in the parking lot at the outer edge of the camp area. I started down the now dark camp road on my own, lost in thought about the day that had passed. I hadn't gone far when I saw someone coming purposely toward me. How Marty knew when I'd be back, I don't know, but he greeted me by taking me in his arms.

Our romance blossomed.

I wrote a letter to my boyfriend in the city, apologizing as best I could.

By the end of the summer, my "boss" on the waterfront and I were in a committed relationship and planning to marry the following June.

Back in the city, we found ourselves at Lake Ontario, standing on what we now think was Pier 4 at the foot of York Street, gazing at the water together rather like we had done all summer. Marty gave me his fraternity pin – a small octagonal pin of black onyx with the Greek letters Sigma, Alpha, and Mu in gold in the centre, and studded all around the outer edges with tiny seed pearls. He leaned over and pinned it on my sweater just over my heart. Being "pinned" is a dreadful expression when I think of it today, but, in the custom of the day, it was quite natural and considered preliminary to being engaged.

It was all moving very quickly. Marty was certain about our relationship and knew he was ready to marry. We had known one another for less than two months (aside from those two quasi-encounters years before). And other issues beyond the speed of this courtship gave me pause for thought. I had just graduated high school and was about to start a three-year diploma program at the University of Toronto. My intended had already completed a four-year undergrad degree in commerce and finance and was going into his third year of law. I had yet to set foot on the U of T campus, while he was already a "big man on campus," involved in all sorts of activities, including debating and athletics and having done a stint as president of the Students' Literary and Athletic Society at University College. I had travelled to a few small towns in upstate New York and had never been outside of North America. He had hitchhiked his way across the United States during school holidays and had spent a summer in Africa with World University Services

(WUS), seeing parts of Europe on the way. No doubt all of this attracted me – but it was also intimidating.

Our engagement came as a great shock to many people – to our parents, to other girls who had seen Marty as a good catch, and, of course, to the person I had been so committed to before going to camp. But it was something that, once put in motion, seemed to move forward of its own accord. To use the Yiddish expression, it seemed *bashert*, or meant to be.

5 Daughter, Stepdaughter, Sister: Relationships Reconfigured

Growing up, I was never aware of my role as a daughter. I think I was dutiful – but then, not much was asked of me. I was not given any unusual responsibilities after my mother died: no cooking or cleaning or laundry. Sometime before my mother died, we began to have "help" in the house. We needed it when her health was failing, and, after she died, we needed someone to look after us and our home. I never thought of it as being privileged. If anything, I disliked the intrusion – no matter how helpful the help – a feeling that has remained through my adult life.

Once my brother had left for university, it was just my dad and me at home. We were good companions. After dinner, we'd watch our brand new, tiny, black-and-white television. There were hardly any stations, but whatever was on, my dad, who was lying on the sofa, had no trouble falling asleep to it. I sat on the floor in front of the set – and did homework while I watched. Neither of us gave the TV our full attention except when Percy Saltzman, "the Weatherman," came on and showed where changes were happening by circling those parts on the map with a piece of chalk. He ended his report with what became his trademark – throwing the chalk up in the air.

Within a few years of my mother's death, my father started to go out socially with other women and eventually began, I believe, to look in earnest for a mate. He was just forty-six when Tillie died, and it would have been distressing to think of going through the years that lay ahead on his own.

In addition to the set-ups arranged by friends and family, Mike had his own contacts through his work: women who were divorced or whose store-owner husbands had already passed away were also on the lookout for a mate. Mike had been a widower for seven years when he found Sally, a widow, the mother of two boys, aged eight and eleven, and the owner of a successful upscale women's wear shop in Kitchener. It seemed a good time for Mike to move on.

Mike and Sally planned to split their time (unevenly) between her home in Kitchener and our home in Toronto. The plan was for them to come to Toronto and stay in our house with me for one or two nights mid-week and for me to go to Kitchener on weekends. A business girl would have the little apartment in our basement in return for looking after the house and me. Why all this change could not have waited for one more year until I was finished high school and was in university, where I could live in residence, was never discussed. I think I was so looking forward to gaining a mother and a lovely new home that I never really thought about it.

The end of our lives at 174 Glencedar loomed. Mike and Sally married, and Mike moved into her large, modern, split-level house with manicured lawns and flower beds, very unlike the horseshoe and baseball grounds at our place. On the other hand, it felt like we were moving up in the world.

Sally's house was not decorated to my taste, but it was definitely elegant. The front entrance opened into a spacious foyer with a patterned black and white tile floor and walls with murals of a leafy pastoral scene. Floor-to-ceiling cream-coloured, heavy drapes hung in the living room and dining room, and there was lush creamy-white broadloom throughout. More dreamy murals covered the walls in other rooms, and pleasant paintings hung everywhere. A formal flower arrangement for the dining room table was delivered weekly.

The dining room in the house in Kitchener

Despite these material plusses, it's hard to believe that Mike didn't realize he was getting into a difficult arrangement. Sally's first husband had died by suicide, and it had to have left scars on her and her two sons. There were likely problems in the family before that event, and so all three brought considerable baggage into the union. Of course, my father also brought baggage of his own, primarily in the form of memories of a beloved wife and mother who had died a tragic death, and perhaps there were also some guilt feelings over leaving me at home more or less on my own. Although I never acknowledged it at the time, I must have felt abandoned (again) during this period – this time, by my father's remarriage rather than my mother's death.

Storm clouds also gathered on the work front. Mike intended to decrease the time he spent on the road and gradually increase his time working in Sally's store. Surely, he thought, he could help with the buying after having sold women's coats to storekeepers for all those years? However, at fifty-three and having always been his own boss, he likely didn't take kindly to Sally's criticisms as he was learning the ropes, and she was likely impatient and unwilling to give up control.

Another sign of potential difficulty was the difference in their financial situations. The eventual sale of our house on Glencedar became a contentious issue when two-thirds of the proceeds were kept for my brother and me (by law) because my mother had died without a will. Mike was still paying off hospital bills from Tillie's illness, as there was no universal health care in Canada at that time.

In the interview my brother did with my dad years later, Mike said that his marriage to Sally "was a horrible mistake – I knew that by the third week we were married." It took much longer for me to feel it had been a mistake.

My last year of high school was difficult, what with being more or less on my own for most of the week and then going back and forth to Kitchener (with my boyfriend) on weekends. Mike and Sally's marriage made for a major change in my life and was a great upheaval for me emotionally. I was not doing much schoolwork, and I worried that I might not have good enough marks for university.

I also worried about what to study in university. I didn't know whether I should do a BA, like most of my friends, or take the course in physical and occupational therapy (P&OT). My interest in P&OT had been sparked when I was sixteen and a volunteer for a few weeks at Woodeden, a camp for "crippled children" (as they were then called), near London, Ontario. My dad had discovered Woodeden while on his travels selling women's coats in the area. He thought I would find it an interesting experience.

If I started out being proud of myself for volunteering at Woodeden, not knowing a soul or anything about children with disabilities, I was soon chastened. Not long after I had arrived, I was given the task of supervising a group of children on the playground. The children, all of whom had some form of physical difficulty, were busy with different activities and everything seemed all right. Then, out of the corner of my eye, I watched as a girl with cerebral palsy, around ten years of age, walked unsteadily about the area. I did not notice that she was getting close to a black iron "horse." The horse was moving rhythmically back and forth as children "rode" on it. In a split second, the girl was in front of the horse as it came forward. It knocked her down. It also managed to knock out one of her teeth. That memory is indelible. Of course, I blamed myself; it was something I could have prevented, and I was terribly upset. I had already taken a stance in life that said I must try to control what I could, especially when it could prevent bad things from happening.

The time I spent at Woodeden made me aware, again, just how lucky I, and everyone I knew, was. During the previous summer at Camp Boulderwood, I saw, for the first time, children whose families lived in poverty. At Woodeden, I saw, also for the first time, children living with physical disabilities. These experiences, along with my own family's illnesses, must have influenced my decision to become a health professional. However, my decision to enter P&OT did not come easily. It's not that I wanted any other professional course. I certainly never thought of medicine, engineering, or law. They might be fine for my brother and my husband, and lots of the boys I went to school with, but not for us girls. Other than Dr Peters, I did not know of a female doctor. What I wanted was an arts course and a BA. In part, I wanted it because of the degree itself – P&OT granted only a diploma – but primarily I wanted it because I wanted to take those kinds of courses. I wanted to study English and history and sociology and maybe philosophy or a foreign language. So, it was a matter of P&OT or arts. I didn't know how to make the choice.

Somehow, I arranged a meeting to discuss my dilemma with the director of rehabilitation medicine, Dr Albin T. Jousse. He oversaw the P&OT program and was also the director of Lyndhurst Lodge, which housed the program for people with spinal cord injury. In addition to his medical training, Dr Jousse had first-hand knowledge of physical disabilities because he himself had syringomyelia, a progressive disease of the spinal cord.[1] A kindly, soft-spoken man, Dr Jousse welcomed me into his office and patiently told me why it would be better for me to choose P&OT: "You can always come back to university to do a BA, or you could even do a BA part-time, but it will be too hard to come back to do an intense professional program like P&OT." Of course, the unspoken reason for why it would be so hard to come back to do a professional course was the likelihood that I would marry and have children and would not be able – or inclined – to return to school full-time. I decided to follow the path he suggested.

The house on Glencedar was sold, and I went to live with Aunt Emma and Uncle Harry Landsberg for my first year in university. Marty was still living at home with his parents, so our lives were similar in that respect. We both settled into school and, by October, we were planning our wedding, which would be in June the following year.

Although Sally never took on much of a mothering role, I think she was trying to do so at the beginning when she helped with my wedding. She came with me to buy my wedding gown, and she arranged with one of her dress manufacturers on Spadina Avenue

My wedding day, 1958

to make the bridesmaids' and maid-of-honour's pale-yellow chiffon, harem-skirted dresses. She held an engagement party for Marty and me in Kitchener, and likely organized the wedding dinner and reception at Beth Tzedec Synagogue in Toronto. My very stylish "going away" outfit, a grey shift dress with a large white collar and bow, came

from her store. I know Marty and I planned our wedding party, who would march, who would speak, and so on, and we picked the music and the band – Benny Louis – but Sally may well have done the rest, along with the "wedding consultant," the famous Miss Dryer from Eaton's Department Store. It was a grand wedding.

Time went on but our mother-daughter relationship never grew. I did not feel I had gained a mother – and Sally probably did not feel she had gained a daughter. When our children came along, the grandmother role did not take hold for Sally beyond the (very beautiful)

With Marty after the wedding

Our daughter, Jenny, at eighteen
months, in an angora wool dress

outfits she bought for them. The white carpets in her homes and the white clothes that she often wore did not bring her closer to our naturally messy babies. There were no offers of babysitting.

Meanwhile it was becoming clear that Mike and Sally's marriage was not doing well. Selling the store and moving from Sally's house to an apartment didn't help, and neither did a move to Toronto. Stress was always in the air. Mike sought to leave the relationship a few times. By then, he was in his late 60s, and divorces in that age group were rare.

I finally realized, after what for me was a particularly nasty occasion, that my efforts at improving my relationship with my stepmother were misguided. It was Mother's Day, and we had given Sally and Marty's mother, Mina, beaded summer necklaces. Mina was delighted with hers. Sally sent me a note. After some introductory remarks, she wrote, "I hope you meant well when you purchased your gift for me, but I hate to see you waste your money on things that you know I would never use. I consider your taste above junky beads – and I'm hoping that you don't consider me in that category – or was that deliberate, and you do?" I was eight months pregnant with my second child at the time, and may well have been overly sensitive, but I was extremely hurt by her words. Mother's Day had been a painful time for me for almost two decades by then. This exchange was heartbreaking.

By 1970, Mike and Sally had divorced. Mike moved into a small one-bedroom apartment in Toronto. It overlooked a beautiful ravine, and that view, along with his renewed independence, seemed to bring him some peace. While he was adjusting to his new status, and with no barriers in his way, he became more a part of our family life – spending more time with our kids, helping out when we had our third child, Nancy – and he also got back together with his old friends. The stress was pretty much gone for him and for us. However, all of that changed less than a year later, when Marty was asked to work with the Law Reform Commission of Canada in Ottawa. With us gone, and my brother and his family in Montreal, Mike would be very much on his own. This time, I felt that I was abandoning him.

Four years later, however, Mike married again. May was also a widow of a small-town Ontario storekeeper, this time from St Catharines. She was a perfect partner for Mike, and they had twenty-two happy years together before his death at age ninety-four. She was a lively, warm-hearted, kind woman with a good sense of humour. She loved Mike dearly, and, in her eyes, he could do no wrong. She paddled with him in his canoe, changed her unhealthy diet to his much healthier one, and even relearned to ride a bike so she could cycle with him. May easily integrated into my family and my brother's family, and she cherished her role with our children. She was a good stepmother. She brought her own family, with whom she was very close, into her life with my father. This new set of relationships was stimulating for Mike, as he now had even more people to whom he could lend his always-ready-to-listen ear. May even integrated into "the gang," Mike's card-playing friends and supporters from way back – something Sally had never managed to do.

My daughter-as-caregiver role didn't fully kick in until Mike and May had a serious car accident. Mike was eighty-nine when he drove through a red light and hit a truck that was making a left turn. Fortunately, the driver of the truck was not injured. Both Mike and May were injured, and from then on their lives were limited relative to their previous level of activity. Time at the cottage ended, and coming to our place for meals increased. I became something of a care manager for the two of them, albeit from a distance. I was the one to consult on various health issues and was also the go-between, arranging the extra help they needed but were reluctant to have. I was the one they would call at night when they were on the way to the hospital because of Mike's angina. It was a difficult time – but so clearly time for me to give back. There was great love between my father and me, and I felt almost grateful for the opportunity to care for him. I've often thought that this caregiving in Mike's last few years made mourning his passing relatively easy: I knew I had done my best.

Like my stepdaughter role(s), my sister role was not straightforward. Growing up, Barry had been an attentive big brother. I have a slight recollection of the time when he had polio. I must have been confused and concerned when he had to be hospitalized. He was in his early teens, and I was about seven. For some reason, he was admitted to the Toronto General Hospital and not the Hospital for Sick Children.[2] At that time,

My brother Barry and me, in front of the house on Glencedar, 1947

children were not allowed to visit patients in hospitals. However, my father, wanting to reassure me that my brother was all right, snuck me in. I stood on his feet and he used his coat to cover the two of us as he walked in. I doubt we fooled anyone for long, but I did get to visit. Barry needed physiotherapy for a time but otherwise did well and came home after a month or so.

After Barry went off to medical school at the University of Western Ontario, we never lived in the same city again. The older-brother advice that had been freely dispensed while I was growing up became less frequent – not because I was any wiser in his eyes, I don't think, but because our social environment had begun to shift. The six-and-a-half years between us started to shrink when it seemed all right for me to be included in some events with his friends. On one memorable occasion, my brother asked me to join with them for an opera performance – probably to fill in for someone who couldn't attend. The Metropolitan Opera Company of New York toured each spring, and Toronto was on its schedule in 1955 with a performance of *Aida* at Maple Leaf Gardens. The Rotary Club transformed the Gardens from a hockey arena to a quasi–concert hall and used the event for fundraising. We sat in the "greys" – the least expensive seats, at the very top of the arena. At one point, I stood up and promptly fainted. It was hot, we were up high, and I probably hadn't eaten much that day. Despite this nasty experience, it was the start of my lengthy love affair with opera.

When I began to date some of Barry's friends, it put me on a different footing with my brother. I was invited to Western for a few football weekends and had an early taste of what university social life was like. It was good for my ego – and probably spoiled me for being more interested in "older" boys.

My engagement to Marty marked another shift in my relationship with my brother. We were used to a dynamic where Barry played the big brother role, leading the way and providing advice. Now I was leading in some respects. I was marrying first and setting up house. Barry and Marty had known each other when they were younger. Marty even remembers being at our house on Glencedar for a party or two that Barry gave. Now they readily engaged in conversation on many topics: on their high-status professions, their university lives, and their love of classical music.

It took Barry a long time to marry. He met Ann – who would eventually become his wife – while still at medical school, but their religious differences took time to work out. Ann was a staunch Catholic and, while Barry's belief in religion was already shaky when they met, he still carried with him the traditions of his early upbringing.[3] Ann grew up in England, in Surrey, near London, and had trained as a physiotherapist. She had come to Canada to work and travel, intending to return to England. But then she met Barry.

Ann was part of a close-knit family, all of whom were religious. For whatever reason, I don't think the family had known any Jews before Barry came along, something that became clear to me a few years after Barry and Ann married. Marty and I were living in England for his graduate work, and Ann's mother, Florrie, had invited us to tea. She also asked her sister to join us. Among the tea sandwiches were some with ham. The sister said, "I'll have one of these – I'm no Jewess you know!" Although I quickly decided that this comment came from a lack of exposure rather than any anti-Semitic feeling, I was certainly taken aback.

At that same visit, Ann's mother showed us pictures from my brother's wedding, to which we had not been invited. I knew Barry and Ann were being married in a civil ceremony but was surprised to see a parish priest officiating. My brother's marriage took some adjusting to; however, my dad and I were accepting and welcoming – we were happy to see Barry, by then thirty, settle down. For our extended family, however, the marriage posed more of a problem. In 1962, marrying out of the faith was still considered a *shonda*, a disgrace, to some of our relatives. Indeed, my grandparents were never told of Barry's marriage: they went to their graves lamenting the fact that he had never married. Uncle Harry, the life-long bachelor who was himself in a secret relationship with a woman who was not Jewish, told Barry that he should not have married Ann.

Ann and I had a good relationship. Our similar professional backgrounds drew us together initially, and we had a number of interests in common, especially with each of us having three children, all of whom were born within the same seven-year period. In later years, as I went back to school and back to work, there was less to keep us connected.

Ann had intended to return to physiotherapy when they settled in Montreal, but rigid licensing issues in Quebec stood in the way. In mid-life she took some courses in counselling and was involved in various community endeavours. However, arthritis, which had plagued her for many years, gradually took its toll and limited her activities. How much depression may have played a part in limiting her horizons can only be guessed at.

Early on, with just one baby each, our two families vacationed in Italy, in Tirrenia, a seaside town near Livorno. By then Barry was a pediatrician, which was reassuring for me with my eighteen-month-old-child. And I think Barry and Ann benefited from having us there as the more seasoned travellers. As the years went by, we made a determined effort to get our families together and have managed to meet somewhere every few years.

Barry's career flourished. Like many researchers, he travelled a great deal, for conferences where he delivered papers and to meetings of various associations in which he held executive positions. And, like most wives, Ann remained home with the children. In his own words, during a speech when he was given an honorary degree at his alma mater, he rued his absences, saying "you always pay a price for the time you are away from home." Nonetheless, he was much loved by all.

If I thought the sister role had threatened my own identity in my teenage years, I soon realized it was nothing compared to what happened once I became engaged to Marty. He was then (and ever after) a high-achieving, smart, and attractive man, already well-known in various social and legal circles. Just as I had been Barry's kid sister, I was soon known as "Marty's wife." Given the times, and the fact that my goal, like that of almost all of my female peers, was to be married – and the sooner the better – this label was not something to complain about. Marrying someone already accomplished and clearly headed for a secure future was especially desirable. I barely registered any sense of threat to my own identity. However, I remember a telegram sent to us at our wedding, and the feelings that washed over me as I read it: "Congratulations to the Gold Medal boy and the Golden-Haired girl." It was a clever telegram, but I know I was rankled by the idea that my appearance should be equated with Marty's academic achievements.

Growing Together

6 Student/Wife/Worker: My Roles Begin to Multiply

Most weeknights during my first year of university, I studied in what is now the Gerstein Medical Library. Marty was usually there with me, and I saw then how disciplined he was; how he stayed focused and didn't seem to tire or get restless when he was studying. We took breaks, usually to go out for a smoke – we were both pack-a-day smokers at the time – but it was usually me who instigated the breaks.

Once we were married, and I was in my second year and Marty was articling, we did most of our studying in our one-bedroom apartment in the Brentwood Towers, a newly developed complex at Davisville and Yonge. Unusual for its time, five buildings were set within a large, landscaped area complete with shrubs and flowers, ponds, bridges, fountains, and even swans. We decorated our place with what is now reverently referred to as "mid-century modern" – with teakwood furniture of Scandinavian design. Sisal carpeting, which was inexpensive (and scratchy to walk on barefooted), covered the living room floor, and we used bricks and plywood boards to construct a desk and bookcases. The apartment backed onto Oriole Park and was just a five-minute walk to the subway and shops. From our south-facing balcony on the tenth floor, and with so

few tall buildings in the way in 1958, we had a spectacular view of downtown Toronto. We could even see the lake on a clear night. The location of the apartment and the way of life it facilitated became the template for future moves: near public transportation and grocery shops, an interesting view, and nature nearby.

I wanted to keep a kosher home, and Marty was happy to go along with it. He certainly didn't care

Brentwood Towers. From an old 1950s/60s postcard, posted on the website of architect Robert Moffatt

about it as much as I – but his Jewish upbringing had been traditional too, so it seemed natural. I ordered meat from "Ben the Butcher" because that was what my aunts did. We had two sets of dishes (one for meat meals and one for dairy), as we did when I was growing up. And we didn't mix milk with meat. However, as for many Conservative Jews – the "rules" could be broken outside the home. Not only would I eat "out," but I would have foods not deemed kosher. I purposely avoided pork chops and ham, but somehow bacon seemed acceptable. Hard to explain for sure.

These early years of marriage were not easy. Being a student and a homemaker – even though it was only for the two of us – was difficult. I was losing touch with my own circle of friends as I moved into Marty's social environment. Moreover, I didn't fit in that well in physical and occupational therapy (P&OT), and P&OT didn't fit that well into the University of Toronto. "Campus life" meant nothing to me. I was in classes all day and then hurried home to get dinner. There was no time for clubs or sports. Meanwhile, my high school friends were mainly in arts and science and in University College. Their course load was lighter, and they could hang out in the JCR, the Junior Common Room. There was never time in my day for that – and, even if there was, I would not have gone, conscious that it wasn't for me.

Hart House – for men only. Courtesy of University of Toronto Archives

One of the few university-based activities I engaged in was to go with Marty to Hart House to hear Boyd Neel's Chamber Orchestra. But from the moment of what felt like a furtive entry to the building, I felt uneasy. I knew that I was allowed in the building only because I was the guest of a male. It was the end of the '50s, and women would not be fully welcome in that building until 1972. Some five years after his death, the conditions of Vincent Massey's gift to the university that had restricted entrance of females to Hart House was changed.

I found the P&OT course stimulating, and I worked hard to do well. It was a heavy course, preparing us to work as either a physical therapist or an occupational therapist or, potentially, for a job that called for both. Our schedule was jam-packed all day, every day. It was physically as well as intellectually exhausting, with lectures in different locations across the entire campus. It was possible to do well in some of the subjects by just "knowing the ropes." In chemistry, for example, if you acquired the lecture notes from the previous year, then you knew precisely what would be on the exam, as the content never changed; you could memorize the answers and pass the exam with having very little understanding of the subject. Boys from the School of Practical Science (aka engineering) tutored us in physics, and we figured out how to come to adequate answers for this course too – also with little understanding. Our (male) profs seemed to assume we could not understand, and we (female) students also assumed we would not understand.

It was different in anatomy, which was taught by Kathleen McMurrich, a highly knowledgeable anatomist who, with her initial training as a physio, was "one of us." I loved anatomy and can still smell the pungent odour of formaldehyde in the lab where we tended our prosected (already dissected) cadavers. Medical students had done the initial dissection, and what was left when they were finished was given to us. Dressed in our white lab coats and armed with dissecting instruments, four of us stood around each cadaver and looked for the origins and insertions of muscles, the course of major nerves, bony prominences, and various landmarks of interest.

Our knowledge in anatomy was tested in written exams but also with a much-dreaded "bell-ringer," where we had to identify anatomical specimens as we moved at the sound of a bell, from station to station where they were displayed. There was no time to linger at any one station, and woe to the person who was still ruminating over the last specimen when it was time to be looking at the next one. Like all my classmates, I was terrified of the bellringers.

We enjoyed our classes in "meds and surg" (medicine and surgery), where top-notch physicians (and surgeons) came to lecture and talk about their cases. It was there (and in anatomy and physiology) that we gained most of our medical knowledge. I was particularly fascinated by our courses in psychiatry, held in the auditorium of the Toronto Psychiatric Hospital (TPH). Lectures were usually on a particular mental illness. Following the clinical description came the case history of an actual patient and then an interview with that patient. The lecturers were prominent psychiatrists on the staff of either TPH or the Queen Street provincial psychiatric hospital: Mary Jackson, Bill Mitchell, Abe Miller. We felt privileged to be their students. Psychiatry was, by far, my favourite course. There was something about the many theoretical explanations and ideologies that made it attractive to me; answers weren't cut and dried – there was an opportunity to think more broadly to problem solve and find a way to help.

About half of our class time in the occupational therapy component of the P&OT course was given over to theory and application. The application component was where we learned several crafts and analysed the cognitive, physical, and emotional abilities they required. These analyses were crucial to our understanding of how to find the right craft or other activity for our patients: one that would suit their interest and require just the right amount of effort and concentration to be stimulating while, at the same time, bringing success. Those courses were fun: weaving, sewing, copper work, leatherwork, and ceramics all gave us a chance to enjoy our creative side. We experienced what it was like to be fully absorbed in a task and (usually) feel proud of something we had made with our hands. There were frustrations as well. When we found it difficult to thread a loom, we appreciated how our patients would feel when they were given an activity that was not graded to their level of ability, where success would not be achieved.

Crafts had a long history of use with people in asylums. They were also used with those soldiers injured during the First World War who required a long period of convalescence. Crafts staved off boredom, taught skills, raised morale, and built self-esteem. Many of my classmates made fun of the crafts and saw no point in them as therapy. Such scepticism had been apparent decades earlier. In 1929, after occupational therapy and physical therapy had been established as separate courses at U of T, the student newspaper, *Varsity*, made fun of their modalities of treatment: "Basket-making was instituted as a course a few years ago [referring to OT's establishment in 1926]. This year sees the opening of a course to train expert masseurs [referring to PT]. Whether or not a tonsorial course will be started next, we do not know." The *Mail and Empire* picked up the story and asked if the university was becoming a trade school.[1] Sir Robert Falconer, the president of the university, came to our defence, saying that the courses were supported by physicians and surgeons, while Dr Primrose, the dean of the Faculty of Medicine, noted that basket making and the massage course were very minor parts of the curriculum and both were both of practical use.

Over the years, occupational therapy came to see crafts as "old-school" and limited their use. Only now with more understanding of why crafts were used in those early years, and how they can be useful today in some circumstances, are they again finding a place. Crafts can still be used to teach cognitive skills of concentration, following instructions, and problem solving. They can also be used to build self-esteem, to divert feelings of pain or sad thoughts, and to encourage socialization.[2] Their value has increased greatly with the current emphasis on health and wellness and the importance of creativity more generally. Nonetheless, many occupational therapists still cringe when crafts are mentioned.

While being educated within the Faculty of Medicine at the University of Toronto made those of us in the P&OT program feel special, we nonetheless also had a sense of being second class. Our program was housed in old army huts on Devonshire Place at the corner of Hoskin, where the magnificent Massey College – designed by architect Ron Thom – now stands. The huts were primitive, and, although they had been renovated, they did not lend themselves to learning. Our teachers were practice oriented: they were highly thought of within their professions but did little or no research. The program itself was overseen by male physicians, whose presence seemed to constrain the autonomy of those who were otherwise responsible for its administration. We were taught to be respectful of the medical hierarchy and to act accordingly, which made it difficult to assert our views.[3] This relationship has changed somewhat over the years but was still apparent just over two decades later, when I became a faculty member. Alas, I am told by new graduates that many feel a similar sense of subordination today, and the literature continues to report the concern.[4]

The program required four months of interning in the summer between second and third year. I spent two months in physical therapy at the Hospital for Sick Children and two months in occupational therapy at the Toronto Psychiatric Hospital (TPH).[5] The former was an emotional experience because of the children I treated: it was heart-wrenching to see them deal with their illnesses and injuries, and to see their parents, so frustrated by their inability to help and so consumed with worry. But my experience at SickKids was negatively affected by a strict and overbearing supervisor. Our interactions brought on a level of anxiety that was paralysing rather than motivating for me. In contrast, I enjoyed all aspects of my experience at TPH. It was thoroughly stimulating and filled with challenge. The hospital itself was an old and unattractive building on Surrey Place just above College, but it housed the sharpest minds around. I was intensely interested in my psychiatric patients and convinced I could help them. I worked hard to establish a good rapport with each patient with whom I worked, and I learned how to modify my ways of interacting to suit each one. I found the case conferences, where hospital staff met to hear about a patient's history and diagnosis and discuss what could help, riveting. I was surprised to find that while I was nervous at having to provide a report on a patient under review, I managed to appear confident.

I worked with some patients on the wards, but I mostly worked with those who were well enough to come to the Occupational Therapy

Department, which was just a few steps away from the hospital in an old church building.[6] Nursing staff generally brought the patients over, happy to see them off doing something of interest.

I took advantage of every opportunity to learn during that placement; I read widely, observed an electroconvulsive therapy (ECT) session, and attended as many lectures and noon-hour case conferences as time allowed. It was 1959, and occupational therapy was a highly valued service in most psychiatric facilities in North America and in the United Kingdom. At TPH, the team of psychiatrists, nurses, psychologists, and social workers, all respected the OT role. It felt good to be doing something worthwhile, to be in an intellectually stimulating environment, and to experience the camaraderie. I knew that I wanted to become a member of that team when I graduated.

Of the sixty or so students who entered the P&OT program with me, only two other women were Jewish, and one of them had to leave for health reasons after our first year. It seemed like most of my classmates had never met anyone Jewish, and I was always a little on edge that something anti-Semitic would be said, not openly but veiled in some way. On one occasion, I was in the cafeteria at the Toronto General Hospital with Vera, a classmate and good friend. We both had Eastern European ancestors – she was Ukrainian and Greek Orthodox. Her dark hair seemed enough to make her look more Jewish than me, as I was quite fair. As we stood in line for our food, we realized that the volunteer serving us was the mother of a new graduate of our program. We asked where her daughter was working. "Oh," she said, "she's at Mount Sinai Hospital." Then, she quickly added, in an apologetic and perhaps embarrassed tone, "It's really alright at Mount Sinai, you know; they treat her very well." My dark-haired friend, knowing that Mount Sinai was "the Jewish hospital," was embarrassed for me. She took her tray and walked on. At that point, the woman became flustered and said to me, "Oh, dear, I hope I haven't offended your friend. She's Jewish, isn't she?" Whereupon I replied, "No, but I am."

This exchange was not surprising. It was still a time of open discrimination at the university and in the hospitals: when higher entrance grades were required of Jewish applicants to medicine, and Jewish doctors had difficulty finding hospital appointments. Mount Sinai, established in 1923 at a time when no Toronto hospital would hire Jewish doctors, was not given teaching hospital status until 1962. The Toronto General Hospital, notorious for its anti-Jewish policies, hired its first Jewish doctor just six years before my encounter at the cafeteria.[7]

Discrimination also extended to other health professionals. In 1931, W.J. Dunlop, who oversaw both occupational therapy and physical therapy for the Department of Extension, wrote to President Falconer asking for advice about what he saw as a "knotty problem." He wrote that, in the previous year, one Jewish physiotherapy student had been placed at the Toronto General Hospital and, while she was "not of very marked Hebraic appearance," some patients refused to have her work on them. He went on to say that, in the current year, there were four Jewish students, and he was concerned that there might be trouble ahead if "the rule against Jewesses in the Hospital [is] enforced."[8]

Some students in my class were from wealthy families that belonged to the Granite Club or the Royal Canadian Yacht Club, where Jews were explicitly not allowed. To this day, when I meet with former classmates, I worry that something will be said that I will see as discriminatory, no matter how innocently (or ignorantly) it is offered. Not long ago, I met with former classmates to plan an alumni reunion, and, as we discussed the costs, someone suggested we could "act like a Jew" to get a better price. I was appalled, but hardly anyone noticed the derogatory reference, and no one (including me) commented on it.

I made some good friends in P&OT. I was very close with Vera – the Greek Orthodox, Ukrainian classmate who had been mistaken as being Jewish – with whom I later worked at TPH. She lived part of the year in Montreal and part in Trento or Milan, or wherever her Italian mathematician husband, Giorgio, taught. Their various homes were small and

With my friend Vera (at right), 1960

simple and beautifully decorated with interesting furniture and art and vibrantly coloured fabrics. The garden at their house in Montreal burst with colour. Dinner was always superb and accompanied by just the right wines. Vera herself was dressed and coiffed in a wonderfully elegant but simple style. We kept in touch over the years and visited one another in Canada and abroad. I became closer with Vera some years after she received a breast cancer diagnosis. When the metastases were no longer under control, despite the various regimes that were tried, I had planned a trip to Montreal for a last visit. I was away at a conference when Marty phoned to tell me she had died. I was terribly upset: it seemed so wrong that I had been busy giving a paper (and feeding my ego) and had not managed to visit in time to provide support and say goodbye.

The P&OT class of 1960 in procession across the front campus

I've also kept in touch with Holly. We had been close friends at school and resurrected our friendship five decades later at a time when her husband, formerly a surgeon, was diagnosed with dementia and I was diagnosed with breast cancer. Our old friendship proved a powerful source of support for both of us over the time that followed. Old friendships have a way of bringing us back to our earlier selves and seem to play a special role, particularly in times of need.

I did well in P&OT. I graduated in 1960 with honours, standing second in my class and winning an award for the highest marks in occupational therapy theory courses. If I had felt inadequate coming out of high school with poor marks, I now felt more confident. I had some proof that I could do better.

Following my graduation and Marty's call to the bar, we left for England. Marty had a scholarship to do a year of postgraduate work, and we looked forward to living in London and travelling around the Continent. I was excited about the possibility of working at the Maudsley Hospital in London, probably the most prestigious psychiatric facility in the world at the time. I had an interview with the chief occupational therapist, and we discussed job options. We decided, however, after Marty had discussions with potential supervisors for his work, that it would be better for him to study at Cambridge. I would have thought about how it would be better for me to be in London at the Maudsley, but I certainly didn't suggest that we consider that in making the decision. We had been married two years by then, and I would not have been thinking much about my future. We were in England for Marty's career.

Fulbourn Hospital, Cambridge, original building, 1856

Not that there would be anything wrong with living and working in Cambridge! Bob and Ruth Ehrlich, Torontonians who were in Cambridge that year, graciously put us up while we hunted for a flat. I found a job at Fulbourn Hospital, the state psychiatric hospital, about eight kilometres outside Cambridge, near Newmarket. I arrived at Fulbourn to see a series of large and rambling old brick buildings with just a few newer structures. The hospital stood on a lush green expanse of land that seemed to stretch on for miles. It had opened its doors in 1858, and an article in the *Journal of Mental Science* four years later described the hospital as progressive. It noted that no mechanical restraints were in use. Patients were kept occupied primarily with work-related tasks. The article went on to say:

> The whole asylum bears the aspect of some large house of industry. The female patients, seated at needlework in their day-rooms, or washing in the laundry, or cooking in the kitchen, or engaged in the various household arrangements, would hardly by a casual observer be recognised as persons of unsound mind. So, also, in turning to the male department. Parties of ten or a dozen working in the garden or engaged in the detail of agricultural labour present little evidence of insanity. In the several workshops of the tailor, the shoemaker, the carpenter, the smith, the basket-maker, the baker, the brewer, are patients daily engaged at their respective trades. Employment and the confidence shown by the implements and tools entrusted to the patients have evidently replaced the old means of coercion and restraint.[9]

Fulbourn had embraced ideas about the importance of activity implemented in the moral treatment era in the early 1800s in both England and France.[10] Patients were treated more compassionately and they were engaged in work-related activities, which, in turn, made their behaviour more manageable. When I arrived at Fulbourn a full century after that description of Fulbourn's patients' activities, gendered work of some sort was still seen as a major factor in patients' well-being: the women mended, did laundry, and cooked or served food; the men worked the land or did maintenance tasks indoors. Those who did not work were either unable to do so because of the severity of their mental or physical conditions or were about to be discharged.

The idea of patients doing work for the benefit of the institution was controversial, especially when they were not being paid. But the need for some form of occupation was widely accepted and doing work-related tasks that would be familiar to many of the patients made sense.[11] Among those patients who were not doing work for the hospital were those who came to the occupational therapy department to do crafts. I worked with them on two of the wards: Adrian, for patients who had been acutely ill but who would likely recover after a short time and be discharged, and Treetops, for those who were chronically ill and had been in Fulbourn for years and would likely never be discharged.

In the short-stay acute-care unit, we used what were then current approaches to treatment, including the therapeutic community, first implemented by the psychiatrist Maxwell Jones after the Second World

War. Fulbourn's medical superintendent, Dr David Clark, further developed the concept a few years before my arrival.[12] In this approach, the hospital environment was used to teach the skills needed to live in the real world that lay outside. Staff and patients met together for regular meetings to plan activities and deal with conflicts and concerns. Group activities facilitated social interaction while also teaching skills for daily living, such as meal planning, banking, or interviewing for a job. The approach was a perfect fit for OT, teaching the skills needed for everyday living.

Treetops housed chronically ill women, much as it had done for decades. A few of those women came regularly to the Occupational Therapy Department and pursued handicraft projects, and I brought craft materials to the others who would not venture off the ward. They greeted my visits with more curiosity than interest, and they were difficult to engage. Early on in my work on that ward, one woman, referred to by all as "Lady Sarah," called out to me from where she sat in a chair that stood against the wall. I came over to see what she wanted. I leaned forward and said "Hello." Maybe I said, "Hello, Sarah." Typically, we would not call a patient by a made-up name like "Lady Sarah." Within seconds, Lady Sarah slapped my face. I don't remember it hurting – but, of course, it stunned me. There was no point in responding. It was not clear whether she was affronted because I had not called her "*Lady* Sarah" or the slap arose from some other unrelated reason. What *was* clear was that she was unaware that she should not have hit me. I remember other patients coming over and being solicitous in their way.

Another occupational therapist or a nurse and I took patients on "outings" into Cambridge periodically. We went by bus into town, and just getting away from the institution and being a part of more normal life was a tonic. Depending on our patients' level of functioning, we adapted our walks to be around the colleges or through the town to look in shops or to visit the market or the Fitzwilliam Museum. No matter where we went, our trips to town always ended with tea, usually at the Whim, a venerable establishment on Trinity Street near the colleges.

Even among the variety of town and gown residents in Cambridge, my group *always* stood out: old "good" clothes dug out just for the outing, frequent mutterings to themselves, and an unsteady gait, along with some foot shuffling, both usually due to overmedication. They were a mixed and somewhat motley crew. But this act of going to town and having tea in a restaurant, this act of normalcy, was treasured by all.

I learned to speak "English" when I worked at Fulbourn – changing my vocabulary to communicate better with my patients and co-workers. Cookies became biscuits, thumbtacks were drawing pins, the trunk of my car was a boot, stores were shops. I came to appreciate the perfect colour of the tea that the head nurse ("Matron") poured at our meetings.

As time went on, I felt very much at home. The occupational therapy staff were young and close-knit. One older woman, a fine craftswoman, worked as a therapy aide and was very supportive to us. The occupational therapist in charge of the whole department was a petite, powerful, and pretty woman, Rosemary Huggins, who was about thirty-eight at the time. A graduate of the occupational therapy course at Dorset House, the oldest such program in the United Kingdom, she was smart and well travelled and spoke several languages. We

With Rosemary Huggins and Marty, Cambridge, around 2014

became good friends and remained so until her death in 2021.

Living abroad was a transformative experience for me. I had barely been out of Toronto before I married. I'd been to New York State to visit my cousin Carol and some friends of my dad's. One of those trips got me to Cooperstown and the Baseball Hall of Fame – something I later lorded over my son, a great sports enthusiast. I had gone on a high school exchange trip to Canandaigua, also in New York State. I had gone to Detroit a couple of times, where I had another cousin, and to Ann Arbor, where I had a good friend. That was it. Living in England and travelling around Europe opened a whole new world for me.

Marty and I travelled during the summer when we first arrived and again the following summer before we left, all in a spiffy red Sunbeam Alpine convertible. It was strange that, having never owned a car and having no money to speak of, we went all out with this purchase. It was irresponsible, but Marty had some scholarship money that we could blow because I had a job, and we rationalized that the tax we saved by bringing the car back with us to Toronto made it a good deal. Something like that! We picked up the car at Rootes Motors on Piccadilly, an area of London where such a flashy sports car fit right in. It was a stunning though highly impractical car.[13] With only a jump seat in the back and a very small trunk, it was hard to take any passengers or much luggage. It had a left-hand drive, which made it difficult to drive in the United Kingdom but would be fine on the Continent and back home. I wore the requisite headscarves and sunglasses to go with a convertible.

We set out that first summer toward Paris. On the first day in northern France, we bought bread and cheese and tomatoes and had a lovely picnic by a quiet river in Chantilly. The next day, we had an unplanned

With the Sunbeam Alpine

stop at a small hotel in Senlis, just a half-hour or so away. I had become desperately ill with a fever and diarrhea. A doctor came. He stood by my bed and listened as I described my symptoms in my best high-school French. After taking my temperature, he exclaimed, in a mixture of French and his best English, "Beaucoup de fièvre … Je pense, je pense . . . one hundred ten." It took us a few panicked moments to realize he had made an error in translation.

I recovered and we carried on through France and Italy. Then we crossed the Adriatic by car ferry to Greece, disembarking at Igoumenitsa. After a short time back on the road, we picked up a hitchhiker, who didn't mind being scrunched up in our so-called back seat. However, a trio of expert Swiss travellers just behind us on the road noticed that our passenger made our already low-to-the-ground car perilously lower. They stopped us to say it would be better if they took the hitchhiker. After a day or so, the hitchhiker left us and we travelled on with our new Swiss friends. They guided us through famous sites as well as out-of-the-way villages. Unlike us, they had planned their travel. Furthermore, they knew how to stop each day at a decent hour and relax over a drink before dinner (also unlike us). We left them at Mycenae so that we could go to Epidaurus, on the off chance that we might get tickets to the opera playing that night at the ancient amphitheatre.

I'm sure we didn't realize at the time just how lucky we were to get those tickets. The opera was *Norma* starring Maria Callas, then one of the world's most renowned sopranos.[14] Our seats (on large slabs of stone) were at the very top of the amphitheatre. Tired from our journey, I am embarrassed to say that we both slept a bit during that extraordinary performance.

We developed a love of opera together from Epidaurus on. Over the years we have planned our travel to include many of the world's great houses: the Met in New York, Chicago's Lyric, the Staatsoper in Vienna, La Fenice in Venice, the Palais Garnier and the Bastille in Paris, La Scala in Milan, the Royal Opera and Glyndebourne in England. While we were sometimes at odds about other cultural events – with Marty liking chamber music and jazz, and me preferring symphony and ballet – opera quickly became a shared passion.

We left our car in Greece and flew to Israel for the first of what would be many visits – and, in many ways, the least impressive. In 1960, Israel was still a struggling state, under-developed, heavily burdened with new immigrants, and uncertain of its ability to defend itself from its many hostile neighbours. In each future visit, we were awestruck by the changes we saw as Israel transformed itself into a modern country while maintaining its place in the Mediterranean and celebrating its history.

Guided by advice from our Swiss friends, our trip out of Greece took us to an astounding monastery perched high on a cliff in Kalambaka, Meteora, and into what was still known as Yugoslavia. Our little Sunbeam made a great impression as we carefully drove through crowds of goats on hillsides and into isolated mountain towns on our way from Sarajevo to Zagreb and on to Ljubljana. By the end of this first trip, I had passed from being a novice to an experienced traveller and would be keen to travel for the rest of my life.

During the year in Cambridge, we took trips to Scotland and Ireland, and in the summer before we returned home, we travelled in Denmark and Sweden and through Germany to Austria. All our trips were done on a shoestring. *The* travel book at the time was *Europe on $5 a Day* and, although we never quite achieved that goal, we were very frugal: cheap hotels, no fancy meals, shared desserts, few purchases. When we had trouble finding hotels that met our criteria, we improvised: sleeping on the hood of our car in a vineyard in Beaune – and in a large bathroom in Sarajevo, one of us on a small cot and the other in the bathtub.

In addition to the obvious benefits of travelling – of gaining new knowledge, adapting to new surroundings, becoming aware of different cultures and ways of doing – we learned how being away from one's everyday environment with all its stresses and expectations could be very freeing. Being on more "neutral" territory was good for our marriage. Discovering new things together led to a future with shared memories.

Living in Cambridge meant we could do a lot in London (just an hour or so away by train) on a day-return ticket. We went to plays and museums and we met up with friends. Phil and Di Weinstein had a flat in Gloucester Mews, and Stan and Alene Daniels were on the fourth floor of a house just off the Brompton Road. Marty had known both Phil and Stan in Toronto and each had known my brother. The husbands were in London furthering their careers, and the wives were, like me, accompanying them. Phil was studying town planning, the field he would pursue when he returned to Canada. Stan had abandoned his doctorate at Oxford and come to London to write music and comedy. When he returned to Toronto, he wrote for the *Wayne and Shuster Show* and then went to Hollywood to write for the *Dean Martin Show*, the *Mary Tyler Moore Show*, *Taxi*, and more, winning multiple awards along the way.

On one of our trips to London, we visited Buckingham Palace. In those days, visitors from the Commonwealth could apply to attend one of the Queen's Garden parties – unless, that is, they were the guilty party in a divorce. The materials that accompanied the application for the invitation stipulated that condition, which was removed in later years when the royal family began to experience its own divorces. We were fortunate to be "invited" to attend two of these Garden Parties, one in 1961 and the other in 1969. Both occasions were delightful: strolling around the gardens, taking tea in one of the many tents set up for the occasion, eating cucumber sandwiches, watching for a glimpse of their Royal Highnesses and other notables in attendance. It was great fun to get into a cab and say to the driver, "Buckingham Palace, please."

After returning home from that year in England, I took a job at the Toronto Psychiatric Hospital, the same teaching hospital where I had so happily interned as a student. I worked in the Day Centre, which was in the same old church building that housed the Occupational Therapy Department for inpatients. Day treatment programs were relatively new in the 1960s, offering a treatment option midway between in-patient and out-patient care.[15] Marge Murphy, a more senior colleague, and I ran the occupational therapy program for the Day Centre. Our program facilitated a more gradual discharge for those who had been hospitalized but still needed support and an opportunity to build more skills for daily living. We used the patients' dining room for social activities: for coffee in the morning, tea in the afternoon, and group meetings. The original pews in the central area of the church had all been removed and the space was left open with worktables at one end and a makeshift volleyball court at the other. Offices for the psychologist, the social worker, the OTs, and the psychiatrists ringed the hall. The space had a comfortable – and comforting – air about it. The original stained-glass windows of the church still adorned the area and gave it something of an otherworldly, calming effect. The Day Centre also had a ten-bed nursing station where ECT could be administered, and where a patient who might be feeling unwell could rest.

Now as a member of the staff at TPH, I had control over my work and could plan programs and initiate change. We ran the program in the Day Centre as a therapeutic community, much as I had experienced on the *Adrian* ward at Fulbourn. We held regular community meetings, and the patients and staff planned all the programs together. We assessed each patient upon admission to learn about their interests and their goals and to get an idea of their level of functioning. Knowing the importance of socialization, especially for patients on their way to being fully discharged into the community, we primarily ran group programs, including current events discussions, groups crafts, music appreciation, and cooking.

We also ran some longer-term projects, including the production of a play. A play provided activities for a lot of patients, and not just those who had acting parts. Patients made posters advertising the play, worked on scenery and costumes, and did make-up. At the performance, they took tickets, greeted guests, and directed them to their

Current site of the Toronto Psychiatric Day Centre building, much as it was in 1961

seats. All activities were carefully matched to our patients' skills and abilities and adapted as needed to provide a level of personal growth. By the end, there was a sense of togetherness and achievement that lifted everyone's spirits and gave many patients a newfound measure of confidence.

Another memorable project involved painting classes given by a well-known artist, Jack Pollock, who owned a gallery just a few blocks away on Elizabeth Street. Jack was a supporter of all things related to mental health, and he gladly provided us with lessons. Our patients enjoyed the experience of finding themselves fully engaged and learning something new. To reciprocate for the painting lessons, the group decided to make a window box for the outside of Jack's gallery. The project provided tasks for patients who worked at different levels, including measuring, purchasing materials, constructing and painting the box, and buying and planting the flowers. Participation in group programs like these provided opportunities to work on problem-solving skills as well as the social skills needed for living back in the community, all in a supportive and safe environment. We wrote up our program for the *Canadian Journal of Occupational Therapy*.[16] It was my first publication.

My work as an OT at TPH fostered my own growth. Comments from patients and staff contributed to my feelings of success. I knew I was doing good work. I was very happy in that job. I would never have thought to leave TPH had I been on my own. But in January 1963, much to my dismay, we returned to Cambridge for another six months so that Marty could satisfy residency requirements for what had now become a doctorate. By then, he was thirty-one years of age and an assistant professor at Osgoode Hall Law School. Soon after our return to Canada, he joined the University of Toronto as an associate professor with tenure in the Faculty of Law, and his trajectory as a scholar was clear. He quickly became a full professor and, in 1985, a University Professor, attaining the highest professorial rank possible. U of T would be his academic home for the next fifty years and counting, and his achievements would make him one of its most accomplished residents.

The trip back to Cambridge was necessary for Marty but not for me. I did not want to leave my job at TPH. Marty and I had not discussed the plan to go back to Cambridge in any depth, and we certainly didn't consider the possibility of me staying back in Toronto: that would not have crossed our minds. Nor did I consider this disruption to my life as unfair. It was unfortunate and sad for me, but there was no question I would go with him.

7 New Roles: Motherhood and Living My Husband's Life

While the first trip to Cambridge was an adventure, this second felt like more of a duty. It was hard to get excited about it. We left Toronto at the end of December 1962 and stopped in Funchal, Madeira, for a few days. We stayed in modest quarters and rang in the New Year with chicken soup while watching fireworks from a rooftop patio – apparently a common tradition. I did not enjoy the tourist activity of being pulled down the cobblestoned hill on a wooden sled (a large two-person wicker chair mounted on wooden runners): that was crazy. But I was feeling very down at the time, and maybe nothing much would have been to my liking.

Renting out the apartment in Toronto, packing up, leaving the job that had brought me such satisfaction, leaving family and friends again, was all stressful. I had let my former boss at Fulbourn Hospital know that I was coming back, and she told me that the only position open was on a ward known to be difficult. That did not appeal to me at all. I was too tired and too unhappy. We would only be away for six months, and I decided to just lie low and wait it out. I'd find something to do.

We rented a second-floor flat on Hartington Grove, just off Hills Road, and a short bus ride from the centre of town. I decided to teach myself to type. I knew it would be of help to Marty, and, in fact, I typed the first draft of his doctoral thesis.[1] And I did some creative writing. I wrote some poems and a few short stories – including one that was built around a noxious odour that I truly thought I could smell at night. In my story, a mysterious chemical smell emanated from the famous Cavendish labs not too far from where we lived. It was an attempt by an enemy group, my heroine suggested, to slowly poison all those bright Cambridge minds. A little scary to think what my subconscious might have been trying to express.

Cambridge in January is cold and damp, and the days are short and dark. I emerged from our flat periodically to shop in the market in the centre of town and go to the laundromat. Otherwise, I stayed in, ruminated on my state, and wrote letters home.

And I read.

I read some of the many classics I had missed – and whatever else I fancied. Where could there be a better place to do that than in England? I huddled in front of the electric fire in our sitting room with my book and my knitting and my cigarettes. I had mastered the art of knitting and reading at the same time – and smoking was such a habit by then – that it required no

Coffee and cigarettes, Cambridge, 1963

attention at all. I had been smoking officially since the age of sixteen (and unofficially since about twelve, when I smoked with my older cousin Vicki in the bathroom at our grandmother's house). Most people I knew smoked, and certainly everyone I knew who worked in psychiatry smoked. By 1963, Marty and I were each smoking about a pack a day – a horrifying thought, knowing what we know today.

I read the Brontë sisters, Jane Austen, George Eliot, Virginia Woolf, Sylvia Plath (and Ted Hughes), Dickens, Hemingway, Fitzgerald, a little Proust, Kingsley Amis, James Baldwin, C.P. Snow, the Durrells, and more. Never a very fast reader, I relished the opportunity to linger over each book, usually not wanting it to end. I bought the books at Heffers or Bowes and Bowes in Cambridge, at a time when books were reasonably priced, and I brought all of them back home to Toronto, where they took pride of place in my bookshelves.

I have little doubt that I was depressed during this period. The early years of marriage had been difficult in many ways. It was hard at first just to be a newlywed and a student. Then it was hard to work in Cambridge without any of the usual supports, and then to start what I thought would be a more long-term position at TPH in Toronto, only to have to leave for Cambridge again after just sixteen months. After almost five years of marriage, I had become less certain about who I was. Being taken back to Cambridge and away from the work that I had found so fulfilling in Toronto made matters worse. Not working fed my sense of isolation and general sadness. Marty, on the other hand, was fully engaged in his doctoral thesis and involved in the life of a graduate student. We were in separate worlds. Mine was constricted and inward looking, while his was expansive, filled with interesting new people, all within an exalted university atmosphere.

Gradually, the quiet time alone with my books brought some solace. I began to see the present in a better frame; it was, after all, just a step along the way, not necessarily the way of the future. Bit by bit, my spirits began to lift; good thoughts started to creep in, along with the warm weather of spring. Among those good thoughts was one about having a baby. It suddenly seemed like the time was right. I was twenty-four – around the average age for women in Canada to have their first child at the time. Ideas about work moved into the background. Motherhood would be a new adventure.

I was excited to learn I was pregnant. I was also a bit anxious, and I was glad to have three friends with whom I could discuss pregnancy and childbirth: Janaki, from Sri Lanka, was expecting her first baby at the same time as I was; Nancy, a nurse from Toronto whom I had met at a nearby laundromat, was expecting her second child soon and had personal and professional knowledge to share; and Jean, an American, who had just had a baby, gave me lots of opportunities to observe the job that lay ahead. None of these women had a mother or close friends nearby to turn to for information or reassurance, so I did not feel any different from them.

Knowing that our days of travelling would soon be curtailed, Marty and I took a brief trip to Spain before we headed home. We drove along the Andalusian coast, swam in the ocean, and ate good seafood. We even watched El Cordobes, the famous matador, fight a bull – something I could not imagine doing today, let alone if I were also pregnant!

On our return to Toronto, we bought a small, semi-detached house on Hillsdale Avenue East, not far from where we had lived in our first apartment. We renovated that house with the help of Jerome Markson, a fine architect, and a friend and who would be involved in our many home renovations to come. We were in the new house by the time Tom, our first child, was born.

Coming home from the hospital, I felt different from others who were having their first child. Their mothers helped get things ready for the new baby, many came to stay during those first weeks to help with the baby – and all would have made a fuss over their daughters. That was certainly not a role for my stepmother, Sally. We hired someone to help for those first few weeks, and then Marty and I just figured it out. We were both nervous in our new roles but also happily awestruck by this new experience. I adored holding and feeding and playing with that new baby (and the two that followed). I was completely absorbed in watching his development (and that of his two sisters). Nursing came relatively easily, and I enjoyed that simple quiet time when I could always be sure of comforting my babies. I had learned about nursing fifteen or so years earlier from a family visit with Dr Peters (the woman who had been my mother's radiation oncologist). I had sat with Vera in

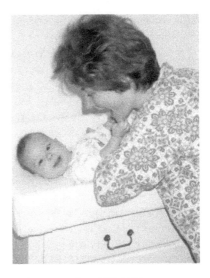

With Tom, our first child, 1964

her bedroom as she nursed her second-born daughter and made a point of showing me what she was doing: cleansing her nipples with sterile water, as one did in those days, then positioning the baby just so, and getting the baby to "latch."

My life now revolved around the new baby and the new home. I sewed curtains for the rooms, I learned to garden, and I made friends with some neighbours. Marty and I settled into being parents and even quit smoking, the US surgeon general's report on smoking and lung cancer having been published just a week after Tom was born. We were charting a new chapter of our lives together and, in that story, I had the leading role. Marty was involved, for sure, and took on tasks whenever asked, but we both knew that I would have control over this child-raising part of our lives. From the outset, Marty

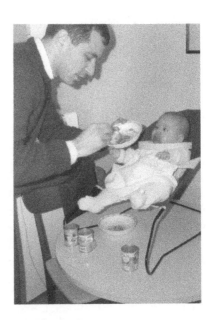

Marty feeding Tom

made me feel that he respected and valued the job I was doing, and that was of major importance.

I was doing well in the mothering business until Tom was nine months old, when I had a sobering and unforgettable experience. We had been in Kitchener visiting my dad and stepmother in the apartment where they were living at the time. When we were ready to leave, my dad came out to the parking area to see us off. I was carrying Tom, who was a big baby for his age. I was wearing high heels and a heavy fall coat. The shoes did not fit perfectly, having been bought on sale in England the year before and, because that October day was warm, I had the coat slung over my shoulders. Suddenly, I wobbled on those improperly fitting shoes and that made my coat fall off one shoulder. I used the hand that was supporting Tom's back to pull my coat up and, in that split second, he flipped backwards. He fell over my arm onto the asphalt surface below. I was the one holding him, and he fell out of my arms. I was the one responsible. How could such an awful thing happen?

Tom cried for a few minutes (max). I screamed, scooped him back up into my arms, and kissed him profusely, the tears streaming down my cheeks, my heart pounding. We gingerly placed him in the infant car bed in the back seat of the Sunbeam Alpine (there were no infant car seats then) and drove as fast as we safely could to the hospital, leaving my father standing alone, shaken, in the parking lot. The nurse at intake asked what happened. By now I was crying almost uncontrollably. The nurse did not seem particularly alarmed. As she took Tom off for an X-ray of his skull, she said, "The baby looks okay to me – but you're a mess." The X-ray showed a slight fracture of Tom's skull – which we were told was probably helpful in that any swelling of the brain that might have occurred with the impact would have a place to go without putting pressure on the brain itself.

The Emergency Room physician thought Tom should be kept under observation for twenty-four hours – either there in Kitchener or in Toronto. We decided on the latter. We phoned Bob Ehrlich, our pediatrician, to say we were our way to the Hospital for Sick Children. He arranged for a top-notch neurologist to examine Tom on our arrival. Nothing new came up with that exam and, after twenty-four hours of observation, we three went home. Tom was back to his old self in no time.

For many years, my father would recall the incident and blame himself for not having caught Tom as he toppled down out of my arms. After all, he said, he had been a rugby player, and he should have been able to catch Tom as he was falling. It was good of him to try to share the blame – but ridiculous. Looking for a place to lay even some of the blame, I have never bought high-heeled shoes on sale again.

It took a very long time before we could find even a sliver of humour in this event. Imagine, dropping your child on his head and him turning out to be ever so smart? Could this be a new technique for improving a child's IQ? To the best of what we know all these years later, Tom was none the worse for wear.

Tom busy playing

When our second child, Jenny, was born a few years later, my world grew again. Now I had a "millionaire's family," with a boy and a girl. I loved going out with the new baby in the carriage, Tom walking by my side, and Tippy, the dog acquired just after Tom was born (and named after my childhood dog), in tow. The greengrocer, just a block away on Yonge Street, beckoned almost every day, feeding my addiction to fresh produce and just-in-time shopping. I had coffee with my neighbourhood friends and joined them canvassing for the Canadian Cancer Society. We played tennis on the nearby public courts in Davisville Park, our sleeping babies parked in carriages just outside the fencing. I enjoyed becoming a part of my local community.

In my quiet times at home, I sewed more curtains, made some mother-daughter dresses for Jenny and me, and knitted sweaters and mitts for everyone. My homemaking skills broadened: I became more adventurous in my cooking, and we entertained more often. I enjoyed the creative outlet these activities fostered, and I liked the compliments I received for my efforts. I worked at keeping the children engaged in activities that would hold their attention and stir their imagination: dressing up, doing crafts, baking with me, making Hallowe'en costumes. I loved chatting with them as we did our activities and was intrigued to see how their speech and thoughts were developing.

The garden at Hillsdale was small and in almost constant shade. Although we planted a few bulbs in the fall, as spring progressed and the trees came into full leaf, the only other flowers that survived were shade annuals like impatiens. But that was fine; rather like my backyard when I was a child on Glencedar, the area was first and foremost a place to play. There was room enough for a plastic wading pool on the wooden deck in summer, and a place to pile up leaves for jumping into in the fall and for building forts in the winter.

The routine at bedtime always included a story, along with not-so-subtle attempts to teach the skills of reading. The picture books we read had repetitive or rhyming words that could be anticipated and said aloud, so there was some subliminal sight-reading happening. We had an illustrated "alphabet frieze" decorating the upper part of their bedroom walls when they were preschoolers, which made them familiar with the sounds of the alphabet: the picture of a banana was soon connected with the letter B. Never seen as a lesson, it was just part of the ritual of going to bed. The ritual also included a "lie down," whereby I (and often Marty) laid down in the bed. We'd have a little chat and then I would sing a song or two. My repertoire wasn't large: "Hush Little Baby," "Toora-Loorah-Loorah," and my own rather direct "Shah-Shah Baby, Time to Go to Sleep." I enjoyed being a mother. I was in a good place. My world was not large like Marty's, or even like it had been for me when I was working, but it was good.

Making good on Dr Jousse's advice back when I enrolled in P&OT, I started taking courses toward a BA right after that first stay in Cambridge. I enrolled as a part-time student at Woodsworth College at U of T and, over the years, registered for courses that I had always wanted to take as well as others that just appeared interesting as I went along (History of Science and Technology, English, Religions East and West, Italian). No focus, no major. I did one course a year, except for the years when we were away from Toronto, and I did that for thirteen years. (I received two credits from my P&OT course to make up the fifteen needed for the BA). I was usually the oldest in the class but, as I had little time or need for making new friends, that didn't matter. I chose evening classes so that Marty could be home to look after the children. I left dinner ready but, otherwise, it was a night off for me and a time for Marty to be in charge. Those hours away from home – just being on my own – were precious, and they connected me back to my student self.

The BA courses were a nice pastime, and, as a wife and a mother of two, I didn't think I wanted for more. It was fine to be a stay-at-home mom in the '60s – but only just. Betty Friedan published *The Feminine Mystique* in 1963, but, when I read it, I didn't realize its potential impact. I thought then – and still do – that, if people choose to have children, *some one* (or some two) should take on a mothering role. At the time, there was no thought of parents sharing the parenting role, which now seems such a sensible solution.

I was not thinking beyond my mothering role to who I might be after those intense early years passed. I wasn't worrying about how hard it might be to get back into the workforce after a long absence. For that matter, I wasn't thinking about myself as an entity apart from my family roles at all. Had I been thinking more about women's roles, I would have found that a landmark course in women's studies ("The History of Women") was being offered at U of T by Professors Jill Ker Conway and Natalie Zemon Davis in 1971. The course was immensely popular and proved to be the solid starting point for a burgeoning field of study. If I had taken that course during my BA, my thinking about my future might well have changed sooner than it did.

By the spring of 1968, we had moved to a larger house, still in the Davisville area, on Belsize Drive. While we probably could have afforded to move into a not so large house in a more prestigious area, in Forest Hill or Rosedale, or at least Chaplin Estates just across Yonge Street, we had become comfortable in our area and saw advantages in raising our family in a less wealthy and more "mixed" community.

We bought the house from its original owner, a widow whose husband had died in the influenza epidemic in 1918, shortly after they had moved in. Buying the house in the winter, we had only her say-so that it had a beautiful garden. In fact, she had more than told the truth. As spring arrived, a spectacular garden appeared: scilla and snowdrops started the show, hundreds of daffodils and tulips followed, and the lilacs, forsythia, and honeysuckle bloomed thereafter. Spirea, peonies, irises, daylilies, and climbing roses took us into summer. Being a well-planned perennial garden, there was always something new coming into bloom, and we often took to "touring the garden" to check into the latest addition.

The focal point of the backyard was a fairly steep hill bordered by shrubs on one side and a rock garden with steps alongside it on the other. Our kids and their friends rolled down the hill in the summer and

sledded down in the winter. At the bottom of the hill was a large flat area of grass bordered on three sides by flowerbeds. A river (Mud Creek) had run through the land some fifty years before we purchased the house,[2] and there was some question as to whether that lower part of our garden was the original configuration and all the neighbouring lots had been filled in, or our lot had been scooped out by the first (and only) owner. The flowerbed at the back rose up to where it was level with our neighbours' backyard to the south.

The flat area of the yard was ideal for games of all sorts: tag, spot, red

Garden at Belsize

A natural skating rink in the backyard

rover, and even a little baseball. Winter occasionally brought just enough flooding for a natural skating rink to form.. It made for that special skating experience that cannot be found on proper rinks: having the place to yourself, staying out late into the night, maybe some light snow gently falling, the stars and a moon lighting up the sky, and all with easy access to hot chocolate.

For this garden, we had an excellent teacher in our Chinese neighbour. Mr. Young had his own well-established garden of flowers and vegetables when we moved in. He knew how to make everything grow and do well. In his limited English, he managed to tell us what we were doing wrong and what we should do to make it right. We took on gardening in earnest and developed a system: go to a nursery in early spring, argue about the merits of perennials (me) over annuals (Marty), and compromise in the end. Come home, plant, and repeat, spending a ton of money from spring through early summer. Of course, there were (good-natured) arguments about where to plant and what madly spreading things needed to be dug out or at least cut back. Marty generally did the planting and transplanting. I did the finer bits, deadheading, weeding, and pruning. Ultimately, we would both have to stop; exhausted, sunburnt, covered in dirt and perspiration. It was exhilarating and somewhat – but not altogether – satisfying. It was never a truly well-tended garden, but visitors who stood on the deck and only saw the overall view always complimented us on how it looked. True to our ways of looking at life, Marty saw the result of our efforts as near perfect; I thought it could be much improved.

The garden provided a rich and tranquil scene, always varying, with new blooms from early spring through late autumn, and snow-laden or icy branches in winter. It was truly an oasis of beauty, and it never ceased to move us. My dad would often sit and gaze at the scene. He'd take a deep breath, and say it was a *mecheyeh* (like a miracle). We felt very fortunate and grateful to have this rich view each day.

We knew when we moved into the house on Belsize in the spring of 1968 that, by the following December, "we" would be on sabbatical. In those years, most professors took advantage of the opportunity to be away during sabbatical leaves, and most wives accompanied their husbands. Marty had arranged for academic visits in New Zealand and Australia before returning to Cambridge for what would be our third stay. He had just published his doctoral work on double jeopardy and was working on a new project relating to law reform.

Our travel bug had been pushed to the side when Tom and Jenny were infants, and this sabbatical seemed a good time to bring it to the centre. It would be a long trip to New Zealand, so why not stop in Tahiti on the way? And on our way back, why not visit some old Cambridge friends, then living in what was still called Ceylon? It was an ambitious trip, and we would have to watch our pennies, but, with Marty's way paid by research grants, it was a great opportunity to see the world. Tom was just turning five and Jenny was two-and-a-half, so missing school was not a problem. I was excited about our adventure.

The trip started out in some diffi-culty. A brief stopover in Los Ange-les turned into a longer stay after Marty and Tom both developed the H3N2 flu (aka the Hong Kong flu). The pandemic had reached California just that month, and the only surprise was that my daugh-ter Jenny and I did not succumb. I found it frightening to be away from home and responsible for our fam-ily's health. However, the boys soon recovered, and we continued on our

Me, Jenny, and Tom in Tahiti, 1968

way, rewarded by a few idyllic days in Tahiti on the way to New Zealand.

I picture myself on that trip, quietly providing childcare, always on the hunt for parks with playgrounds, packing and unpacking as we moved from place to place – from Auckland to Wellington and Christ-church, then on to Melbourne, Sydney, Canberra, and Perth. It was dif-ficult, keeping the children engaged and being on my own most of the time while Marty worked on his research or met with colleagues. How-ever, it was winter at home, and hot and sunny where we were. I was still young – only twenty-nine – with a lot of energy and patience. I was frustrated from time to time, but not unhappy.

The visit to our friends in Sri Lanka was the only time during our travels when I would not be aware of my tagging-along status. It was also one of the few times in those three months of travel when I was in the com-pany of other adults. We had known Sam, as well as Sena and Janaki, in Cambridge, and came to know Nirmala after Sam married her sometime later. The husbands had been students with Marty in 1963. We stayed with Sena and Janaki at their lovely home in Colombo. Their son, Nishi, and our son, Tom, were born just a few weeks apart, albeit at opposite ends of

From left: Nishi, Janaki, Jenny, me, Tom, and Sena at their home in Colombo

the Earth. Nishi had toys, of course, and he and Tom and Jenny played happily by day and slept together in the same room at night. I did not have to worry about the children at night because there was a maid on guard; indeed, she slept on the floor in the room with them. There were peanut butter sandwiches for the children when they could not manage the curries. For us, the food was delicious and made us devotees of Indian food for life. Our hosts took us to jewellery stores for rings and bracelets set with the fine gemstones for which the country is known. Nirmala graciously took us to visit several Hindu temples. In Kandy, I watched while Tom, Jenny, and Marty rode on an elephant. Riding elephants was not my thing – not for political reasons but for preserving my own life.

It was good that Marty did not have any official business in Sri Lanka: no lecturing, no research, no meetings. Instead, we were just a group of friends getting together. Sadly, these two couples – one Hindu and Tamil, the other Buddhist and Sinhalese – were not able to maintain their close friendship during the many political upheavals that were to follow. We kept in touch with both couples over the years

Snowdrops and crocuses, looking toward the back of King's College Chapel, Cambridge, 1969

and visited them in Vienna or in New York where they each lived while working for different United Nations agencies. But all six of us were never together again.

Back in Cambridge by mid-March, for what was our third stay, it was spring. Snowdrops and crocuses were in full bloom, and the daffodils were peeping through the ground. There could hardly be a more beautiful place in the world. We found a good flat on Fen Causeway near Newnham Croft, the school Tom was to attend.

I could not work, given the children and the effort needed to make a temporary new home for the four of us. Jenny (tearfully) attended a local playschool for a few hours twice a week, and Tom could go to school on his own once we crossed him over the busy road at Fen Causeway. That gave me just enough time to bike to the market in the centre of town. We all had bikes that year. Tom had his first two-wheeler, and Jenny had a tricycle with a special carrier at the back for her teddy bear.

I loved the market in town. I had my favourite produce stall where the proprietor and I would talk about the origins of the various fruits and vegetables, some that I had never seen in my part of the world or knew by a different name: his courgettes for my zucchini, my eggplant for his aubergine.

There wasn't much socializing that year, given our babysitting needs, but on one memorably disagreeable occasion (for me), the four of us were invited to lunch by Marty's former supervisor, Professor Glanville Williams, in his rooms in Jesus College. It was a kind gesture, for sure, but so stressful for me as I tried to ensure that the children behaved during the meal. After lunch, we strolled the gardens of the college, the children and I keeping ourselves well behind Marty and his supervisor so they could continue to talk. The whole outing was unpleasant. There was nothing in it for the kids or me. Why were we there?

Back home in Toronto by the fall, I was expected to take part in the Faculty Wives' Association. With all good intentions, and similar to what other universities did at the time, the association endeavoured to help women adjust to their wifely roles in the institution where their husbands were employed. Faculty wives' associations were a concrete example of how the social order saw women like me – as having an identity based on our husbands' positions. At the Faculty of Law, we wives organized our own group and met informally at one another's homes. I'm not sure why we were not involved in social causes on campus, as some wives were elsewhere, fundraising for scholarships or fighting for better student housing, for example.[3] Our "meetings" were more social and less activist oriented; a member would speak on a topic of current interest, such as abortion rights, or teach us something like quilting. I remember the evenings as being a little awkward but pleasant. However, as more wives returned to work, the membership dwindled, and by the mid-70s the group folded.

Despite having the "ideal" family of a boy and a girl, and knowing the world was aiming at zero population growth, we decided to have one more child. We liked being a family. I enjoyed mothering and was good at it. Tom and Jenny looked forward to having a new sibling.

After Nancy's birth, and now an old hand at the new baby business, I was busy with the Home and School Association at the local school

Tom and Jenny with their new sister, Nancy, Toronto, 1971

and back at university working on that BA with one course a year. Renovations on the new house (also by Jerome Markson) had finally come to an end, and life settled down to a steady rhythm once again. But by the summer of 1971, there was another upheaval, when Marty was asked to join the newly formed Law Reform Commission of Canada. He took a leave of absence from the Faculty of Law for what was supposed to be a three-year stint. We rented out our newly renovated house in Toronto and moved to Ottawa.

This was a difficult move. There was nothing in Ottawa to attract me – or almost anyone else – in those days. Some of the now wonderful museums were still being designed, restaurants closed by 9 p.m., and there was not much of a cultural life. I was reluctant to leave my father, who, then separated from his second wife and living on his own in Toronto, needed some support. I didn't want to leave other family and friends, and I didn't want to leave my volunteer work at the local school or my university courses. But at the same time, I knew it was a good opportunity for Marty and not something he could turn down. There was little to discuss.

Life in Ottawa for me was something of a cross between Cambridge and Toronto. I made friends with other moms and a few neighbours, but our social life was mainly a matter of which of Marty's work acquaintances invited us where. Those get-togethers meant intense and seemingly weighty conversations among the husbands and relatively superficial ones among us wives. We were invited to the occasional diplomatic gathering, but, again, the wives chatted among themselves. I could often overhear conversations that the men were having and wished I could participate, as they were usually about politics. I liked the other women and enjoyed our chats, but we were always aware that we were not the reason for the gathering. My feelings of being an appendage were starting to grow.

I remember talking with Peggy Laskin, the wife of Justice Bora Laskin (then a new member of the Supreme Court of Canada and soon to be named its Chief Justice). Bora had taught Marty at law school, and Peggy and I had become friends despite the difference in our ages. I think Marty and I had endeared ourselves to the Laskins because, ten or so years earlier when we were travelling in Italy on our own, we had met up with their then-teenaged son, John. We took John along with us (scrunched in the back of that Sunbeam Alpine) to see synagogues in Rome, and his parents were impressed.

Peggy and I talked about our roles as wives. Her husband had already achieved a high level of importance in Canada, and mine was about to do so in the coming years. Although we didn't label it this way, we knew we weren't living our own lives – we were living our husband's lives. Our primary role was to look after the family, be a support to our husbands, and attend their social functions. Although Peggy was a generation older than me and had long been accustomed to her role, she empathized with my frustrations nonetheless. Many women today are essentially living their husband's lives, however good those lives might be.

Whatever Ottawa lacked in its cultural life in the '70s, it more than made up for with its outdoor activities: skating on the Rideau Canal, cross-country skiing in the Gatineau, hiking and biking close at hand. It was a great place for families. Our rented house on Maple Lane on the edge of prestigious Rockcliffe was spacious and gracious, and the neighbourhood was beautiful, with its tall, stately trees, large houses set back from the street, and few if any sidewalks. I had never lived in such an upscale area. We were near the governor general's home – or the "governor jello's house," as our kids called it. Hearing the French language regularly was a new and welcome experience for us. Marty was given French lessons for a while – but, regrettably, he never took to the language.

When we arrived, Pierre Trudeau, who had become prime minister in 1968, was still a newlywed, having married the much younger Margaret Sinclair just a few months before.[4] There was an air of excitement – and romance – about the town. However, fear and

Tom, pulling Nancy on a sled, with Jenny and me, Rideau Canal, Ottawa, 1972 anxiety were also present, with the final vestiges of the War Measures Act, invoked during the FLQ crisis, not disappearing until the fall. Although the crisis had wound down by the time we arrived, some soldiers were still stationed in Rockcliffe, keeping a close watch over the homes of key members of Parliament.

Loneliness and a sense of isolation were regular companions for me during much of that year. Our house was too far from grocery stores for me to walk there with my new baby in the carriage, and I hadn't made many friends. I felt my isolation most acutely during a week in March, when Marty had gone to Toronto for some meetings, and I was on my own. Nancy, just thirteen months old, had what seemed like a cold, but soon developed into croup. Although croup is a scary illness with its sharp, barking cough, I had suffered through it with Tom and Jenny and was not too worried. I knew what to do: turn on the shower and sit with the child in the bathroom with the door closed, as they inhale the steam; take the child outside for a drive in the cold air if necessary, and be prepared for a long night or two.

I tried all the usual remedies for the first few days and nights but when there was no improvement, I took Nancy to the pediatrician. He warned me to monitor her condition and take her to emergency if she worsened. The next day – Thursday – was bad, and by that night, with no improvement in sight, I decided to take Nancy to the hospital. I was in phone contact with Marty, and with Bob Ehrlich, our Toronto pediatrician, and with my pediatrician brother. But there I was in Ottawa, on my own.

Tom and Jenny were only eight and six at the time, and I could not leave them alone. I felt I knew the mother of one of Jenny's classmates just well enough to ask her to help in my emergency. Luckily, her husband was home and could stay with their children so that she could stay with mine that night and take them to school the next day.

I bundled Nancy up for the drive to the Ottawa Children's Hospital in the dark of night. There was a ton of snow on the ground and the temperature was desperately cold, making the drive even more frightening. Staff admitted Nancy quickly and put her into a crib fitted with a "croup tent" – a covering that extended above her head and shoulders and into which cool moist air was pumped. As Friday wore on, Nancy's condition had not improved. Picking her up and walking around with her didn't help. She coughed and coughed. I was frightened to see this darling baby look more and more sickly. The attending physician requested a consultation with the chief of surgery in the afternoon. He examined Nancy and said that she might need a tracheotomy. We could wait and see how she progressed, or we could decide then and there to have it done. As it was already near the end of the day, waiting meant that, if the tracheotomy did need to be done, it would be done as an emergency procedure, probably by a resident, while the chief of surgery was en route to supervise. If the tracheotomy was done then and there, the chief of surgery would do it, and it was almost guaranteed to be a smoother procedure. Of course, only time could have told if the surgery was necessary. Marty was on his way home, but the decision was mine to make. I decided to go ahead.

When I saw Nancy in the recovery room an hour or so later, she looked fine. Her breathing was no longer laboured. Despite the opening into her trachea, now fitted with a metal tube, surrounded by white gauze, and taped down, she looked very cute – the nurses had tied her dark hair into two little ponytails complete with red ribbons! Within no time, she seemed her old self – unhappy only when the tube was being suctioned, which had to happen at regular intervals.

When it was time to remove the tube a few days later, the concern was whether she would be able to breathe all right on her own. Once she passed that test, the only remaining issue was to keep her lungs clear. The physio had been doing "hacking and clapping" on her back to loosen the secretions in her lungs and lessen the chances of pneumonia. With my physio skills not that far away, it was agreed we could take Nancy home early if I was prepared to place her over my knee and do the hacking and clapping myself. I gladly agreed. My baby did not seem bothered by her mother's new role, and she soon recovered fully. Her tracheotomy scar is barely visible today. When she was a teenager, and such matters were of concern, we reassured her that Elizabeth Taylor had still been considered the most beautiful woman in the world, despite her scar from the tracheotomy she had undergone after a serious bout with pneumonia.

This health crisis was dramatic but short-lived, and it had a good outcome. It was not nearly as serious as what so many mothers face when their child is ill. Nonetheless, it was an intense and frightening ordeal for me. As the Canadian historian Jane Errington noted in describing women's roles in the early nineteenth century, much of the work that women do, including caring for sick family members, remains hidden.[5]

By spring, when we had finally adjusted to life in Ottawa and were beginning to enjoy it, we found ourselves preparing for our return home. That three-year stay we had planned for turned into just one year, when Marty was appointed dean of the U of T Law School. Being dean, was certainly going to be a new and exciting role for Marty. I don't know if there were expectations for me, or whether I put them on myself, but I took on the role of "dean's wife" with a mixture of interest and apprehension.

8 Multitasker: Full-Time Mother, Part-Time Worker, Grad Student, and Dean's Wife

With Marty's new position, it seemed a given that I would do more entertaining. To that point in our marriage, we had had friends and family to dinner and hosted small parties of one sort or another, including gatherings for Marty's students. But this level of entertaining would be different. There would be more of it, and it would be on a larger scale. Along with whatever else we might do, we decided to host an annual "garden party."

We invited about eighty people each year. The guest list included everyone from the Law School, a smattering of judges, and various university officials, some of whom (like John and Gay Evans) had become good friends. I did the invitations (no email then), planned and prepared the food, and made sure the house was in order. Odette, the woman who cleaned for us one day a week, helped me make open-faced sandwiches on cocktail rye to add to the store-bought asparagus rolls and cucumber sandwiches. We set out nuts and olives, pâté and French bread, and fruit platters and cheese. I ordered frozen miniature ice creams in the shape of fruits and nuts, which our daughters passed around in little wicker baskets. The ice cream (and our daughters) were always a big hit. Our son helped direct guests to the garden when they arrived. We hired a bartender from the Faculty Club to serve the wine, and we prayed for good weather.

The garden party was a considerable investment of time and effort. I enjoyed creating the event and liked the praise I received. However, I've since wondered about the value of my labour when we entertained. How much would it have cost if everything had been organized by someone hired for that purpose? If all the food had been catered? If it had been at a commercial venue? And what if I could have just "appeared" at the party along with the guests?

Marty expected me to accompany him to various functions, and I never questioned whether I should go. I sat through many Law School events – my least favourite being skit night, where it was impossible for an outsider to understand the many in-jokes. Most of the social functions, usually dinners, involved the legal community – academics and practitioners. I enjoyed getting to know that community, but the talk was law talk, and it was usually of little or no interest to me. Seated between two lawyers – always men in those days – there were times when they would talk over me to each other.

Events we attended at the president's house were always enjoyable, especially as I came to know more people. The house and the gardens were lovely, topics of conversation were more general, and the food was good. There were some special events, like the dinner given by the Ismaili community in Toronto to honour a visit by the Aga Khan. There was no reason for that invitation – it just came with Marty's position. For that occasion, as for all the others, I spent time organizing the right clothes and having my hair, and maybe my nails, done. I enjoyed getting dressed up and looking as good as I could, but I clocked a lot of hours and spent a lot of money doing so.

With the new job came more work for Marty on committees and commissions, and he was often away in Ottawa or Montreal for a day or two. If he was speaking at a conference or giving a lecture somewhere interesting, the children and I might go along. We could share his hotel room, which was already paid for, and only have to pay for our food and transportation. At the time it seemed a good deal – a chance to get away, stay in a hotel, not cook or make beds. But it never really worked. Marty tried to be attentive to us, and I always felt guilty if he was missing something he should have attended.

Marty loved his position as dean. It made use of a lot of his skills: his creativity, his ability to plan and organize, to focus and concentrate, and problem solve. When he gave speeches at events, he always managed something humorous and clever. Already a highly accomplished scholar, he was somehow even more productive during the years of his deanship. He was thirty-nine when he was appointed and had a lot of energy, keeping in good shape with regular games of squash. He still came home for dinner most nights, sometimes early enough to toss a ball from across the road to one of our kids who stood in our driveway. But soon after we finished dinner, he went back to the office or into his study. And he worked on the weekends too. Once he sat down to work, he became fully absorbed and oblivious to what was going on around him, so I never worried about keeping the children quiet. His ability to concentrate allowed him to work almost anywhere. When he drove the kids to Sunday school, he'd drop them off and then settle in at a nearby coffee shop and work there for a few hours until it was time to pick them up.

There were many celebratory events for Marty over the years: many book launches, award ceremonies, and special honours. When, in his speeches, he thanked me for being a great support, I always felt awkward. I hadn't done much to deserve the thanks, other than to keep out of the way and allow him to keep at it. It wasn't the place or yet the time to thank me for the work that I, like most wives of academics, were expected to do to help their husbands advance – caring for the immediate and extended family, keeping house, entertaining, attending social events, sometimes proofing manuscripts, and even doing some editing. There is now a rich literature on the topic of what seemed "normal" for a faculty wife to do – at least in those days.[1]

Despite my extra roles, my years as the dean's wife were also good years for me. As the school year began for Marty in his new position, I was busy settling us back into our home after the year in Ottawa. Tom and Jenny were at our local school (Davisville), just a block or so away, and I was home with Nancy, then a year and a half. Within a few months, I had become deeply involved with the Davisville Home and School Association.

Home and School Associations in the '70s were relatively powerful groups with a lot of autonomy – particularly in upper-middle-class areas of the city like ours. We had regular meetings with the principal of the school and voiced our concerns and made suggestions to improve the learning environment. We could put forward plans for change. I found a comfortable and energizing role for myself in the Home and School Association. I knew I had skills that would be useful, those organizing skills I had learned in the clubs in high school and in my sorority, and I could see places where they were needed. Before I knew it, I became vice-president and then president. Group leadership skills, learned in my occupational therapy education, came in handy when I presided over our meetings. I don't think I was a particularly popular president of the Home and School: I was always anxious to get things done and never great at delegating. I wasn't authoritarian, but I was probably impatient with others who were not prepared to take on a lot (or too much), as I did.

We did a lot. We were one of the first schools in the city to develop an "After 4" program. We ran it with a cadre of volunteers, offering activities such as floor hockey, drama, arts and crafts, and music. The program benefited the mothers as well as the children. At a time when after-school care was not readily available, having an After 4 program meant that mothers who worked outside the home could delay picking up their child to the end of the workday. Stay-at-home mothers, like me, who ran the program also benefited. We had the satisfaction of knowing we were contributing, and we had an opportunity to socialize. That socialization helped to counter the isolation experienced by many women who stayed home with their children.

One of our more inventive programs was our "Community Resource Bank." We asked local businesses and various neighbours to allow groups of children to come and see their work in action. Local establishments, including the corner bank, a muffler shop, and a fish and chips restaurant, welcomed the children, while individuals who had interesting jobs outside of our neighbourhood came to classrooms to talk about their work. Our intention was to expand the children's horizons with these learning experiences and also to build supportive relationships within the area. The '70s was a time of growing concern among some that we needed to protect children from strangers who were presumably lurking about our streets. Neighbourhood Watch programs told children to go in an emergency to a house that had their sign in a window. We resisted that approach, preferring to act as though *all* our neighbours were friendly and that we would all look after one another. By having the involvement of so many parents and some local businesses, we were nurturing a supportive environment.

In my involvement with the Home and School, I worked closely with my neighbour Gertrude, a family physician, who had also chosen to stay home while her children were young. We had many talented parents in our school's catchment area, and we took full advantage of them. We had health professionals, teachers, a linguist, some artists, actors, restaurateurs, and a social worker. We had enough French-speaking moms to run a noon-hour French class at a time when French was not yet taught in all of Toronto's elementary schools, and we had enough people from the theatre world to stage a play.

We also developed a program to work directly with children who needed extra help. Teachers identified the children and sent them to meet with us for one-on-one time, primarily for extra reading. Everyone was happy with the program: the teachers, the children we tutored, and the parents of those children. In some cases, the children were from families who couldn't help their children with their academic work. In other cases, it was a matter of the child being more willing to do extra schoolwork with someone other than their own parent.

And, of course, we held a Fun Fair. Our Fun Fair drew the neighbourhood together and put out a special welcome to ethnic groups in our community who proudly provided the food we sold at our International Café. The Plant Booth facilitated the sharing of plants from one garden to another, and the Trash and Treasures Booth gave the children – and some adults – a chance to spend just a little money to have something to take home. There were also games, with those that involved unceremoniously dunking an adult being the most popular.

Everything we did at the school depended on the availability of stay-at-home moms. They were the only adults who could be involved on a regular basis. We were volunteers, but we were also workers – unpaid workers, of course, putting in hours at our kids' school in addition to the unpaid hours we worked to keep our homes and our families functioning and flourishing.

I also volunteered at the Metropolitan Toronto School for the Deaf, which was housed in a building adjacent to Davisville Public School. Along with its own elementary school program, the school ran an integrated nursery school, for hearing and non-hearing children to attend together. My daughter Nancy attended that program when she was three years old. I used my rusty therapy skills to do some perceptual-motor work with a few of her classmates.

The school was riddled with ideological (and methodological) conflicts at the time, with the oral method not only taking precedence over sign language but with sign language being prohibited. To facilitate the oral method, the children wore large amplifying aids, suspended from a thick cord around their necks and kept in a white cloth pocket that lay against their chest. How effective these aids were at making sound more audible was not clear. I realized, though, that they were somehow attractive when Nancy, who was fully hearing, fashioned a pretend aid so that she too could wear one around her neck.

Having become aware of how valuable occupational therapy could be with schoolchildren, I had been meeting with four other occupational therapists to find ways to promote our role in the public school system. We developed a formal proposal (*Occupational Therapy for Schoolchildren with Special Needs*) and presented it to the School Programs Committee of the Toronto Board of Education in 1976, and to the Committee on Special Needs of Students with Disabilities of the Metropolitan Toronto School Board the next year. While our proposal might have raised awareness of a potential role for occupational therapy, nothing concrete followed. However, working with this group led to my being asked to take on a job one afternoon a week leading a perceptual-motor class at a private school for children with learning disabilities. I remembered enough from my P&OT days to understand, from a theoretical perspective, what I needed to do, and I had the support of the previous person in the job to help with the practical aspects. I was not very confident in this teaching role, but I worked hard to prepare my weekly session and I found the work interesting.

That little job, plus the volunteer work, plus some education-related courses toward my BA – which, by the mid-70s, I had finally finished – led me to think that, if I ever wanted work in the area of occupational therapy in elementary schools, graduate work in special education would help prepare me. The usual path to graduate school was a four-year honours degree, and most graduate programs were not interested in applicants like me whose preparation did not exactly fit the criteria for admission. OISE – the Ontario Institute for Studies in Education – which was then separate from U of T, was a bit more flexible. It had been established in 1965 to provide teachers with further education, and its environment was appropriately adult-oriented. Of course, I did not consider doing graduate work outside of Toronto. I did not even consider York University because it was so much further away, and the travel distance would add to my time away from home.

OISE accepted me into the special education program with my three-year BA and my three-year P&OT diploma. I set out to do a master's of education, a non-thesis, course-heavy program that is considered a "terminal" degree (i.e., a degree from which one could not go on to a PhD). I thought an MEd was all I would need. However, after completing a few of the MEd courses, I decided to keep my options open and switched to the master's of arts thesis program. The coursework was lighter, and the idea of doing a thesis seemed interesting.

It would have been enough for me just to start graduate school, but, for whatever reason, it also seemed like the right time for me to try to go back to work part-time as an occupational therapist. I'm not sure how I thought I could add yet another role to my life: Marty was still dean, the children were still young – six, ten, and twelve – but, with all of them in school, and after thirteen years at home, the time just felt right to move on.

Because I wanted part-time work, there was only one employment option for me: to work with Community Occupational Therapy Associates (COTA), a new organization that offered occupational therapy services through the Home Care Program of Metropolitan Toronto. Without the option to work part-time, I would not have gone back to work. I was prepared to pay (and privileged to be able to pay) the "motherhood penalty" – to work *and* keep doing the emotional labour within my family.[2] The work at COTA would be interesting, and, as a self-employed worker, I could schedule my own hours. It was the ideal place for me.

Home care services were intended to speed up hospital discharges and change the site of non-acute care from the costly, and often unnecessary, hospital setting, to the community. Occupational therapy had a major role to play in meeting these objectives. Patients, or "clients," as they were beginning to be called, were seen where they lived – in their own homes or in boarding homes, or long-stay institutions. As COTA therapists, we assessed our clients in those real-life settings and worked with them to develop goals and establish interventions. We could help people with illnesses and disabilities to do what they wanted to do and needed to do to lead satisfying and productive lives. Home care was a much-needed service in the '70s, even as it continues to be today; however, despite successive governments acknowledging its value and promising to expand it, it remains an underused option within our health care system.

I was very apprehensive about returning to work after so much time away from the field. Refresher courses were just becoming available in my profession, but a regulatory college was not yet in place to require them. To add to my worries, my work experience had been with psychiatric patients, and at COTA, I would also be seeing clients with physical disorders like stroke. However, COTA offered a good orientation and mentoring program for new hires, and I hoped that – along with my own reading – would be enough. After a few months, I started to feel comfortable in my new role.

With Nancy just in Grade 1, I arranged my working hours so that I could be there for her when she got home for lunch. If I saw clients or had meetings in the morning, I rushed home at noon. I often found Nancy waiting anxiously for me on our front porch. My heart sank when I saw her there, and I still have a bad feeling thinking about it. I was now a full-time multitasker: trying to be a full-time mother, a part-time worker, a part-time student, and still a dean's wife.

COTA was an extraordinary work experience. I worked in a geographically defined area of the city and saw a varied roster of clients – adults with stroke, young people with psychiatric illnesses, some older adults with dementia, and children with developmental delays. I looked forward to the work each day and generally came away feeling I had made a difference. Some situations could be dealt with in one or two visits, but others called for several visits in a week for several weeks or even months and were very intense. Sometimes I had to convince the home care discharge planner to extend my visits beyond what had been originally requested. "Mary, I know my time is up, but Mrs. Brown [who had had a stroke and whose right arm and hand were paralysed] is doing so well. She's able to manage the cooking with just a little help from her husband. I just need some time to figure out how she can do some gardening again, now that the weather's good. I need two more weeks. With any luck, I can get her to attend the gardening club at her church." There was an implicit understanding between the COTA therapist and the discharge planner that, whatever those visits cost the program, it was not only better for clients and their families, but also less expensive for society.

Many of my clients were challenging. One new mother, whose husband left her the day their only child was born, became a long-term but highly successful client. A somewhat unstable individual with low self-esteem before this upheaval, she needed help to deal with this shocking event and to adjust to the role of a new – and now single – mother. My job was to support her and to problem solve with her to develop her mothering skills and build her self-esteem. I worked with her for over a year through crisis after crisis, until the successes began to take precedence, and she was able to manage with less and less support, get a part-time job and find daycare for her daughter. I was surprised and delighted one Hallowe'en several years later, when she appeared at my door, proudly showing off her lovely daughter, then aged about seven.

Another client, a newly divorced woman with two older children and a job as a health professional, had been hospitalized with depression and was trying to return to her previous roles. She needed support to carry on with her responsibilities as a worker and a mother and to adjust to her changed marital status. I visited her regularly, acting as a sounding board as she struggled to adjust to her new status, and, on occasion, being there to hear the children's concerns. After some time at home, working with me to figure out her new status in life, she too returned to work. Ironically, our paths crossed many years later, when she was the one to care for one of my family members who was hospitalized.

Both of these women had been diagnosed with a mental illness and required appropriate medication and ongoing medical contact, but it was clear that they could manage their life roles if they had support, encouragement, and guidance. That their official diagnoses would not doom them, that they could function despite illness, contradicted the more common biomedical approach, which focused only on the illness. Forming a strong interpersonal relationship with clients was key to becoming an ally in their journey to recovery.

I had several clients at COTA who had suffered a stroke, and I quickly learned how life altering that condition could be. The shock of finding oneself suddenly and significantly impaired was devastating. Relationships, careers, one's sense of self – all were affected. Doctors often painted gloomy pictures for recovery and warned of the possibility of a second stroke. Perhaps they were trying to be careful not to give too much hope, but patients were generally furious at that approach. Indeed, it may have spurred some on to show just what they *could* do. One man, highly accomplished and well known in the world of music, related how his doctor told him that he should be happy he was alive and should be content to sit at his window and look outside. He was disgusted by the suggestion and determined to prove him wrong. While he was not able to return to his former vocation, he recovered well enough to resume some of his previous roles and find new ones that were related. My heart went out to these people, and I worked hard to help them adjust and find a way forward. I saw my job as instilling realistic hope for the future and helping my clients find a way to move forward.

Being self-employed meant billing for my time, and I found that difficult. I certainly didn't think I should be paid for the preparation I thought I needed, which others might consider to be excessive. Then there was the time I spent with a client to establish rapport and build a relationship, without which, I believed, little could be accomplished. How could I bill for that cup of tea we shared? Like many self-employed people, I charged the amount of time I thought was appropriate rather than the time I took. No matter how much, it was a paycheque, something I hadn't seen in many years.

I made most of my home care visits by car and came to know the city well, relying on my *Perly's* book of street maps, where co-ordinates for any address in the Greater Toronto Area could be found. I took off my shoes when I entered a client's home as a gesture of respect for the place I was entering, and I checked my shoes before putting them back on after some visits when there was a good chance that cockroaches might have crept in. The radio kept me company while I was on the road, and Peter Gzowski's *Morningside* on the CBC kept me thinking. If there were calls to be made near my home, and I wasn't carrying much, I walked or rode my bike. I did my progress notes and my billing at night at a desk in our bedroom when the kids were asleep. I was very happy with my job.

One special project came to me via the Stroke Recovery Association of Ontario. They knew that stroke survivors needed ongoing support and stimulation after discharge from rehabilitation, and they hired COTA to establish a social-therapeutic group for that purpose. Happily, the task of developing and implementing a program fell to me. Before starting the group, I interviewed potential members in their homes to understand their needs and learn a bit about them so that my support would be relevant. Most members had suffered damage within the left hemisphere of their brain and were aphasic (had difficulty speaking) to varying degrees. All but a few were paralysed on the right side of their body, with their arm and hand more affected than their leg. A left hemisphere stroke was a heavy blow. It fit the description of punishment from God as set out in Psalm 137.5: "If I forget thee, O Jerusalem, let my right hand lose its cunning and my tongue cleave to the roof of my mouth." To not be able to speak or use one's dominant hand was a cruel affliction indeed. Those whose stroke occurred in the right half of their brain had similar physical impairments. Although their speech was usually intact, they were emotionally labile, often had visual and motor planning deficits, and were paralysed on their left side, with their arm and hand typically more involved than their leg.

Many of my clients expressed sadness, anger, and frustration, whether in halting speech or with tears or other body language. They often seemed to have an air of embarrassment about them in response to what had become of them. Despair was barely below the surface. Stroke survivors who became members of my social-therapeutic group had tried to come to terms with their lot. The time that had elapsed since they suffered their stroke didn't seem to influence their level of adjustment. Some who had their stroke years ago were still searching for a more complete recovery, while others who were more recent survivors seemed ready to adjust to their limitations and find ways to move on.

The Brown School Stroke Group, as we were called, met at the elementary school of that name in Toronto once a week for two hours in the afternoon. Wheel-Trans buses or family members brought the members to the school and took them back home when our session was over. We started our session by sitting in chairs arranged in a circle and exchanging greetings. People shared personal and general news to the extent that they were able to speak. All our members could comprehend speech quite well so that, even if they couldn't speak, they benefited from socializing. Sitting in chairs, we did some simple exercises to help maintain flexibility and promote balance. Then we had a special activity each week – a speaker, a movie, a party, a concert, or an outing. Planning the next week's activity was a part of each session.

Our members became close with one another, and with me; over time, we developed a warm and supportive environment. Indeed, members' spouses, who were meant to have some time off from caregiving during our sessions, occasionally stayed to be with the group, enjoying the sense of belonging it gave. We often faced challenges to our plans: bad weather interfered with our plans to go out somewhere, a speaker cancelled, or a member suffered a second stroke. But we carried on. That was a core value for the group: to acknowledge the difficulty and to carry on.

Although members of the group had finished their formal rehabilitation, my role allowed me to make home visits now and again to see if anything further could be done. Sometimes I ordered a dressing aid or other device that made self-care tasks easier when only one hand worked. Sometimes I arranged for an adaptation to the home itself to make it safer and more accessible for the person with the stroke or easier for the person giving care. Sometimes I facilitated a connection with resources in the community – to attend church services, for example, or to get out to a gym program that would accommodate them.

With Ann, a member of the Brown School Stroke Club

I found the situation for one older couple that I visited particularly heartbreaking. Immigrants from Scotland many years earlier, they had no children and no family members in Toronto. It was the wife who had had the stroke, and she had great difficulty adjusting to her now second-rate homemaking abilities. Her aphasia meant she could not express her feelings: she could only look at me with her sorrowful eyes and nod if I happened to describe what she was thinking. Ann was anxious for any help I could offer that would improve her situation. Homemaking, which had been her strong suit, was now greatly impacted by her useless right arm. Ann's husband, Ian, was equally sorrowful but tried to put on a happy front. He invariably welcomed me with, "Ah, Judy, come in, come in. Let me take your 'cat and hoat'" – all said in his delightful Scottish lilt. A lonely couple, completely devoted to one another, they were extraordinarily grateful for my visits, and I always found it hard to leave them when it was time for me to go.

The Brown School Stroke Group added to the overall satisfaction I had with my job at COTA. I felt fulfilled. It was nice to have a regular paycheque, albeit a small one; to have colleagues with whom to share ideas and concerns; and to be able to talk about my work when I was with others. Community-based occupational therapy made so much sense theoretically and personally. I had landed in a good spot.

Things were good at home too. The kids were growing up, and with that came so-called rites of passage for them. From the age of about nine, our children attended Hebrew school on Sunday mornings and once or twice a week after regular school, in preparation for their bar or bat mitzvahs. These coming-of-age events (at thirteen for the boys and after twelve for the girls) were anxiety producing (for them and us) but also proud moments for all. The kids sang their "portion" in Hebrew – the part having been selected from the Torah reading for that date as determined by the Jewish/lunar calendar. The congregation included about 200 people on those Saturday mornings, half of them regular attenders, and the rest composed of guests who were there just for our event. We had a buffet lunch following the service for our guests, with just a few speeches – and a party at home in the evening.

Aside from our celebrations not being overly lavish, they were different in another major way: at least half of our guests were non-Jewish – an odd occurrence for a Jewish celebration then, and probably even now. Living, as we did, in a non-Jewish area, with our kids in local public schools and Marty in academia, it was natural to celebrate with our non-Jewish friends, work colleagues, and neighbours. The kids' classmates were impressed with our beautiful synagogue and by the fact that they had a friend who could read Hebrew.

Toward the end of the '70s, as Marty's term as dean of the Law School was drawing to a close, plans were afoot for yet another sabbatical. The prospect of this trip was, again, difficult for me. I was finally a part of the working world. I was partway through my master's degree. I was beginning to carve out a separate identity for myself again. I did not want to leave my father, aged seventy-six, my courses, my job, or my house. I don't remember us discussing whether we should go; it was more a matter of just how we would go about it.

It was 1979, and likely our last big family trip. We would be away for a year – a month travelling in Europe, five months in Israel, and six months in England. We would leave Toronto in late June and travel through France, Italy, and Greece. In August we would arrive in Israel, and toward the end of December we would return once more to Cambridge to spend the remainder of the year. It was exciting, for sure, but it also put the new life I had been carving out on hold.

I reluctantly left COTA, with the plan to return in a year.

9 Variations on a Theme: Different Environments, Same Situations

Finding schools for the three children in two different countries was a major challenge, as was finding suitable accommodation for the five of us. Simply packing up for a year was a logistical nightmare: hot in Israel and relatively informal; rainy, damp, and more proper in England – that meant a lot of baggage.

While still in Toronto, we bought a small blue Renault and arranged to pick it up in Paris. Unlike that little red Sunbeam Alpine convertible that we drove on our first trip to Europe, this car was for a family. However, we were a family on the move with luggage to keep all of us for a year, and it was crowded. We put some of our bags in the trunk and tied the rest onto the roof andevery night when we stopped, we took everything into the hotel. In the morning we brought it all out and packed it away again.

Jenny and Nancy guarding the luggage, 1979

We did some sightseeing in Paris: the Eiffel Tower, Nôtre Dame, Sainte-Chapelle, the Louvre, and the Luxembourg Gardens. The children showed polite interest in all the sights, but there was true excitement only when we showed them the sign that said Avenue de Friedland on a street running off the Arc de Triomphe.[1]

We left Paris as soon as we could for the countryside. Our only definite destination was to spend a few weeks in Puyloubier, a small town in the south where we had rented a little house owned by a neighbour in Toronto. Otherwise, we just meandered. It was hard to find a room that could accommodate the five of us in a hotel that we could afford. Wanting to see or do just one more thing in the day often meant that we were still driving well into the evening, already hungry and tired when we started hunting for food and a place to sleep. We developed a routine for the search: two children waited in the car with me, in the dark, while Marty and one child (they took turns for this privilege!) stopped at the various hotels, checking the rates and the condition of the room. With all of us now cranky, we would eventually drag ourselves and all the luggage into that room and then set out to find some food. Patience often wore thin. Clearly, we had forgotten what we learned twenty years earlier from our Swiss friends about stopping early.

Avenue de Friedland street sign, Paris

Still exhausted and stressed from leaving Toronto, I sometimes found myself sitting with my face pressed against the car window, quietly in tears, as we drove through the countryside. I did not try to hide my unhappiness, but neither was I prepared to discuss it, not knowing myself just what it was that was so upsetting. Reaching Puyloubier – nestled at the foot of Mont Sainte-Victoire, where we could see what Cezanne saw when he painted there – helped a little. It was a magnificent view, and it couldn't help but be uplifting for the soul.

The location of our little house was perfect for day trips to the Mediterranean, to the beach at Cassis, and the nearby Calanques. The house itself was somewhat primitive, but we had been warned about that, so it was not a shock. I got used to washing the floors and, like everyone else, dumping the water in the trough in front of the house.

One of the children went off each morning to buy fresh croissants for our breakfast, and after a week or so, we were beginning to feel at home in the village, saying *bonjour* to a few neighbours and even trying our hand at *boules* in the grassy area just opposite. What could be better?

Then I saw scorpions on the stairs.

Cleaning floors, Puyloubier, 1979

I was having trouble sleeping one night and went to the floor below to get something to drink. And there they were on the stairs. I was particularly horrified because we were all sleeping on mattresses on the floor, which would make it easy for the scorpions to crawl onto us. I knew that scorpions were not unusual in the south of France, but I also knew that their bite, while generally not deadly, could be serious. As usual in such situations, Marty and I hid the danger from the children. As was also usual, Marty tried to minimize the problem, saying "I'm not worried" – as if that would satisfy me! Deep down, he knew that such a statement – as on those many other occasions in our lives – would do nothing to calm me. It was time to move on.

After stopping at Aix and Avignon – where we danced on the bridge, singing "Sur le Pont d'Avignon / On y danse, on y danse" – we drove south to Monte Carlo. We tried without success to sneak Tom, good at math and interested in gambling, into the casino. From there we went on to Pisa, Florence, and Rome, and eventually over to Brindisi, where we took a car ferry to Corfu. We stopped there at a beautiful beach and took a break from sightseeing before driving across Greece to Piraeus, where we boarded a boat to Israel.

No moment in all my travels before or since has ever been more moving than arriving with my family by boat in the port at Haifa. It was sobering to think about the many waves of immigrants, including members of my own extended family, who had done the same, especially after the Second World War. And here we were with so much security in our lives in Canada, visiting Israel by choice, not fleeing persecution, not forced to start life all over.

From Haifa, we drove straight to Netanya to the apartment we had rented, one that had been advertised in the *Canadian Jewish News* earlier that year. It was perfect. On a quiet tree-lined street, just at the edge of the city, overlooking the Mediterranean ocean. From the master bedroom, we saw the sea and heard the waves. At night, the view was majestic and the rhythmic sound of the waves lapping the shore lulled us to sleep.

The layout of the apartment was all that we hoped. The girls shared a room, which was reassuring for them, and Tom had a room to himself. We even had two bathrooms – a luxury we did not expect. The apartment was close to the main part of the city, which meant I could walk to the grocery stores and markets, practise my very limited Hebrew with shopkeepers, then come home and cook new foods. Best of all, the kids could be at the beach minutes after their return from school.

We enrolled all three children in the American International School, then located in Kfar Shmaryahu about a twenty-minute drive from Netanya and near the north end of Tel Aviv. We drove the children to school and picked them up each day, carpooling on occasion with an American missionary family who lived nearby. The school was excellent. Our kids learned a lot and became friends with children from all over the world, children whose parents were with their country's embassies, or working with Christian or Muslim religious organizations, or with a business in Israel – almost all, like us, there temporarily.

The atmosphere in the school was welcoming, and the gardens in the surrounding area were lush and tropical. But the presence of a bomb shelter in the basement of the school and the regular air raid drills were a sharp reminder of the ever-threatening political situation. Israel Defense Force planes practised overhead each day, their deep roar a constant reminder of the need to be on guard. This tension was a part of life that Israelis live with daily – one that was, and is, completely foreign to a Canadian. I always felt on edge.

On some occasions, Tom, almost sixteen, stayed late at school for an activity and came home by bus on his own. That had me very worried. It was a time of considerable unrest in the country, and bombs exploding at bus stops and in bus terminals were not uncommon. In the seven months of 1979 preceding our arrival, there were bombings in Tel Aviv and Jerusalem, as well as one in Netanya.[2]

Marty drove back and forth to Jerusalem or Tel Aviv most days for his research and to teach. I went with him now and again, but I was especially nervous, as it put me at a greater distance from the children. With bomb shelters everywhere, including in our own apartment building, it was hard to dismiss the possibilities of a terrorist attack. Of course, what I *should* have been nervous about was the more immediate life-threatening danger on the roads. Driving in Israel in 1979 was crazy, and the accident rate was high. The explanation was that most Israelis were very stressed: they worked several jobs to make ends meet, drove fast to get places quickly, and were always sleep deprived. Indeed, on one occasion, our little Renault was rear-ended on the Tel Aviv–Jerusalem road. We were not injured, but the car was a mess.

Not wanting to have my master's studies completely interrupted during Marty's sabbatical, I arranged for two practicum visits in Israel that could count toward the requirements for my degree: one at the Feuerstein Clinic in Jerusalem and the other at Micha, a nursery school for deaf children in Tel Aviv. At the clinic, I sat in on an assessment of a child with a learning disability by the renowned psychologist Professor Reuven Feuerstein. I quickly became convinced of the value of the clinic's approach, whereby they assessed not only what a child knew and could do, but also what a child *could learn to do* once the assessor found a good learning strategy for that child. The approach makes enormous sense, not only for children with learning disabilities but also in many other clinical situations. The visit to Micha was interesting, and different from what I had seen at home at the Metropolitan Toronto School for the Deaf. I wrote up my reflection papers for my visits and mailed them off to my course instructor at OISE.

We took several trips within Israel during our stay: to Masada and the Dead Sea, to Tel Dan and Banias in the north, and to Mount Sinai, which was then in Israeli hands. Tom went to Sinai with his class from school, and the rest of us, along with an older Christian couple from France, went in a hired car with a guide, all on the same weekend. Our little group stopped at a Bedouin Camp, had a delicious dinner, and then slept in a tent for a few hours before driving to the foot of the mountain. By 3 a.m. the next morning, we were climbing Mount Sinai,

From left: Marty, Nancy, Jenny, and me, Mount Sinai, 1979

hoping to reach the top in time to see the sunrise. It was not an easy climb, with the cold night air and darkness all around. Having made what was considered a late start, we arrived at the top of the mountain just after the sun did. Tom and his classmates were already on their descent by then and our paths crossed.

At some 2,200 metres above sea level, the view from Mount Sinai with the brilliant sun cresting above adjacent peaks was breathtaking. Climbing back down the mountain with the steep descent and the rising heat was challenging, and we welcomed the sight of the Monastery of St Catherine with the "burning bush" at the bottom. Despite all the biblical references, we gave little thought to Moses or the Ten Commandments during our visit to Mount Sinai. We were simply mesmerized by all that we saw around us.

Our social life in Israel was much like at home: we mixed in legal and academic circles. The gatherings would be initiated by Marty's colleagues, all of whom were law professors, judges, or practising lawyers. No one seemed to know how to talk about anything that would include non-lawyers, and it was easy for me to go through a dinner hardly saying a word. It didn't help that politics were not to be discussed. Israeli politics are too partisan – and too disturbing. With many of our contemporaries having children about to enter the army for three years (the boys) or two years (the girls), talking politics was understandably off-limits.

Years later, when Marty had a conference in Jerusalem over the December holiday, my then twenty-year-old daughter Nancy and I went along. We went places on our own while Marty attended sessions, but on the day when Shimon Peres, then head of the opposition Labour Party, was to address the conference, we wanted to hear him. Marty thought it would be all right, even though we were not registered for the conference. And it probably would have been fine if the speech had been given in an auditorium where we could have just slipped in. Instead, Peres spoke at the end of a lunch for the attendees. So, Nancy and I stood in a passageway, watching as the desserts passed us by, listening to the speech from afar. I was wrong to expect that anyone would make a move to have us sit. Nonetheless, it also felt wrong that we could not share this special event in a more dignified way. It seemed to underscore the idea that, as a wife, I was welcome only when I was helpful to the cause. The experience was so distasteful that it prompted me to consider all such events more carefully in the future. Rather than being an onlooker, trying to catch a word here or there, I was coming to feel it would be better to not be present.

One special bonus of our stay in Israel was getting to know some of my relatives who had settled there after the Second World War. A cousin on my maternal grandfather's side lived with his wife and child in Netanya and worked in a diamond factory. They invited us for lunch, and I was moved by the experience of eating foods cooked in the same way as my grandmother, who had settled a world away, would have cooked them. Their simple living quarters reflected the difficult existence of most working-class people in Israel. I was uncomfortable when they came to visit us in our more spacious apartment, as it made the financial disparity in our lives so apparent.

We also met with two sisters, Doreen and Maisie, who were my father's cousins. Their father had emigrated from Rokiskis in Lithuania to South Africa when my grandmother and my dad came to Canada. The sisters came to Israel in the late '40s during the War of Independence. Doreen married Mendy, an American who had come to Israel as a teenager. They lived at Ma'ayan Baruch, a kibbutz near the unstable northern border with Lebanon, where clashes at the border town of Kiryat Shmona – just seven kilometres away from the kibbutz – affected their lives almost daily. Their kibbutz followed the ways of communal living: members did not own property and were assigned their work. Most daily activities were shared, including childcare and mealtimes.

When we visited Mayan Baruch, Mendy told us how, during the War of Independence, he had been part of the operation that carried 250 sleeping children out of a kibbutz into safety. The story is told in the book *Exodus*, by Leon Uris, albeit in somewhat fictionalized form. The protagonist, Ari Ben Canaan explains the operation: "Four hundred men from every settlement in the Huleh will be led up the west face of the mountain by David Ben Ami. If everything goes according to plan and they are not discovered, they should be here by daybreak tomorrow. Two hundred and fifty of the men will each carry a child down the mountain tomorrow night. The balance, a hundred and fifty men, will act as a guard force."[3] We felt the drama even as Mendy recounted the story, which had occurred some three decades earlier.

Maisie and her husband, Basil, lived with their three children at Kfar Monash, a *moshav* near Netanya, where life was communal but less so than on a kibbutz. Each family, while contributing to the whole enterprise, had their own home and preferred form of work. Basil and his son-in-law raised chickens, and Maisie taught English at one of the schools.

Visiting with Maisie and her family, we heard the unspeakably sad story of how their son, Offer, aged twenty-three, had died while on a training mission with the Israeli Air Force. We could not comprehend the hardship, and our hearts went out to our newfound relatives. We stayed in touch with Maisie and Basil over the years and visited them on subsequent occasions.

This stay in Israel, meeting extended family and exploring the country, was an extraordinary experience, binding us more closely to the land and its people.

We left the sunshine of Israel for the cold, damp, and dark days of December in England. It didn't take long to settle in, as we knew our way around Cambridge after so many stays. This time, we lived in graduate-student housing at Clare Hall, in buildings beautifully

designed by the British architect
Ralph Erskine. Our flat was spacious and well equipped, and the
grounds were lovely, backing on
open country, away from the town
and nearby busy road.

Each of our children was in a different school, and they all made
their way on their bikes. Even
Nancy, just turning nine, rode her
bike once she learned her way and
we thought she was safe. Neigh-

Our flat at Clare Hall, Cambridge, 1980

bours around our courtyard at Clare Hall were friendly and interesting;
one family was from the United States, another from Israel, and a third
from Finland. I played tennis on grass courts there for the first time, on
the courts just behind our flat. My partner was from China; her husband,
like mine, was a Visiting Fellow at Clare Hall.

I found two special education practicum placements for myself in
Cambridge: one in the Adolescent Unit in the Department of Psychiatry
at Addenbrooke's Hospital, and the other at the Roger Ascham School for
Physically Disabled Children. I did a third placement at St Elizabeth's
Centre, a school for epileptic children in the village of Much Hadham, a
few hours away by bus. Each placement had a unique population and
unique ways of meeting their children's learning needs. I again wrote
up the visits and sent my reports back to my instructor in Toronto. I was
glad to be able to continue with my program in this way and grateful to
have been able to arrange the placements.

Lots of family and friends came to visit us in Cambridge. We gave
good tours, walking around the colleges, and punting on the Cam River,
going as far as Grantchester on occasion. Marty's mother and my father
and stepmother May visited in the spring, which was tiring for them
but wonderful for us, seeing them after we'd been away for almost a
year. We all celebrated Passover together with a Seder in our flat.

One of the friends who visited us that year was a former colleague of
Marty's from the University of Toronto Law School. Mark MacGuigan had
left academia for politics and at the time was Canada's minister of external affairs. Mark had come to Cambridge on some business or other, and
we arranged to take him punting. We were having a pleasant time out
on the Cam River, just making conversation, when he asked if we came
down to London very often. We said we did. Then he asked if we would
like to come for a party at Canada House to celebrate the one-hundredth
anniversary of the Canadian High Commission. We said sure. Then

he rather casually added that Queen Elizabeth and the Duke of Edin-
burgh would be attending the party, and we would likely have a chance
to meet them. As I had been a royal watcher since childhood – when I
kept a scrapbook of the queen's wedding and then her coronation – it
was a very exciting invitation, which we gladly accepted.

That was a night to remember for a few reasons. We were sent an
official invitation with instructions to arrive at a time well in advance
of the arrival of their Royal Highnesses – always a matter of protocol. Once at Canada House, we were told not to go up to the Royal
couple when they arrived, but to stay put wherever we were; they
would split up and come to us. We mingled and had a drink, and,
when the Royal couple arrived, they did, indeed, split up to move
around the room. We were off chatting with a small group of people
from Cambridge and Oxford when Queen Elizabeth was brought over
to us. It was 1980, and Prince Charles was a student at Cambridge, so,
after some niceties were exchanged about that, I asked her how he was
enjoying himself. She said something about it being difficult because
of all the tourists coming around to look and how he had to change
rooms to avoid that. A straightforward response. Then, someone who
was at Balliol College in Oxford mentioned that they had just started
to admit women to their college. Then, another person, (jokingly)
asked the queen, who was what was known as "The Visitor" at Oriel
College, whether she thought admission standards would drop when
women were admitted there. There was some restrained chuckling as
we waited for her reply. While Marty and I recall the interaction and
the participants involved somewhat differently, we are united on how
the queen replied. She laughed quietly and then said, "Oh you're just
a male chauvinist pig"! Needless to say, we were all taken aback. Did
we really hear that?

After the queen moved on, Prince Philip came by. He was even more
handsome than I had anticipated but seemed rather dismissive in his
manner. After someone put out their hand to shake his, he said, "What
is it about Canadians that they always have to shake hands?" That was
pretty much it. And he moved on.

Life in Cambridge was, for me, pretty much as it had been on our
previous visit just over ten years earlier. With Clare Hall having a residence for families, one might think more efforts would be made to foster inclusion. Periodically, the college did attempt to welcome family
members with a communal lunch; however, all the grad students and
fellows still wanted to "talk shop." I attended a few of the lunches, but,
once again, I felt like a fish out of water and soon gave up.

All the comings and goings associated with Marty's career meant that we lived in Cambridge on four occasions: for a year in 1960–1, for six months in 1963, five months in 1969, and another six months in 1980. I have mixed feelings about those times. One cannot help but be entranced by the stunning beauty of Cambridge. Having the privilege to simply be in that ancient place with its majestic buildings, to stroll the backs, visit the gardens, listen to concerts in the chapels, punt on the river, while also having the experience of living in a small English town, is extraordinary. But at the same time, it was not the place for a wife, not in the '60s on my first three stays, or in the '80s on my last. Still watching our pennies in those years, it was hard not to feel slighted when Marty dined at High Table – enjoying a full-course dinner with sherry to start, wine during, and port to follow. There was certainly no cooking or washing up for him to do, and no childcare duties, on those nights. Privileges for the elite in academia are not that different than for the elite in other walks of life, and the elite were, and are still, mainly male. Wives can never truly *share* in the perks that their husbands receive, nor should they. Who *should* be entitled to perks, or whether they should even exist, is a different story.

The year away had brought extraordinary experiences for all of us. All three children made friends and did things they would never have done at home. The connection with family members living in Israel and the connection with the country itself had a profound effect on all of us. The learning that all travel brings, with exposure to other environments and cultures, was immeasurable. And the memories are embedded for all five of us. While I might have felt hard done by at times, I could never have turned down the chance for this experience.

We returned to Canada in the summer of 1980, and I returned to my job at COTA, now with the title special projects coordinator. The work with clients was as satisfying as ever, and, with my new title, I was developing more skills: planning programs, writing grant proposals, and making public presentations. For example, during the early '80s, COTA thought children who needed occupational therapy to help them function better at school should receive it within the school setting, much as the home care program provided our services in the home. I prepared a brief entitled "Occupational Therapy: A Support Service for School Children with Special Needs" and presented it to the North York Bill 82 Planning Committee and the Special Education Committee of the Toronto Board of Education. It was similar to the presentations I had made with our private group of occupational therapists in 1976 – but now the time was right.

Once Bill 82, the Education Amendment Act, 1980, was passed,[4] the publicly funded school system in Ontario became responsible for the education of *all* Ontario students, including those with special needs. School boards were required to provide special education programs and services. With that law, occupational therapy (along with physiotherapy) became not only a desirable service but an essential one.

I added yet another task to my multi-tasking self in 1980, when a colleague at COTA asked me to take over her part-time teaching job at Seneca College, a community college in Toronto. It was just one night a week and just for one term, and, after encouragement from Marty, I agreed. The course was in rehabilitation counselling and included some lectures on rudimentary anatomy and physiology. I had my colleague's notes from the previous year, which made the endeavour possible. Nonetheless, I was doing something I had never done before: standing in front of a class of young adults, presenting material (newly relearned by me), and setting and marking assignments and exams. Unbeknownst to me at the time, it was a test run for the academic career that lay ahead.

With my fieldwork completed and all the coursework done for my master's, it was time to focus on my thesis. I was fortunate to have John Kershner, a cognitive neuroscientist, as my supervisor. He suggested I do something on the hypothesized sex-differences in neurocognitive tasks, an area of interest to him that worked well for me. I could study how males and females with Broca's aphasia (difficulty expressing speech) carried out a spatial task in comparison with males and females who were considered "normal," and were matched for sex, age, and level of education. Sandra Witelson, the Canadian neuroscientist, had just published her work on sex differences in hemispheric functioning in *Science*,[5] and it had attracted a lot of attention. I drew my sample from the stroke population, and I drew on my clinical knowledge of stroke to support my work. Our results offered an explanation for the poorer performance of females with Broca's aphasia on linguistic and spatial tasks and contributed to knowledge of sex differences in hemispheric functioning. I thoroughly enjoyed the entire research process and found it fascinating.

I graduated with my MA in the spring of 1982. A month later, I was sitting on the side of my bed lacing up my running shoes to go out to play tennis with neighbours when the phone rang. It was my former teacher, Thelma Cardwell, then the acting director of the Division of Occupational Therapy at U of T. She asked if I would join the faculty and start teaching in September.

I had never thought about being an academic. In my various students days, there were subjects I wanted to study in greater depth, and always new areas that I wanted to explore. In my eight or so years of clinical work, I took the time to learn about the diagnoses of those who whom I was working. I always knew I enjoyed teaching – from the little girl I tutored in reading when I was in Grade 8 to the kids at camp that I taught to swim and from teaching my own children to read to my brief stint teaching rehabilitation counselling at Seneca College. But it never occurred to me that combining my curiosity in health sciences and my enjoyment of teaching could result in an academic career. Indeed, I had still not thought about having "a career" at all.

Still Growing

10 Academia: Tiptoeing into a New Life

The fact that I didn't see myself as an academic did not seem to matter much in 1982, when I joined the Division of Occupational Therapy. It was a small program, none of the faculty was above the rank of assistant professor, and no one had tenure. Teaching was the raison d'être, and thoughts of research seemed few and far between. Among the most senior faculty, products of diploma courses from the 1930s and '40s, only one had a degree, and that was a BA. When I was hired, there was no discussion of research or of a tenure-stream position. My job was to teach.

Although the experiment, which had started in 1950, of having occupational therapy (OT) and physical therapy (PT) together in one program had ended in 1971, and each of our disciplines now granted their own degree, we were still housed together and shared some functions as well as a few classes. We were both at 256 McCaul Street, along with Art as Applied to Medicine (now known as Biomedical Communications), and were all in the Faculty of Medicine. For OT, it was the fourth of our "temporary" homes since the start of the diploma course at U of T in 1926.

The building was off the main campus of the university, just below the southwest corner of College and McCaul. A non-descript, five-storey building it had been a warehouse before rudimentary renovations tried to turn it into a place of learning. The physical plant had an erratic heating system and poor ventilation. People with physical disabilities could not access the elevator independently. The classrooms had old-fashioned desks, the so-called lab space had minimal equipment, there was no research space, and no student or faculty lounge. Faculty "offices" consisted of a modular desk and a chair in an open concept. To complicate matters, the Salvation Army ran a homeless shelter next door. They turfed out their (all male) residents each morning just as our (almost all female) students arrived for class. The mix was not good.

256 McCaul, the Division of Occupational Therapy, just south of College, much as it was in 1982

When I arrived as a faculty member, I encountered a not-so-subtle message about the place of women in the university. The building for the Faculty of Nursing, where the population was also primarily female, was not much better than ours. When Northrop Frye described Hart House in 1962, saying, "it dramatized the kind of life that the university encourages one to live: a life in which imagination and intelligence have a central and continuous function," he knew full well that the life the university encouraged was intended for men, and was one that women could not share.[1]

Women were very much in the minority within the faculty of the university when I joined. Even today, at a time when women make up *more than half* of the student body, female faculty still remain in the minority. This imbalance is seen particularly in the highest ranks, where male full professors continue to outnumber female full professors.[2] Similarly, salaries of female faculty remain lower, despite continuing efforts to close the gap.[3]

When I was hired, I followed the common practice for women of simply accepting the salary offered. It did not cross my mind to negotiate.[4] I had no idea how critical the starting salary was for going forward at the university – how across-the-board percentage increases would build on my initial salary, as would whatever annual merit increases I might earn. Not only did I accept the offer, but I was grateful for it. Just having the job and a full-time salary (with a pension and other good benefits) was well beyond my expectations.

Teaching loads were extremely heavy in my division, at least by today's standards. None of us had a "40–40–20" job description that would be considered typical (i.e., 40 per cent research, 40 per cent teaching, 20 per cent administration). Teaching was, for the most part, of the "jug-to-mug" variety: we prepared a lot of information, and we gave it to the students. It was didactic in tone and content and provided little opportunity for students to think critically. As is common in many young (by university standards) disciplines, and where the discipline lacks confidence regarding its place in the institution, we provided way too much material for each class. In addition, we taught the same material twice – once to each half of the class. The entire class was not all that large, just forty or so per year. But classes were split, and we taught the same material to two groups of twenty. Which class had the better learning experience – the one at the first of the week, when our thoughts were fresh and the adrenalin was pumping, or the one that came second, when our thoughts were more practiced, and we were more relaxed – would be interesting to know. Either way, repeating the lectures was not the best use of a teacher's time.

When I started to teach, male physicians provided the lectures on medical and surgical conditions, and on psychiatric conditions – just as they had when I was a student about twenty-five years earlier. There was often some repetition, which was understandable, as the lectures were generally one-off, and the physicians were not always apprised (or did not want to be apprised) of what the students already knew or what the previous week's lecturer had presented. That lack of coordination was annoying to students, but no one was going to tell doctors how or what to teach, beyond offering some general parameters. There was a clear power dynamic between us and them, and, although there might be some camaraderie, a respectful distance was maintained. We addressed most physicians, our academic colleagues, by their title and surname, while they called us by our given names. Thirty years later, the patriarchy that I knew as a student in the late '50s was still alive and well, although perhaps not quite as pervasive.

The trade-off for having less-than-perfect content in these lectures was the pretense of being part of a special in-group where experts (the physicians) shared their knowledge, *almost* as though we were all members of the same club. Sociologists James and Mary Maxwell wrote about the early relationship between medicine and occupational therapy in their 1994 chapter "Inner Fraternity, Outer Sorority."[5] The Maxwells acknowledged the almost charitable role played by the medical elite in sponsoring the emerging profession from the time of its appearance in Canada during the First World War. That this relationship continued for decades was due in part to the role the physicians had chosen to play in overseeing the new profession and bringing it along into health care, but also, in part, to the occupational therapists themselves who were complicit in maintaining the patriarchal relationship. These women worked in a subservient manner in the hospitals and in the university from the start.[6] Change was incremental, and, to this day, occupational therapists have trouble making their voices heard within the health care system. They have trouble explaining that they have what the medical model needs to promote health and well-being.

By the late '80s, the role of physicians in the program was much reduced, as our own faculty took over teaching much of what had been their material. We knew enough about relevant medical, surgical, and psychiatric conditions to give the students what they needed to know; we could avoid repetition, and we could make the lectures relevant to OT practice. We emphasized the occupational therapy role and de-emphasized the diagnostic labels and the reductionist approaches to treatment that came with them. As OTs, we were not in the business of fixing broken parts. We wanted to help people with illness and disability do what they wanted and needed to do to get on with their lives.[7] We were as concerned with adapting the occupations, and the environments within which the occupations were carried out, as we were with having the person with the illness or disability adapt. We could effect change in any or all three areas – an approach now referred to as the person-environment-occupation model.[8]

Another bit of housecleaning that occurred in the late '80s was to remove all of the craft equipment. Although it was clearly not appropriate for students to spend valuable class time learning to do a range of crafts, such as weaving or pottery, as I had done as a student, the students' *experience* of becoming fully engaged in an activity – the experience that we wanted them to provide for patients – was also denied. The idea of "flow," described by psychologist Mihaly Csikszentmihalyi as "a feeling of great absorption, engagement, fulfillment, and skill – [and] during which temporal concerns (time, food, ego-self, etc.) are typically ignored,"[9] could not be examined unless special labs were set up to do so. Even then, the learning was more theoretical and intellectual than experiential and emotional, a learning environment that early twentieth-century education reformer John Dewey would have thought inappropriate.

Along with the disappearance of the craft equipment in the classroom came the gradual disappearance within the profession of the role of crafts in therapy, once its mainstay, especially in asylums. The idea that being engaged in a craft could be useful preparation for vocational training or even a return to work, or that it could divert patients' attention from their pain, their worries, or, indeed, psychotic thoughts, had become almost heretical. If there was still a place for crafts, it was for physical purposes – that is, to mimic exercise. For example, crafts were used to strengthen muscles, increase joint range, and promote flexibility, particularly in the hands, arms, and shoulder.[10] There was nothing wrong with this practice, but it seemed to come at the expense of the more complex reasons for the use of crafts, or "occupations," in mental health.

Theoretical explanations for why crafts were useful in mental health were ignored, even though some had been around for over a century. The "two-thoughts hypothesis" of the American physician Edward Jarvis suggested that engaging patients with mental illness in occupations could bring on periods of sanity. In 1862, he explained his theory of how being engaged in an activity could build sane thoughts and suspend the mental disorder, stating, "as no two particles of matter can occupy the same point in space at the same moment, so no two absorbing thoughts or emotions can occupy the mind or heart at the same instant of time."[11] Thus, by extending the time of engagement in an activity, saner thoughts could prevail.

In 1910, Narziss Ach, a German psychologist, stressed how engaging in occupations could build self-esteem and a sense of agency: "Through the success and through the knowledge that 'I am the cause of this success,' the awareness of ability, i.e., the knowledge that 'I have accomplished this through my volition, I can do this' emerges." In a footnote to his publication, Ach stated that this effect could be found in "the so-called occupation therapy."[12] This early reference is rarely mentioned in the literature, despite its being directly relevant to the goals of occupational therapy.

In 1936, the Canadian endocrinologist Hans Selye proposed that, to relieve stress, "you must find something to put in the place of the worrying thoughts to chase them away."[13] That something had to be an activity that was absorbing. In cognitive therapy, which first became popular in the 1960s, Aaron Beck focused on identifying – and then refuting – intervening thoughts, which in depression tend to be automatic and negative. He recommended successful engagement in activities to refute those thoughts so as to undermine the patient's belief that they are not capable.[14]

The apparent value of diversion to mental health could have been well-supported theoretically by the time I started teaching had we looked; instead, the profession simply dismissed the idea of diversion– and the use of crafts – altogether.[15] While we paid some attention to the use of art, particularly with mentally ill patients, we did not consider its importance for everyone, tapping creativity and nurturing the spirit, as the artist and social reformer William Morris had recommended.[16] Now that art and craft have become more mainstream in the pursuit of health and well-being, occupational therapists are having to catch up.[17]

As I prepared to teach for the first time in the fall of 1982, I worried about a lot of things. I worried about my material, about being able to answer students' questions, and about how I would be perceived relative to the popular lecturer who had gone before me. I also worried about what to wear. In order to look professional and professorial on that first day of teaching, I bought a tailored, rust-brown wool suit, with a slim-fitting jacket and straight skirt. I wore a colourful, printed silk, long-sleeved blouse under the jacket, and I wore high heels. The outfit felt just right. Silly as that may sound, it helped.

My family was intrigued by my new full-time worker role. Marty made peanut butter and jam sandwiches for me for my lunch – albeit only on that first day. Tom, who was an undergrad at U of T, now had two parents on campus with him, which may or may not have been a good thing. Jenny, in high school, and Nancy, in elementary school, seemed to like the idea that I was now a teacher.

I drove to the university that first day and each day thereafter, even though I lived near public transportation and could have used it, as Marty did. But having the car made me feel less anxious: if anything happened with one of the children, I knew I could get to them in a hurry. I could also get to their school performances, pick them up and take them wherever they needed to be after school, and shop for what we needed for dinner. Having the car helped with the juggling – and the potential for feelings of guilt. Like many women who go back to work, I did not want anything about my mothering and homemaking roles to change. I wasn't trying to be a supermom – I just needed those roles to still be me.

After an initially shaky start, most classes went well. My primary course was "Adult Psychosocial Dysfunction" (aka mental health). I also taught a course on communication skills and interviewing, which gave me a chance to convey to students the paramount importance of establishing a good rapport with clients, how to be an active listener, and how to form a therapeutic relationship. These interpersonal skills were essential to all interactions with clients: without them, no meaningful goals could be set or achieved. I taught other courses over the years, but these were my main areas. I rather enjoyed the experience of holding forth in the classroom – once I got started. I experienced major anxiety beforehand, but a pretty good feeling during and after. Still, it took a long time for me to accept that I actually could do this new thing.

Although I thought about what I needed to do well in advance of each lecture and did some preliminary work, it was usually not until late the night before the class that I felt fully prepared. I could never just present material from the year before. Aside from there being new material to incorporate, I always thought there was a better way to present the material. I was not trying to be perfect, just better. For me, the late-night (final) preparation brought the material to the forefront of my mind, which was helpful for the next day. After a while, I stopped being too hard on myself for doing that last-minute final preparation and accepted that it seemed to work for me.

The saying that teachers keep a chapter ahead of their students always seemed directed at me – especially in the early years. Although I had had considerable clinical experience and knowledge in the areas where I taught, that didn't stop me from feeling like an imposter. Imposter syndrome – the feeling of being a fraud not worthy of the successes you may have, along with the fear of being found out – is common, but it is more prevalent among women. Women apparently fear failure more than men do, a tendency that some scholars explain by women's lack of socialization for risk taking, especially for risk taking by choice. Although times have changed, the gendered imposter syndrome is alive and well today.[18]

Just as I was adjusting to my teaching role, the issue of research activity (or lack thereof) came into sharp focus. Apparently, the whole Department of Rehabilitation Medicine (composed, at the time, of speech-language pathology, physical therapy, occupational therapy, and the medical specialty of physiatry) was not generating the expected level of research. The dean of the Faculty of Medicine, Dr Fred Lowy, was concerned. In January 1983, he gathered all of us together in the large ground-floor classroom at 256 McCaul. After some preliminary remarks, he told us, in so many words, that if we could not produce more and better research, we did not belong in the university. Everyone was stunned. The meeting, which took place just four months after my arrival, is vivid in my memory.

I took Dean Lowy's message to heart, and a year later I started my first research study. My previous clinical work in mental health provided my research question. Why was it so difficult for some patients to cope with illness and disability and adjust to altered life circumstances, while others seemed to manage whatever life throws at them? It was a complicated matter. We have always known about this almost dichotomous clinical outcome when two people suffer the same event, but little was known about why it happened. By the mid-'80s, research into the social determinants of health was providing some insight.[19] The concepts of social support and coping skills were always on the lists of determinants of health in some form. When I worked with people who had suffered a stroke, the dichotomy was the same as elsewhere: there were those who could manage and those who could not. I was interested to know more about why this might be and decided that research into the psychosocial factors affecting stroke outcomes would be a good start.

Stroke had been much in the news in Toronto in 1982. The world-renowned Canadian pianist Glenn Gould died that fall, just seven days after suffering a massive stroke at age fifty. I was a great fan of Gould, having heard him play in person and owning many of his recordings. I attended the public memorial service held at St. Paul's Anglican Church, and, like everyone in the sanctuary that day, I was overwhelmed when Gould's hauntingly slow, last recording of the Goldberg Variations filled the room at the end of the service. Tears welled up in my eyes. I couldn't help thinking about how his life would have been had he survived his stroke, and how difficult it would have been for the health care system to offer him much hope.

Just three days after Gould's death came the news that John Robarts, the former premier of Ontario, had taken his own life after surviving a series of strokes. He had described his difficulty coping, saying, "It's such a long, bloody struggle."[20] Along with what I knew about the difficulties experienced by my stroke patients when I worked at COTA, the stories of these two high-profile people reminded me how universal such suffering was. These thoughts added to my reasons for wanting to do research in the area of psychosocial adjustment to illness and disability.

For my first foray into research, I had a wonderful collaborator in Mary Ann McColl, who had joined our faculty in 1984. We both had clinical experience working with people who had suffered a stroke, which gave us a good starting place. She had the methodological smarts, having recently graduated from a master's program in epidemiology and biostatistics, and I had my master's thesis in a stroke-related area.[21] She was the more logical thinker, a highly organized writer who got things going and kept us on track; I was the more tangential thinker (but in a good way, I like to think), bringing caveats and additional possibilities into our discussions. We worked well together over several years developing a body of work on social support: observational studies, experimental studies, and assessment tools, as well as some theoretical work on depression and disability.

Social support was a hot topic at the time. Sydney Cobb and others had suggested that it could play the role of a mediator in determining health outcomes.[22] The early work on stressful life events by Holmes and Rahe set the stage for our hypothesis that a stressful event such as a stroke, with its potential for negative sequelae, including depression, could be buffered by social support.[23] Our first study, supported by a modest grant from the Dean's Fund in the Faculty of Medicine in 1984, was enough to get us going, and other larger grants followed. Our first publication titled "Social Support and Psychosocial Dysfunction Following Stroke: Buffering Effects in a Community Sample," appeared in the *Archives of Physical Medicine and Rehabilitation* in 1987.[24]

Seeing the apparent benefit of social support in our cross-sectional study of this population, we wanted to determine if it was something we could try as an intervention. We used social network therapy and the work of the Canadian psychologist Benjamin Gottlieb to help us develop and evaluate a social support intervention.[25] With the aid of another grant, we tested its effectiveness after stroke in a randomized trial. We hired occupational therapists to work with the stroke survivors in our experimental group. After workshops on how to assess participants' existing support networks and how to map out additional supports that seemed needed or were wanted, therapists worked with the participants (and their families) to help build that support. The control group received the usual post-stroke rehabilitation but no social network therapy. We were disappointed to find that, although we saw the expected differences between groups, they did not reach statistical significance, either on social support measures or psychosocial outcomes. However, we gleaned many important insights regarding the issues that needed to be addressed in future studies, such as the right time to attempt to (re)build social support post-stroke, and whether it was necessary to screen out those with already high levels of support for this type of intervention. We also learned, more generally, how necessary it was to educate society about the importance of giving and receiving social support.[26]

In the 1990s, we were joined by another colleague in my department, Rebecca Renwick, and we expanded our program of research to people with HIV/AIDS. We wanted to see if coping methods and social support acted as determinants of quality of life in that population. The study, published in *AIDS Care* in 1996, teased out the types of support and coping that were related to quality of life.[27] It also revealed the surprising finding that several aspects of quality of life were affected positively once the diagnosis was confirmed. Our funding for this study enabled us to develop and validate an instrument to measure social support for this specific population: the Social Support Inventory for People with HIV/AIDS (SSIPWA).[28]

Our next step was to focus on quality of life for women with HIV/AIDS, knowing that they were about to succumb to the virus in greater numbers, but our grant application was unsuccessful. Not wanting to give up on this topic, I managed to get ten departments within the Faculty of Medicine to join us in an application to the faculty's Rosenstadt

Fund to sponsor a lecture series on women with HIV/AIDS. At the same time, we collaborated with representatives from Voices of Positive Women for funds to host a panel of women living with HIV/AIDS. The lecture series and the panel were open to the university at large. Alas, attendance at both was dismal. Our focus on women with HIV/AIDS was not yet of interest in the university community. Yet, a decade or so later, women represented 26.2 per cent of all HIV-positive test results in Canada, more than doubling the proportion of cases before 1999.

We published eleven papers on our work on social support during this period, all in what would be considered good journals (e.g., *Social Science and Medicine, Archives of Physical Medicine and Rehabilitation, AIDS Care, Occupational Therapy Journal of Research*). In all, we developed and validated three population-specific inventories for measuring social support: one for people who had survived a stroke (the SSISS), one for those diagnosed with HIV/AIDS (the SSIPWA), and, more broadly, one for people with acquired disabilities (the SSIPAD, and we published two book chapters, one dealing with depression and disability and the other with the quality of life for people with HIV/AIDS. Postcards from around the world requested reprints of our work – a lovely feature in research circles at the time, one that has disappeared with the advent of online access to journal articles.

As I became more involved in research activities – writing grants, running studies, presenting at conferences, and writing papers for publication – I struggled to develop my research skills on my own. My master's program had prepared me for research to some extent, but it was clearly not enough. I began to think that doing a doctorate would be the best route. I also knew by then that a doctorate would put me in a good position to apply for a tenure-stream appointment, should one ever become available.

I was forty-six, and, for the first time in my life, I had a plan to actively pursue a career.

When I was trying to decide whether to apply for the PhD program, I told myself what I have since told others: apply – and worry about whether to go or not once you have been accepted. As it turned out, I was accepted. With that knowledge in hand, I did not dither about whether or not to enrol. By now my children were twenty-one, nineteen, and fourteen. Tom was away at McGill University in Montreal doing law, Jenny had just started her undergrad at U of T, and Nancy was safely launched in high school. My mothering role was lighter than ever. Our parents were doing well and did not need any help from us. Marty was almost as busy as when he was dean, but times had changed, and I was not expected to be at his side as much in his work-related social activities. He took on a little more at home, becoming an expert at cooking salami and eggs. He was a reliable and willing grocery shopper and took over my task of paying the bills. My being busier than before may have made him even more productive, as I kept out of his way and was not urging him to do other things with me.

By the summer of 1985, I was back at school, at OISE, where I had completed my master's degree. Given my roles as a wife, a mother, and a daughter, it did not cross my mind to go outside of Toronto for my doctoral work. Besides, I had enjoyed OISE and found the environment just right for me as a mature student. The courses for my degree were few, my classmates were supportive, and my supervisor and doctoral committee members were excellent. A faculty of education was a good fit for me.[29]

Meanwhile, I kept teaching full-time, despite the rules that said you couldn't work more than ten hours a week and be in a full-time doctoral program. It seemed to me that, because I didn't teach in the summer, I could take one OISE course, which would make my doctoral course load more manageable for the rest of the year. This could fit within the *intent* of the rules. I could complete the program within the expected time and not be slowed down by the fact that I was working. That first summer, I took one half-course and I enrolled in two other courses for the following term. I also had permission to audit a neuroanatomy course in the Faculty of Medicine. I was off to a good start.

Life has a way of interfering just when you think you have sorted things out. I had only just begun the winter term when my daughter Jenny had a major car accident and all our lives turned upside down.

11 Difficult Times: Family Troubles and Work Troubles

Now in her first year at the University of Toronto, our daughter Jenny was in Quebec on Christmas break. She was driving to Mount Tremblant to ski with three passengers: a girlfriend, my brother's fifteen-year-old son, Alexander, and a friend of Alexander's. It was January 2nd, 1986. Late that morning, the police phoned my brother, Barry, who lived in Montreal, to tell him there had been an accident. Barry called our house and reached Marty, who happened to be at home. I was at my desk at work when Marty called me with the news. I instinctively cried out such that colleagues rushed to see what had happened. One of them insisted on driving me home, realizing I was too distraught to drive myself.

There was black ice on the auto route near St Jérôme. Once a car hit that ice, its driver instinctively hit the brakes, which made the car spin off the road. Each car ran out of control in this way, until some eighteen cars were involved. Jenny saw the car ahead of her put on its breaks, and she put on hers; her car spun around, and the passenger side of the car landed in a snowbank in the median. Unhurt, she scrambled out the driver's side onto the road to assess the situation. When the next car hit its brakes and spun around, it hit her and sent her flying twenty feet away. The same car hit Alexander as well as Jenny's friend as they were getting out of the car, and both of them sustained injuries. Alexander's friend, having remained in the car, was unhurt. Jenny suffered a broken leg (a "bumper fracture" of her left tibia and fibula), injuries to her left knee, a broken right ankle, a concussion, and a scalp laceration.

An ambulance took her to the hospital in St Jérôme, where they stitched up her scalp. From there, she was taken to the Royal Victoria Hospital in Montreal. I boarded a plane in Toronto and arrived at the Royal Vic while Jenny was still in Emergency. She was somewhat disoriented, complaining about the pillow under her head being lumpy when in fact it was the stitches and the swelling on the back of her head that were causing the discomfort. She kept saying, "Mom, is it you? Will you stay? It hurts so much." Then, in a pleading sort of tone, she would add, "It wasn't my fault." I told her that I knew it wasn't her fault, and that of course I would stay. I tried to reassure her that everything would be all right. Inside, I was heartbroken for her and terrified of what might be in store.

Jenny's broken leg would turn out to be a complicated injury. By the time she reached the hospital in Montreal and was readied for surgery, her leg had developed an acute "compartment" syndrome. The syndrome occurs when the intact tissue (the fascia), enclosing the groups of muscles, nerves, and blood vessels surrounding the broken bone, cannot expand to accommodate the increased pressure caused by the trauma. The pressure prevents adequate blood flow to and from the compartment. The combination of poor blood supply and the now surgically opened wound put her at risk of osteomyelitis.

An orthopaedic surgeon operated on Jenny's left leg that day. He reduced the pressure and fixated the fractured bones internally with metal plates and screws. He left the wound open to drain and then a day or so later, with Jenny back in the operating room, he took a skin graft from her thigh and closed the wound. Her leg was then encased in plaster above and below the knee. Her right leg was also in plaster below the knee to fixate her broken angle.

It was lucky for all of us that our son, Tom, was living in Montreal at the time. After seeing that Jenny was all right, he drove to St Jerome to speak with the police and deal with the car. His good friend and roommate, Mark, sat with me during the lengthy surgery.

The Royal Vic, an imposing, if somewhat run-down-looking, structure, had a celebrated history since its founding just over a hundred years earlier. I felt Jenny was in good hands, medically, if not psychologically. I left the hospital at about 3 a.m. that first night. Jenny was still sleepy from the anaesthetic, and I thought she would not wake for a while. With nowhere to lay my head, and exhausted from the stress of the day, I needed a break. Unfortunately, Jenny awoke soon after I left. She realized she was in a hospital and called out for me, and then a doctor, and then a nurse. When no one came she thought she was still lying on the side of the road and shouted more loudly. A nurse finally appeared, only to scold her. She told Jenny to stop shouting, that she would wake everyone up. It was not a helpful response.

The driver of the car that hit Jenny sent a bouquet of long-stemmed red roses the next day. We put them aside, unable to appreciate his gesture.

I stayed at Jenny's bedside for a week, then went home to sort out my teaching responsibilities and my doctoral courses. Marty and Nancy, who had been eager to see Jenny, came to Montreal when I left, and Tom continued to visit throughout the ordeal. I took an overnight train back to Toronto. The regular rumbling of the train along the tracks lulled me to sleep as I took my first real break from standing guard – that act of vigilance that mostly mothers perform when there's a sick family member.

I came back to Montreal and stayed for another week until Jenny could be discharged to Sunnybrook Hospital in Toronto for follow-up care. I slept at my brother's home in Westmount and felt comforted being with him and Ann. After long days at Jenny's side, I found some respite in the walk from the hospital to their house, even in the bitter January cold.

The flight home with Jenny was a saga in itself. It was as if Air Canada had never transported someone on a stretcher. The crew clumsily carried her, vertically, head down, through to the back of the plane, where they placed the stretcher across the tops of a few empty seats. I wrote a nasty letter telling Air Canada I thought they should be able to do better but had no reply.

Soon after she was admitted to Sunnybrook, it became clear that the fracture site was infected and needed to be re-opened and allowed to drain. After another week in hospital, more antibiotics, and instructions for cleansing the site twice daily, Jenny was allowed home on crutches. In early February, we tried, with great effort and the use of a wheelchair, to get her back to university for a few hours a day, thinking that being with her friends might cheer her up and keep her in touch with the life she had been leading before the accident. But, by mid-February, her leg had become more painful, and she spiked a fever. She was re-admitted to the hospital and diagnosed with acute osteomyelitis – a potentially life-threatening infection of the bone. It was the night before Nancy's fifteenth birthday.

Intravenous antibiotics were restarted. Dead tissue and bone, a result of the compartment syndrome, were removed during successive visits to the operating room. Bone grafts taken from her pelvis were used to stimulate the healing process, and more skin grafts provided temporary closure of the otherwise gaping wound. Watching her go into the operating room, over and over again, broke our hearts. Although she always seemed calm and resigned to whatever had to be done, she kept her teddy bear by her side, just in case.

During one of our many conversations with the orthopaedic surgeon, he explained in some detail the battle between the healthy new tissue and the infected dead tissue and the uncertainty as to which would win. He raised the possibility of amputation as a worst-case scenario.

Finally, on April 23rd, after a total of some ten visits to the operating room, Jenny seemed to be on the mend.

Meanwhile, many Ontario doctors were protesting the recently proclaimed Bill 94 (the Health Care Accessibility Act, 1986) designed to bring Ontario's health care system in line with the Canada Health Act of 1984 and to ban doctors' ability to extra-bill.[1] Some doctors were threatening to strike. They sported buttons on their white coats that said "Kill Bill 94." The atmosphere was tense. The doctors' actions prompted Jenny to write a poem about how they made her feel. Two of the verses excerpted below sum up her mood:

> To suffer once more through a meal hardly filling
> While the doctors all worry if they'll get extra billing,
> And storm into our rooms with a word seldom kind
> Oblivious so long as their paychecks get signed.
>
> Antibiotics, they'll make you better
> (Who cares if they're turning your skin into leather)
> Now give me your arm, we'll find one more vein
> And blow six on the way, but don't mind the pain.

Through all of this, and for several years to come, Marty dealt with a myriad of insurance and legal issues arising from the accident. One potential lawsuit might have had a preventative effect: Quebec's transportation services were alleged to have been negligent in not properly salting the road on the day of the accident, or indeed on other days, as the highway was known to be poorly maintained in winter. Unfortunately, that action did not proceed because Quebec's no-fault insurance legislation precluded the Ministry of Transportation from being held liable.

What a time of fear and stress. Fear for Jenny's life and that of her leg. Stress for her because of the trauma she had experienced and the disruption of her first year of university and what should have been an exciting new chapter of her life. Stress for Marty and me because of the incessant worry and decisions that had to be made. Nancy, instead of getting the attention she needed as a young teenager, took on a more caring adult role, while Tom watched most of it from Montreal, gave support where he could, and visited often.

Jenny took a job at her old camp that first summer while still on crutches, and, in the fall, she returned to university full time, having salvaged two credits from her first year. The last step in her treatment was to implant tissue expanders on either side of her ankle to begin

With Marty at Jenny's graduation, 1990

the lengthy process of creating enough new skin to graft over the disfigured, but now fully healed, area. More than two years after the accident, the reconstruction was completed, and her leg was finally healed. It was a special day when she finished her undergraduate degree in 1990. Both Marty and I were thrilled to march at that convocation ceremony.

Once the immediate danger to Jenny's life had passed, and we knew that a lengthy process of recovery was ahead of us, we tried to resume our lives and just deal with events as they arose. We were confident we could kick into heavy caring mode as needed. For me, resuming my life meant returning to my teaching and my doctoral work. The teaching was much as before. However, my doctoral work was now at a new stage. I needed to decide on a thesis topic.

Before entering the doctoral program, I had attended a behavioural neuroscience conference in Toronto, where I heard about a study that piqued my interest. Dr Jason Brown, a neurologist from New York University, described his research with people who had had a left hemisphere stroke. These individuals usually had some degree of aphasia and weakness or paralysis of the right arm and leg (hemiplegia). Some people also had agraphia – that is, they were unable to spell when using their *left* hand, despite its being motorically intact. For stroke survivors with both aphasia and agraphia, the ability to communicate was thus profoundly affected: they could not speak, and they could not write what they wanted to say.

Brown's study showed that spelling improved if the letters were formed while using a prosthesis. The *paralysed* (dominant) arm rested in the plastic trough of the prosthesis and the hand sat on top of its curved end. A hole in that end part of the prosthesis held a felt pen. When the intact shoulder muscles were used to move the prosthesis – along with the pen – the person with agraphia could print the letters of

some simple words with their paralysed arm. Brown's explanation for
this phenomenon, what he called
"hemiplegic writing," was rooted in
microgenetic theory. It suggested
that words that came from a devel-
opmentally older level of language
could be accessed by the similarly
older, lower-level motor system at
the shoulder joint. Brown claimed
that "use of older proximal motor

A prosthesis facilitates writing movements
for a hemiplegic arm

systems [i.e., movement by the shoulder muscles] facilitated access to
submerged or preprocessing levels in language and action structure."[2]

The condition of agraphia fascinated me, and I thought it would be
a perfect topic for my thesis. It combined my concern for people who
had suffered a stroke, the interest in brain and behaviour that had
surfaced during my master's program, and an ongoing fascination
with the English language. I set out to replicate and extend Brown's
work. I ordered a prosthesis from him, and I recruited five stroke survivors with chronic, non-fluent aphasia, who also had agraphia, from
the Toronto Speech and Stroke Centre. I designed linguistic tasks to
operationalize Brown's concept of higher-level and lower-level language processing. I used a single-subject A-B-B-A design, where each
participant acted as their own control, doing the same tasks with the
hemiplegic right hand and prosthesis (A) and with the unimpaired
left hand (B). Although I assessed my participants' motor ability to
form legible letters and words with the prosthesis, my primary interest was in the linguistic properties of what they could and could not
write. I also asked them to complete what was considered a "disconnection" task, to rule out other explanations for the effect Brown had
found.

I met with participants in their homes as often as necessary for them
to get through my set of tasks. Everyone was pleased to participate,
even though they had difficulty with some of the tasks and became
frustrated. I asked my participants to *write* (not print) sets of linguis-
tically different words, including abstract and concrete nouns, verbs,
homonyms, and pseudowords (made-up words that could only be
spelled phonetically). I also asked participants to try to write a sentence
to express a thought of their own. The results of this task in particular
were exciting for a few of my participants who saw that they could
indeed share some thoughts this way (e.g., "my sweater is new"). I was
excited too and wished I could continue to work with these individuals

Attempts by four participants to write sentences using the prosthesis

in therapy rather than as research participants.

My results confirmed earlier findings by Brown of superior performance by the hemiplegic right arm and prosthesis combination. As both hands demonstrated better performance on so-called lower-level tasks (e.g., spelling concrete nouns such as "dog"), the results lent some support to his microgenetic theory and the use of more primitive structures to access lower-level language. However, that explanation did not account for better performance by the right (hemiplegic) side on higher-level tasks, such as writing pseudowords, which could only be accomplished through phonetic spelling.

I thought the results of my study suggested that "automatic writing," first proposed by the Russian neurologist Alexander Luria, could be responsible for the effect I was seeing. By requiring my participants to write, rather than print, I facilitated their use of a much-practised skill. They used their intact shoulder muscles to move the prosthesis in ways that enabled the pen to form words much as they would have done before their stroke. Interestingly, in today's world of computers, where cursive writing is no longer a highly practised automatic skill, my explanation would likely not be tenable.

My thesis supervisor was Professor Linda Siegel, a psychologist with expertise in the cognitive aspects of learning disabilities, and a fine scholar. One of her requirements for me as a student was that I submit an abstract of my study to a major neuropsychology conference. I was surprised when my abstract was accepted, and, as a result, I would be presenting my preliminary findings at the International Neuropsychology Society conference in Washington, DC, in 1987. Talk about the imposter syndrome! What was an occupational therapist doing at a neuropsychology conference, anyways? It was a stressful but exhilarating experience. It was also the first and last time I ever ran out of time when presenting my work. The feeling of complete shock when a "room monitor" (the person responsible for keeping presentations on schedule) holds up the "one-minute" sign, and it seems utterly impossible to finish within that time, is something one never forgets.

About six months after I had started the PhD program, a rare tenure-stream position became available in my division. The ad stated that a PhD was *preferred*, not required. With the profession at a stage where few people had that degree, it seemed that my being *enrolled* in a PhD program, along with my four years already on the faculty, would make me competitive. The position was advertised broadly, according to proper hiring practices. It was assumed by many (myself in particular) that there would be few applicants and that I would be selected for the position – or that the position would be held for me until I received my doctorate. The profession was small, and we would surely know about someone out there with a doctorate who might want to apply.

As it turned out, someone with a doctorate and other good qualifications was out there and did apply, and that individual was selected over me. I was devastated. It wasn't just the failure to be selected that was a disheartening. Since tenure-stream positions available to women were rare at the time – and almost unheard of in occupational therapy – it was unlikely that another would become available any time soon. Anne Innis Dagg recounts her fruitless search for a tenure-stream position at the University of Waterloo and the University of Guelph, despite her stellar accomplishments as a researcher and teacher. She was turned down for a permanent teaching appointment in biology at Wilfrid Laurier University, without even being accorded an interview. At the start of her search, having earned her PhD, Dagg had "hoped to become a tenured professor like my father [Harold Innis], my husband, and my brother." For Dagg, these disappointments resulted in her taking her future into her own hands and becoming a "citizen scientist," where she made enormous contributions to the knowledge of giraffe as well as other subjects.[3] When I was turned down, almost two decades later, I could not claim sexism was at work, given that my competitor was also a woman. It seemed, however, that the door to academia, where I was finally starting to feel comfortable and planning a future, had now closed.

I was not prepared to stay on in the occupational therapy program at U of T under these circumstances. Just as I did not think to do my doctorate anywhere other than in Toronto, given my family roles, I would not consider applying for a position in another city.

I would need to totally rethink my future.

To compound my situation, all of this was happening in the early spring of 1986, just a few months after my daughter's car accident. She was still undergoing some procedures, and our family was still adjusting to our new circumstances. It was an extraordinarily difficult time, and I was just so tired of trying to cope. The best way out seemed to be for me to resign from my position. I knew I was probably overreacting, but resigning seemed the only answer. Having finally started to plan for my own life, it already seemed doomed.

I wrote a letter of resignation. The director of the Division of Occupational Therapy (Robin Schaffer) was dismayed by my action but not surprised; she also had not foreseen any serious competition for the position. And I told my students about my decision to leave. It seemed the right thing to do, given that they had known so much about my life that year already when I had had to cancel or rearrange several classes because of my daughter's accident. Despite their knowing little about how appointments within the university worked, and unbeknownst to me, some students wrote a letter, gathered their classmates' signatures, and sent it off to the chair of the department, Mickey Milner, with a copy to the director of the division. They noted my role in their development as health professionals, and my "personal empathetic and caring qualities." They stated that my loss would be a detrimental to the program.

I think it was the students' actions on my behalf that made me decide not to just slink away. Yet it was hard to know what to do. There had not been anything unfair about the process. It was just that I had (mistakenly) thought that no one more qualified would apply and that the position would be held for me. I was certainly angry with myself. Why did I take this risk? Why didn't I protect myself from this potential disappointment?

After discussions with Marty, and after taking a few days to calm down, I contacted a few people within the university administration to see if there were any options open for someone in my position. Having travelled in social circles that included people higher up in the administrative echelons because of Marty's position, I was not afraid to contact them now for advice. They listened and made helpful suggestions. Apparently, it was possible to have a tenure-stream position protected for a period under certain conditions, but, even if the committee had understood that they had that option, it was reasonable that they should have selected someone who was already fully qualified.

Deliberations at the university continued, however, and it was decided that a new tenure-stream position would be provided and that it would be protected for me – on the condition that I complete my doctorate within the next three years. In addition, my professors at OISE were required to send a written report to the department chair annually to ensure that I was progressing as required. While that requirement could have appeared somewhat demeaning, it seemed fair to me under the circumstances, and I was grateful. However, I was left with the feeling that perhaps I hadn't come by the position fairly, that I was just a squeaky wheel that ultimately got its oil.

I worked away on my thesis and took an unpaid term off from teaching to finish writing. I hibernated at home during that hot summer, did not socialize, and stuck to my computer with our dog Skipper by my side. I was in a hurry to finish so I could meet the conditions that had been set out by the university. I also hurried so that I would be done before I turned fifty, which, by then, was not many months away.

The story had a happy ending. I defended my thesis in December 1988, just three and a half years after entering the program – a relatively short time, given all that was going on in my life. The defence

Writing my doctorial thesis, 1988

itself was stressful, of course, but also quite exhilarating. My teaching experience helped me give a good presentation of the work, which impressed the committee. I found the questions they put to me challenging, but I was able to defend my reasoning adequately.

We planned a party at our home for the night of the defence. It might have been chutzpah on my part to pre-judge the outcome of the defence, but Marty had to leave the next morning for Ireland, and, if we delayed the party, he could not have attended. Besides, I had been shown the examiners' reports of the written thesis and knew they were positive, and I knew I had the support of my committee. Something very untoward would have had to happen for me to fail my oral defence. We invited people to come for "a drink and dessert." Marty organized the drinks, and I organized the email invitations and dish rentals. I ordered desserts and prepared a smoked salmon platter and its trimmings. I set out flowers and tidied the house. It was just like the old days of entertaining – only this time it was for me!

It was a great party, although it started in a worrisome fashion. Guests were due to arrive at 7 p.m. We had invited a lot of people: family, friends, my work colleagues and a few of Marty's, people from OISE and COTA. Excitement in the house ran high as we all got ready. Less than an hour before the guests were due to arrive, the five of us were in the kitchen eating a quick supper of Kentucky fried chicken. We scraped our plates into the small garbage bin fixed to the inside of a door just below the kitchen sink. Skipper, our poorly trained but lovable beagle, enticed by the smell of the chicken bones, pounced on the door to get at them. I instinctively smacked the dog – something I would ordinarily never do. But, given the worry with dogs and chicken bones, and in my stressed state, I did. Skipper then instinctively bit me on my wrist – something he would never have done under ordinary circumstances. And he drew blood. When the guests arrived, I was sporting a (white) bandage on my wrist along with my lovely new white angora sweater. When the party ended, Tom took me to the Emergency Department at Sunnybrook Hospital, where a few stitches tidied up the wound. I fully forgave the dog, who had been my faithful companion throughout the time I was writing my thesis – sitting at my feet or sleeping in a nearby chair. It was harder to forgive myself for having hit him.

There was interest in my study when it was published, including a note with the ominous title "Reply to Friedland," by Dr Anton Leischner in the same issue of the journal, *Aphasiology*, where my paper was published.[4] Leischner's quarrel seemed to be with Brown's naming of the effect as "hemiplegic writing," rather than his own earlier naming of it as a "graphic disconnection syndrome."[5] So the critique was not really aimed at my work. Phew!

I gave several talks, mainly to therapists working with stroke survivors, about the study. I found the effect of using the prosthesis fascinating. It seemed to offer some hope for a path to communication that had not been fully explored, and I thought about going further with the prosthesis. However, I considered myself lucky to go as far as I did in an area more rightly the purview of neuropsychologists and speech-language pathologists and decided to quit while I was ahead.

I settled back into my teaching and psychosocial research. The family was all doing well. Everything was good.

A few months after I completed my PhD, our director, Robin Schaffer, announced that she was taking an eight-month sabbatical leave and asked me to take over as acting director. Some supports were in place, and she would look after the budget – something I dreaded. I didn't think it would add much work for me and I agreed. To my surprise, I rather enjoyed the job. It was taxing but interesting, and I learned a lot. I liked being in a leadership position, running meetings, writing memos, meeting with people. It wasn't the power – because there wasn't much of that – but there was a sense of control that I liked. Just before the time was up for her return, Robin decided to resign at the end of the next six months. Her position became open.

From my experience as acting director, I had a good idea of what the job entailed. With some encouragement from Robin, other faculty members, and my family, I decided to apply. I hadn't had a great deal of academic experience at that point, having been hired just eight years earlier and having been preoccupied with my doctoral work for almost half of that time. Furthermore, although I had had a good three-year pre-tenure review, I did not yet have tenure. I had a PhD, teaching experience, and now some administrative experience, but nothing more. However, I was motivated to apply because I saw opportunities for making change that would be possible with that position and more difficult without it. Once again, the likelihood of someone coming from the "outside" seemed remote, but this time I certainly knew it was possible.

As it turned out, someone from another university did apply.

12 Big Fish, Little Pond: Director, Division of Occupational Therapy

As part of the selection process for director of the Division of Occupation Therapy, the search committee asked us – the two candidates – to give a seminar on our research and to talk about our vision and goals. Like many other women, I felt uncomfortable competing, but there was no choice in the matter.[1] In my seminar, I talked about my research on stroke. I highlighted the social support research I had done with Mary Ann McColl to show the importance of the social environment in buffering the stressful life events initiated by a stroke, and I spoke about my work on agraphia to illustrate how an individual's communication skills could be helped through the use of a writing device. The two approaches to intervention provided good examples of how occupational therapists effect change: by modifying the environment (with social support), and by modifying the occupation (with the help of the prosthesis). Being so invested in the plight of those who had been participants in my studies (and earlier in my clinical work), I gave a spirited presentation.

When the search committee asked about my vision for the future of the program, I spoke about wanting to attract students with a desire to make change, students who wanted to contribute to society and whose diversity reflected the population we served. I stressed the need for lessening the burden of service tasks on faculty so we could spend more time on research. From what I had seen, service duties – in a predominantly female faculty like ours – were particularly heavy.[2] I also spoke about the need to have less didactic teaching, and a curriculum that emphasized the roles of advocate, educator, and counsellor. We needed to prepare students for work in the community where they could help people with chronic illness and disability to adjust to daily life. We needed to move out of the hospital, where the work was more medicalized (and more appropriate for physical therapists), and into the places where clients lived. I wanted our discipline to be more visible within the university and society, to make our voices and our opinions heard.

I stressed the need for a shared vision and set out how I would consult with others to make that happen.

I also stated that occupational therapy should be a free-standing department within the Faculty of Medicine (and not a division of the Department of Rehabilitation Medicine) and that we needed a graduate department. These two goals were important but seemed especially lofty at the time.

As for my own research, I stressed that my goal as director would be to facilitate the research of others and that those efforts would come first. It may have sounded altruistic, but, in fact, it was pragmatic. My administrator role would not leave me a lot of time for my own research, and, as I was not then and would likely never be a "star" researcher, building the division's research capacity seemed a much more important, and viable, goal. I felt good about my seminar and good about my interview.

The search committee met for their final deliberations in our conference room a few days later. I was at the photocopying machine, just opposite the conference room, when the committee happened to take a break. One of the committee members rather nonchalantly walked over to me. She put her hand on my shoulder and asked, in a tone that was somehow too solemn and solicitous, how I was doing. And at that moment, I knew I had not been selected for the position.

Once again, I, as the sort-of-shoo-in candidate, was turned down. But this time I was prepared. Besides, it was easy to accept that the candidate who was selected was more qualified: she had a better record of scholarship and more administrative experience. I even thought how good it would be to have her as my boss. There was no need to panic this time: I was in a tenure-stream position and could just carry on.

It was January 1991, and I had my first sabbatical leave. Marty also had a leave, so finally, "we" would be on sabbatical. All three of our children had flown the coop: Nancy was taking her third year off and doing courses at the Sorbonne; Jenny was in Law School at the University of Toronto, and Tom, having graduated from law at McGill, was about to be called to the bar in Ontario and Quebec. It was a perfect time for us to be

With four occupational therapists outside a mental health facility in Vellore, India, 1991

away – other than for the fact of the (First) Gulf War. We took a brief trip to Paris to see Nancy and then, a few months later, after things settled down a little in the Middle East, we went to India. Marty and I both gave some lectures, and I visited occupational therapy schools and health care facilities. From India, we went to Hong Kong for more visits, then to Japan, and finally to Hawaii to rest up before returning home. It was a great trip.

We were still in India when news came that the person who had been offered the job of director had decided against it. I was asked to take on the position. I took a deep breath, swallowed my pride, and said "yes."

Pushed by my husband and my son, I tried to negotiate salary and conditions for my new position. Having had a late start in academia (at age forty-three), a low starting salary (when I didn't think of negotiating), and some part-time employment while doing my doctorate, my salary was low compared to several others in my division. I would receive a small stipend for my administrative role, but that would not affect my base salary.[3] I wasn't aware of how my salary compared to male faculty members in a similar position, but the gendered differential in pay in Canadian universities was significant at the time.

Over the years, the University of Toronto had established several committees to investigate what they considered salary anomalies for female faculty who were full-time. In 1984, the university established the Ad Hoc Committee on the Status of Women. Its report, *A Future for Women at the University of Toronto*, published that same year, made forty-eight recommendations, many of which would not see the light of day for years to come. It recommended, for example, a code that would define demeaning sexist and racist jokes and remarks as unacceptable in university contexts and publications. It put forward creative solutions, such as a bridging year for women whose studies were interrupted due to marriage or childcare, and it suggested there be a call for recruitment of more mature women.[4]

Ontario passed its Pay Equity Act in 1987, spurred on, perhaps, by Justice Rosalie Abella's statement in the report of the Royal Commission on Employment Equity that provincial laws did not reflect a commitment to equal pay for work of equal value.[5] Now all public sector employers were required to value jobs usually done by women and compare them to those usually done by men in an objective and consistent way based on factors such as skill, effort, responsibility, and working conditions. The act stipulated that "a female job class must receive compensation that is at least equal to the compensation that is paid to a male job class of equal or compatible value."[6] For the university, that meant comparisons across parameters that included the amount of postgraduate education, length of employment, and types of responsibilities. After a review was made of the salaries of men in the Faculty of Pharmacy who had been selected as our comparators, we received lump sum awards in two successive years and, in 1991, our base salaries were adjusted. All faculty in the Division of Occupational Therapy (we were all women) achieved a significant pay increase.

It seems, however, that attempts to address pay equity do not last long. The median wage gap in the salaries of full-time university teachers in 2016–17, as reported by the Canadian Association of University Teachers (CAUT), was $13,750.[7] In 2019, a salary increase was implemented for 800 female tenured or tenure-stream faculty at U of T after it was found that they earned 1.3 per cent less than "comparably situated" faculty members who are men, once experience (including experience prior to hiring), field of study, and other relevant factors were considered.[8]

The issue of how society *values* different forms of work is complicated but significant. Melissa Moyser, who analysed Statistics Canada data for a 2017 report entitled *Women and Paid Work*, suggests that, "given female-dominated occupations largely resemble work women have traditionally performed in the household, the fact that women in these occupations tend to have lower wages than men in male-dominated occupations at the same skill level speaks to the devaluation of women's work in both the private and public spheres."[9]

At U of T, some female faculty members who were clearly valuable by *any* academic standard remained underpaid for years. Ursula Franklin, the esteemed physicist and professor of metallurgy and materials science, spearheaded a class action lawsuit against the university, claiming systemic discrimination in the compensation of its female faculty. Franklin and three other retired female professors sued U of T for back pay and pension adjustments. They claimed that they were paid an average of 20 per cent less than men over several decades. The university settled in 2002, and as many as sixty retired female professors received enhanced benefits.[10]

An argument presented by faculties that choose to (and can afford to) pay higher salaries (as evidenced by Ontario's Public Sector Salary Disclosure Act (aka the Sunshine List) is that, to keep professors who could make much more money elsewhere – for example, in business – salaries need to be comparable.[11] I do not find this argument convincing. If a higher salary is the major driver for someone already earning a good living, then that individual does not place a high value on working in an academic environment. And if that is true, then how can they be so valuable to the university?

When I assumed the role of director of the Division of Occupational Therapy, with full knowledge of our budget because of my earlier role as acting director, I soon realized that we were not highly valued within the university. Our working conditions were poor. Our faculty complement was low, administrative support was minimal, and our space at 256 McCaul was not conducive to the academic outcomes we were expected to achieve. As was common for female faculty, we spent a lot of time on service and teaching. We sat on committees internal and external to our program, as well as committees for our professional associations. We reviewed and revised curriculum content regularly, used a variety of methods to teach and assess student learning, and made extensive comments on the papers we marked. We spent time advising students and took the time to work collaboratively. And all of this meant less time for research.[12]

I tried to establish a friendly and supportive environment when I chaired faculty meetings. I started with some informal information sharing and inexpensive refreshments. I shopped for the refreshments myself, not having a budget for catering or a person to help. I knew that faculty elsewhere – for example, at the law school – did not operate in the same way. We were a small program with large service duties in addition to our teaching and research. It seemed as though we were doing what the institution asked but that, within our less-privileged work environment, no one was looking out after us.[13]

Feeling second class was nothing new for occupational therapy. Along with almost 60 per cent of all health professionals, we are considered "allied health."[14] We became allied health after the Second World War, when a combined department of physical medicine and rehabilitation was established in many hospitals and universities across North America. The distinction was then made between doctors of physical medicine (the physiatrists) and the other health professionals on the "team."[15] The term "allied health" is used broadly and often defined as including non-nurses and non-physicians. Health professionals tend to see it as confirming a lesser value. Not that the lesser value idea was ever hidden for occupational therapists. In 1950, when the then dean of the University of Toronto's Faculty of Medicine, Dr J.A. MacFarlane, was announcing the amalgamation of physical and occupational therapy he said that he hoped "the course as planned will give her [the graduate] the necessary training and background and will enable her to take her place with confidence in this increasingly important *ancillary* service of medicine (my italics)."[16]

Medical dominance over occupational therapy was very clear at U of T in the early years, when Helen LeVesconte, who directed the program from 1933 until 1967, pointed out that our discipline was "medically prescribed, medically supervised, and medically controlled."[17] This subservient relationship was not surprising, given that physicians had played such a central role in our beginnings. It was physicians who had formed an advisory council for the Ontario Society of Occupational Therapy in 1920, physicians who helped establish the occupational therapy diploma program at U of T in 1926, and physicians who presided over the Canadian Association of Occupational Therapy from 1926 until 1967. Ruby Heap, in her study of physiotherapists, describes how a similar relationship came about, whereby "a female-dominated occupation, [became] subordinated to an allied but more powerful male profession."[18]

Researchers have analysed the issue of medical dominance in health care for decades and have examined the complex structures that help to maintain it.[19] Meanwhile, it remains complicated for various health professions to meet the needs of many patients when the physician is the gatekeeper for referrals. Boyce, writing within the context of organizational health reform in Australia's health care system, is optimistic and suggests that, while "medical dominance" over the allied health professions has marginalized those professions or made them "invisible," there is an opportunity for change when allied health (where professions are *allied to each other*) manage themselves.[20] Interprofessional education also attempts to address the issue, although they typically do not adequately address issues of power.[21]

Many who have studied this issue conclude that the professions of occupational therapy and physiotherapy needed the support and blessings of physicians when they were being founded.[22] But it is difficult to explain why the paternalistic relationships continued for so long. For example, Thelma Cardwell, the first president of the Canadian Association of Occupational Therapists who actually *was* an occupational therapist, and not a physician, was elected forty-one years after the association was founded, and Beth Pierce Robinson, the first editor of the *Canadian Journal of Occupational Therapy* who was an occupational therapist and not a physician, was elected some thirty years after the journal was established.[23]

Straying from medicine or, more correctly, returning to our roots – has taken a long time. It's odd that, in the very early days of occupational therapy, there was recognition within the medical profession of the advantages of a broader approach to treatment. When psychiatrist Adolph Meyer (often referred to as the father of occupational therapy) was promoting occupational therapy in 1922, he referenced the strength of the psychobiological model, acknowledging the need for a psychological as well as a biological perspective on illness. George Engel's classic critique of the medical model promoted the biopsychosocial model in 1977, stressing the need for psychological and social perspectives in addition to the biological. Most recently, Huber and colleagues have promoted the health and well-being model, which takes a different approach altogether and suggests that what matters is the ability "to cope and self-manage in the face of physical, psychological and emotional challenges."[24] So, the idea that one need not fix broken parts to contribute to medicine – or, perhaps more properly, to health – has been around for some time. Proposed changes to medical school curricula that reflect the importance of the knowledge of other professionals, and the fact that those professionals may have greater expertise than physicians in some areas are encouraging.[25]

The feeling of being second class within the Faculty of Medicine was temporarily assuaged for me early on with one noteworthy experience. When I started my new position, I was given a lovely welcome by the then dean, Dr John Dirks. He held a small dinner for me in the Gallery Grill at Hart House and asked me to invite a half dozen or so colleagues. He asked about our goals and our aspirations, and he listened to what we had to say. It was a collegial evening. In the years that followed, I don't remember being made a fuss over again like that. Dirks was the first of four deans I served under during my time in a leadership position; however, his term ended the same year I began as director. A controversy erupted when, to address budgetary concerns, he dismissed a large number of non-academic staff with little notice. It was a tempestuous time in the Faculty of Medicine, and Dirks resigned. Harvey Anderson, with a PhD in nutritional biochemistry, took on the role of acting dean. Had Anderson continued in the position, he would have been the first non-physician ever to assume the role of dean of medicine at U of T. Many of us wondered if the environment might have become more inclusive if he had been selected. Might there have been a shift such that even those in "allied health" would have become more integral to the Faculty of Medicine? Within the year, Arnie Aberman, a physician, was selected for the role, and, just before my term ended, David Naylor, also a physician, began his. The first female dean of the Faculty of Medicine, Dr Catharine Whiteside, followed, but by then my term had ended.

At the same time as I was starting to lead my division, I was trying to take care of a professional concern of my own: I had to get tenure. I had been in my tenure-stream position for three years, and it seemed important for me personally and for my division that, as director, I be tenured. I was granted permission to go forward one year early. Fortunately, the review process went smoothly. I received tenure and was promoted to the rank of associate professor in 1992. It was good to get that out of the way.

As division director, my most pressing concern was to increase the research capacity of our faculty. I encouraged faculty to push ahead with writing grants and publishing, if they were able. I advised junior faculty members not to spend too much time presenting their work at conferences. I thought then, as I still do, that such presentations usually involve more effort than anticipated. With most conferences running concurrent presentations, it's possible to have very few people turn up to your session, no matter how good it might be. Presentations do not guarantee publications and, without the latter, the work does not enter the literature, where it can be referred to and built upon. Of course, having peer-reviewed abstracts accepted for conferences is a boost to the ego, and conferences are fun to attend and good for networking. I did not mean to discourage people altogether from presenting their work; rather, I wanted faculty to carefully weigh the short-term rewards against potential long-term gains.

I strongly encouraged faculty members to enter doctoral programs, when that seemed appropriate. There were only three of us with that qualification when I took over, and it limited our grant-getting ability and our research capacity in general. I was sympathetic to concerns about finding the time, especially for those with family responsibilities. However, it helped that everyone knew I had been in the same boat when I did my doctorate (albeit with older children). With regard to choosing thesis topics, I stressed the need to be truly interested in, if not outright passionate about, their topic, as I thought it the only way to survive the process.

I saw my work with students in difficulty as an integral part of my job. Few supports were available to them within the university at the time, and gaining access to the services that did exist was difficult. Our students had to deal with a jam-packed curriculum and, as in any first-rate university, with classmates who were all high achievers. At the time, ours was an undergraduate program, and many of our students were away from home for the first time and had few supports. Living in Toronto and attending such a large university could feel very lonely. Anxiety and depression – usually, but not always, at subclinical levels – were common among university students then, just as we know they are today.[26] I tried to reassure students, all of whom had come to us with high marks, saying, "If we let you in, we'll see to it that you get out." I made referrals to health or accessibility services where necessary and helped students in difficulty seek accommodations and support. Invariably, the students were able to continue or, in a few cases, take some time off and then come back to finish. Some faculty members criticized my approach, saying I was "doing therapy" when I should have been "more professional" and following set procedures. I never had any regrets about the help I gave students. While not against having procedures available, I preferred to consider each case individually and problem solve from there. I wanted to "do therapy" only in the sense that I wanted students to see me as their ally, not their adversary.[27] I could never understand the almost militaristic attitude that still exists under the guise of teaching in some situations. I believe I played an important role in helping students see that problems could be overcome. That notion was something they needed to understand, both for themselves and for their work with patients in the future. My message was that help is available, and the world can be fair.

I needed to direct some of my time and resources to address the requirements for an accredited health professional education program "to meet competency expectations and to support future professionals in their area of expertise."[28] Non-professional programs in universities do not have to meet such requirements nor do some professional programs, such as law, that keep their academic and practice programs separated. We underwent two successful, but very resource-intensive, accreditations by the Canadian Association of Occupational Therapists (CAOT) during my leadership.

I also needed to give my support and attention to organizations that directly related to our being a professional program. I worked with our organizations at the national and provincial level and with our regulatory college. And I tried to stay connected at the local level with the hospitals and community agencies where our students did their fieldwork. In a professional program like ours, maintaining strong connections with the world of practice was essential.

I felt some stress at meetings with our professional organizations, largely as a result of one unpleasant experience. At a meeting with professors from other OT programs in Canada, we were discussing the high fees we'd have to pay to join a larger umbrella organization. The person chairing our meeting suggested "We could try to Jew them down." People around the table gasped. I was astounded that she could have thought it was okay to use that phrase at all – let alone with me there, and her knowing I was Jewish. My face turned red. I was speechless and didn't know where to look. We took a break from the meeting. Some members of the group came over to me and shared their dismay. Someone must have spoken to the person who had uttered the phrase. On our return to the meeting, she gave an open apology, saying that she should not have said what she did. Still, it had a chilling effect on me going forward.

My new position required that I spend a great amount of time in meetings. University-wide committees were expected to have wide representation, including women. Disciplines like mine were often called on to help meet that criterion – this at a time when women faculty were very much in the minority and there were not that many of us to go around. I didn't mind committee work, but some of it seemed almost unrelated to the eventual decisions made at higher levels. For example, I sat on the Leyerle Committee on the Health Sciences. After many meetings and intense discussions, we finally reached an agreement on a change that would affect the future configuration of many of the university's health-related programs. Yet, in the end, the university maintained the status quo.

Another frustrating committee was the Task Force on Accommodation of Persons with Disabilities, a necessary but not high-profile concern within the university in those early days of accommodating students with disabilities. Our recommendations often met with scepticism about the need to give some students special consideration, and even with concern that they were being given an unfair advantage. While such attitudes have since changed, they have not entirely disappeared.

Within my own division, I took on roles of my own choosing, including the Admissions Committee and the Recruitment Task Force. I felt I needed to know more about these areas and where change might be needed. I continued to run the Degree Completion Program designed in the '70s to help diploma grads upgrade their credentials after occupational therapy became a degree program. By the '90s, most diploma graduates who wanted the degree had gained it, but, just as we were preparing to discontinue the program, we had an influx of diploma-trained graduates from abroad, primarily from Hong Kong Polytechnic. They had had excellent training at home, and we decided to continue the program mainly for them.

I limited the amount I taught, but I was sure to do enough so I knew the students and they knew me. I was fortunate that Bonnie Kirsh was willing to expand her role in our program and take responsibility for my course in mental health. She had just finished directing the program at Queen Street Mental Health Centre and was a perfect choice, bringing a clinical and an academic background. Bonnie would go on to be a major voice in mental health, not only in our program but nationally and internationally.

My research was ongoing and, rather than it being a burden, I found that it provided a welcome change from my administrative duties. With a grant from the Ontario Mental Health Foundation, my colleague Deirdre Dawson and I studied relationships among functional status, symptoms of post-traumatic stress, and post-concussion syndrome in survivors of motor vehicle accidents. Since the time of my daughter's car accident in 1986, I had been interested in how such a sudden, traumatic event affected daily living, physically and psychologically. The event seemed similar in some ways to what soldiers experienced who were being diagnosed with post-traumatic stress disorder (PTSD), with the difference that soldiers are likely more aware of the risk to their lives when they go into war than are people who get into their cars on a daily basis. Most of us do not anticipate a major accident, even though we know, intellectually, that accident rates are high.

With concussions almost inevitable in a car crash, we were interested in the potential for some symptom-overlap with PTSD. We published our study, "Function after Motor Vehicle Accidents," in the *Journal of Nervous and Mental Disease*.[29] Carla Ruffolo, one of my graduate students, analysed some of our data to examine this population in regard to return to work.[30] As PTSD and concussions have each become pervasive, and motor vehicle accidents continue to occur, I regret that we did not do more with our data.

In my role as director, I was becoming more and more aware that being a division within the Department of Rehabilitation Medicine was not conducive to our growth as a discreet discipline. Neither occupational therapy nor physical therapy could initiate change without first going through the chair of the department. He (it was always a man and usually a physician) needed to be concerned with doing what was best for the whole department, which, at times, included physiatry and speech-language pathology along with physical therapy and occupational therapy. The chair could not just focus on one part of his department, nor could he fully understand each discipline's issues. As a result, few decisions could be made quickly and without compromise. It was difficult to pursue a vision of our own with so little control.

In many ways, we were already doing what was expected of an independent department. We handled our own student admissions and recruitment, made bursary allocations, organized convocation, and hired all faculty and staff. We prepared all the paperwork for tenure reviews and promotions, and the materials for the marks meetings. Given our limited support staff and small numbers, more service activity was required of faculty members – and that meant less time for research.[31]

We were not the first to notice the limitations our structure imposed. A task force had been struck in 1989 to look at the issue of departmental status for occupational therapy and physical therapy, but discussions did not progress. Soon after I became director, Molly Verrier, my counterpart in PT, and I decided to pursue the matter in earnest. We submitted a joint proposal for departmental status for each of our programs at the end of 1992. Achieving such a structural change required a multi-pronged campaign: to convince the dean, to get buy-in from other departments who did teaching for us (such as anatomy and physiology), to get approval from the Faculty of Medicine Council and, ultimately, from the Governing Council of the University of Toronto. It was a daunting task. And it would take time.

It was good that our proposals were submitted at the end of 1992 because, a few weeks later, there were other more serious things for me to worry about. I had become pretty good at juggling my work and family roles, and I could manage as long as nothing unusual occurred. My children were all living on their own, and although we frequently had my parents and Marty's mother for Friday night dinners, all three were relatively healthy and active, and we were not involved in their care in any way.

Then, in the middle of a clear day in mid-January 1993, my eighty-nine-year-old father drove through a red light at a major intersection in North Toronto and hit a truck as it was completing its left turn. Thankfully, the driver of the truck did not suffer any injuries. However, Mike broke several vertebrae in his neck, and his wife, May, who had been in the passenger seat, was also seriously injured. Although Mike was in especially good shape for his age, the neck injury was potentially very serious. By the time the police informed us that there had been an accident, Mike and May were in an ambulance headed for Sunnybrook Hospital. The police seemed to be preparing us for the worst. My brother flew in from Montreal.

I took a taxi to the hospital and remember telling the cab driver – a fairly new immigrant from Nigeria – all about what had happened. Poor man, I think I even told him about how close I was with my father, given my mother's death so many years before. I arrived in time to see my father being taken from Emergency to his room, his head and neck held in place within a "halo" brace. The brace kept the cervical area of the spine immobilized to facilitate the healing of the fractured vertebrae. Vertical black bars extended down from a halo-like metal circle over his head (hence the name of the brace) to the lower section of the brace, which sat on his shoulders. Mike could see those vertical bars as he lay on the stretcher. When he saw me, he quietly – and rather sheepishly – asked "What am I in for? What did I do?" He was convinced he was in jail. I explained that he was in the hospital, that he had had a car accident. Mercifully, he did not ask whose fault it was. I'm not sure if I was more worried about his physical health or his mental health at that moment. What would he do with the knowledge that he had caused the accident, was responsible for his wife's injuries, and, but for the grace of God, could have killed the driver of the truck?

It would be a lengthy recovery, and the outcome was uncertain. Because the vertebrae were only partially fractured and damage to the spinal cord was incomplete (a condition known as Brown-Séquard syndrome), there was hope for some return of function, but it was hard to predict if he would ever walk again.

Mike's ninetieth birthday, Sunnybrook Hospital, 1993

A month later, my brother and his family came from Montreal so we could all celebrate Mike's ninetieth birthday in the hospital. We hung a "Happy Birthday" sign on an X-ray screen and had a birthday cake. Mike was still in the halo brace, but he managed a bite or two of the cake. He was clearly depressed, and we were all worried. It was not a happy celebration.

When both Mike and May were in Sunnybrook, occasional visits between them could be arranged. Once they were stable, however, both were moved on: Mike to Lyndhurst, a rehabilitation centre for people with spinal cord injuries, and May to St John's Convalescent Hospital. Mike remained depressed but stoic; he was remarkably sanguine throughout his time in bed. I visited regularly and would often find him just staring at the ceiling. After a while, we would get into a conversation – about the family, about the news of the day, but rarely about what might or might not lie ahead. There was not much I could do for him, other than to keep him in a supply of his beloved library books.

Once Mike was allowed up, he was a different person. He was determined to walk again. After many weeks of physical therapy, he had progressed from the parallel bars in the gym to a walker. Gradually both Mike and May recovered enough to return home with some services.

Of course, Mike lost his driving licence. He seemed to know that he was at fault and that his days of driving were over. There was a tacit understanding among all of us: he did not ask about the accident, and we did not offer any details. I was surprised that there weren't recriminations about how badly hurt May had been or comments about how lucky it was that the driver of the truck he hit had not been injured. At some level, I think retrograde amnesia from the event prevented him from acknowledging his culpability.

My brother and I felt particularly guilty about this "accident" – a word that has all but been banished from the injury prevention literature. We had been worried about Mike's driving for several years, worried that his reflexes had begun to slow and that his attention was not as sharp as it had been. In fact, he had long since failed what is referred to in the literature as "the grandchildren test" – the time when parents make the decision not to allow grandchildren to drive with a grandparent. All of that should have been a signal to us that he should no longer have been driving. Period. But like most "children" in this situation, we were conflicted. We knew it would limit the otherwise active life that he and May enjoyed. To ask him to stop voluntarily would be difficult. It would hurt his ego and impact our relationships. This whole area of driving cessation, so problematic for seniors, their families, and their family doctors, would become a topic of my own research a decade later.

On the last day of that same January, one of my students was also in a car accident. Colleen Tate, a first-year student, was on her way back to Toronto after a weekend at home in Petawawa. She was a passenger, sitting in the back seat of the car, when a crash occurred and she was killed. All of us were devastated. Colleen had been in our program only since the previous September, but she had already shown herself to be exceptional: always cheerful and supportive of others, a good student who not only kept up with the work but was known to work ahead. With the help of the university chaplain, we held a service for Colleen in a classroom at school. A memorial award was established in her name, and I kept in touch with her parents over the years. With my father's accident at age eighty-nine, it seemed crazy that he had survived, and nineteen-year-old Colleen had not. I also thought about how lucky we were with our daughter's car accident when she was the same age as Colleen.

Crises of one sort or another seemed to go with the territory of my job and my family life. When the two coincided, it was especially hard. There is only a brief window for daughters/mothers to feel relatively free of family responsibility in the time between tending to their young children and caring for aging parents. Aside from the guilt feelings that surfaced when it seemed as though a family member was being short-changed, I seemed to manage. There was less sleep and more take-out food, and more arguments, I'm sure, but it worked.

Good things happened too. In December 1993, a full year after proposing our structural changes, independent departments of occupational therapy and physical therapy were established, and the Department of Rehabilitation Medicine was terminated. By then, occupational therapy had been a part of that department for forty-three years and had been led by people outside our own discipline. Our journey through a series of dependent relationships was finally at an end.

With our transition to a department came a new way of looking at our place within the university. From a temporary course within the Faculty of Applied Science during and just after the First World War, through twenty-four years in the Department of Extension, where our existence was always provisional, to our being combined with physical therapy in 1950 and taken into the Faculty of Medicine, we were finally standing on our own two feet. Paralleling many of the changes in the role of women generally, our new status had the potential to dramatically change our subordinate role.

13 Little Fish, Big Pond: Chair, Department of Occupational Therapy

In my role as chair of the Department of Occupational Therapy, I would be interacting with people at higher levels of the university's administration than I had when I was director of the division. I would see the larger picture and be more aware of issues and opportunities. I thought that would be somewhat intimidating, but good.

Our new department was now equal, at least in principle, to any other department in the Faculty of Medicine, or in the university for that matter. Equal to the Department of Surgery or the Department of Philosophy. That felt really good. Of course, we would have to live up to that new designation for it to mean anything, but at least we now had a licence to try, and to do so on our own terms.

On a personal note, the change to departmental status brought me yet another potential stumbling block. Apparently, I could not just be given the new position as chair. The job had to be advertised according to university rules. I was still not comfortable with the whole idea of competing for a position and was relieved when the search turned out to be perfunctory. On March 1st, 1994, I officially became the chair of the first Department of Occupational Therapy at the University of Toronto. It was an exciting time: liberating, validating – and challenging.

As a department chair, I was something of an anomaly in the university, coming in at the level of associate professor rather than as full professor. An anomaly among male faculty, that is. As recently as 2016, more than twice as many male faculty members as female faculty members held the rank of full professor at the University of Toronto.[1] For me, having been granted tenure only two years earlier, promotion to full professor would be several years away, if it happened at all.

Before signing a new contract, I entered into salary negotiations, but with minimal success. My salary base was increased only slightly, and my stipend remained the same. The latter did not reflect the higher level and increased responsibilities of my new position. It's hard to know why that should have been the case. Among the many reasons offered for why female salaries are lower is one that is rarely discussed or studied: a belief that, if a woman is married, and her husband is earning a good living (as in my situation), then she does not need to have a good salary for herself. This idea is not too far from the unstated idea that, if a husband is earning a good salary, there is no reason for a wife to work.[2] It assumes that the only reason for work is financial and that other benefits that come from work – such as satisfaction, stimulation, and socialization – are not needed by a wife.

On the upside, I was pleasantly surprised when Dean Aberman gave me a research budget of $25,000 annually; this was just like other department chairs had, but we in the Division of Occupational Therapy never knew anything about it. I was told I could use the money to support my own research or that of the department, at my discretion. I chose the latter thinking that although the amount would be small – around $2500 for each full-time faculty member – it would be highly valued and equitable. It could go toward paying for a part-time research assistant, or a stats consultant, or conference travel. It seemed the right thing to do.

Other undertakings were not commitments but would be supported; for example, to expand and improve our space, at 256 McCaul, and to replace our elevator. Like other female administrators, I was more comfortable asking for things for the department, or for other individuals, than for myself.[3] The elevator upgrade did not happen overnight. It took one of our clinician-faculty members, Joan Lewis, getting stuck in our elevator in her wheelchair for action to be taken. Joan wrote a letter about her experience to the dean, and, soon after, a state-of-the-art, fully accessible elevator was installed.

Lobbying for better space was a never-ending activity. Plans would be drawn up and then scrapped. We met with various officials to no avail. We watched as space we had thought might become ours went to others. Ultimately, the matter rested until my successor was able to include that demand in the terms for her hiring.

The transition from division director to department chair substantially increased the range and number of my activities. I had additional roles within the Faculty of Medicine and the university. For some committees, I was the Faculty of Medicine's appointee – for example, on the board of governors for West Park Hospital. I continued with some of my earlier service roles because I thought representation from occupational therapy was important. I sat, for example, on the university's Accommodation, Resource and Advisory Group Committee, whose goal was to have improved accessibility for students by the time the Ontario Disability Act came into effect in 2005.

I attended the monthly "All Chairs" meetings for the Faculty of Medicine, as well as the meetings for the chairs in the Clinical Sector, of which we were a part at the time. Most of these meetings focused on medical students' education or residents' hospital positions, but I found them interesting just the same. I thought it was important to understand this major aspect of the faculty's business and to learn more about the ever-changing health care system in general.

The meetings were held in the Medical Sciences Building on the main campus. Molly Verrier, the chair of the Department of Physiotherapy, and I usually walked up together from our building on McCaul. We tried not to be late, so as to not draw any additional attention to our presence at the meeting; it was enough that we were usually the only women. We'd enter the dean's conference room and move quickly to one of the twenty or so chairs around the large table, being sure to sit separately from one another. As it was, especially early on, people often mixed us up, even as they often mixed up our professions: OT, PT, Judy, Molly – what's the difference, they seemed to be saying.

Even though most of the topics under discussion at these meetings did not affect us directly, we would, at times, contribute ideas or provide a different, usually broader, perspective on an issue. However, we learned early on that whatever we said would likely be met with a polite, but pat response – "Yes, interesting" or simply, "Hmmm . . . thank you." And then, a little later, the inevitable: a man, and most likely a medical doctor, would say something very similar (if not the same), and discussion and positive comments would follow.

This phenomenon is familiar to women in various settings and is nothing new, infuriating though it may be. Deborah Tannen, the linguistics professor who first wrote about it in 1995, says not much has changed.[4] In a series called "Women at Work" in the *New York Times*, twenty years later, Sheryl Sandberg and Adam Grant pointed out, that "when a woman speaks in a professional setting, she walks a tightrope. Either she's barely heard, or she's judged as too aggressive. When a man says virtually the same thing, heads nod in appreciation for his fine idea. As a result, women often decide that saying less is more."[5]

As a department chair, I also attended "PDD&C," the meetings for principals, deans, (academic) directors, and chairs in the university. Held in Simcoe Hall, the stately building that houses presidents and their staff, where the walls are hung with huge portraits of presidents, chancellors, and former chairs of the Governing Council, the council chambers has an intimidating air about it. A highly polished, oblong oak table sits in the centre of the room, with about thirty elegant chairs surrounding it. A further ring of a hundred or so chairs sits back from

Council chamber, Simcoe Hall. Courtesy of University of Toronto Archives

that area. That's where I generally sat – in that outer ring. Unless, for some reason, attendance was small that day, or someone invited me to join them at the table, I would not think to sit there. The meetings, which were presided over by the provost, covered a wide range of topics related primarily to policy. There were questions and comments, but little real discussion took place at these meetings, as they were primarily for sharing information from the top down. I found them interesting, and I enjoyed being a part of this inner circle, despite feeling no sense of real belonging to it.

By the mid-'90s, in response primarily to government funding cutbacks, department chairs were expected to engage in fundraising and try to increase donations from alumni. I liked being in contact with our alumni, but I did not like asking them for money. As is common for a largely female faculty, we had a broad base of financial support, but contributions were small.[6] Donations could not compare to those from alumni of programs in business or law or engineering, where grads earned much larger salaries and could afford to be more generous. Moreover, I found it frustrating that, when our graduates married, donations were more likely to be directed to their spouse's (usually wealthier) department or alma mater. As elsewhere in the world, the rich within the university get richer, and the poor get poorer. In my rather socialist view of life, it seemed that the only equitable way to deal with fundraising was for the university to take more control and, at the very least, target central fundraising efforts to meet the needs of those who were less able to raise funds on their own but who had the greater need. The university had little appetite for my approach then and probably even less now, when corporate entities as well as wealthy alumni are major donors and support the faculties where they have connections or where they want to have an impact on future directions taken. The naming of many buildings and endowed chairs reflects this new reality.

Our department had one noteworthy fundraising success during my time as chair. When a former director of our division, Thelma Cardwell (the person who had hired me) retired, we decided to endow a lecture in her name. She generously supported the endeavour herself, which got us off to a good start. Inviting others to donate was easy because Thelma was much loved and respected, and well known nationally and internationally. The Thelma Cardwell Lecture, established in 1997, brings our alumni, faculty, and students together each year to learn and socialize.

Being chair of my department was certainly time consuming. The days were filled with meetings and various administrative tasks, and I stayed at the office until seven or eight most nights. Because our building was off-campus and did not seem safe, I wouldn't stay after dark unless someone else was there with me. That person was usually Molly Verrier, my counterpart in the Department of Physical Therapy, whose office was next to mine. On the nights we stayed especially late – often until eleven or so – we would leave the building together and see each other safely into our cars. Sometimes Marty would come with me if I wanted to stay late or go in on the weekend. He was happy to sit in the conference room doing his own work. If I did leave the office at a reasonable hour, I took a lot of work home with me. I was tired, for sure, and admit to often feeling overwhelmed, but, on the whole, I rather liked the pace. I found the work stimulating and satisfying. I thought I was making a useful contribution, and that felt good.

Marty and I often discussed my workload in relation to what would have been his even heavier job as dean, twenty years earlier. We acknowledged that our styles of leadership were different and that the more collaborative approach, generally preferred by women and expected in my department, took more time. But as many of our discussions showed, comparisons between my role and his, or the occupational therapy program and law – whether with respect to salaries, student supports, administrative personnel, physical plant, or the wealth of our alumni – only confirmed the extent to which my department was disadvantaged. While my marriage to Marty meant that I learned a lot about the university, it also meant that I became more aware of what I considered inequities.

One task that kept Molly and me working late was creating a graduate program, where OTs and PTs who were qualified at the bachelors' level could do a research master's degree. At the time, a postgraduate degree was available to our graduates only if they enrolled in related fields such as physiology or education – just as it had been for me some fifteen years earlier. We wanted graduate programs for each of our disciplines, but, with so few resources, it seemed best to mount a joint program. We submitted a proposal, and, after the usual process of approvals at the various levels of administration, the Graduate Department of Rehabilitation Science was established in 1995. Molly was its first chair, and she made a major contribution to its development in the years that followed. We both taught in the program for the first few years and enjoyed working with one another. The program now offers a PhD as well as an MSc and is known as the Rehabilitation Sciences Institute. It draws students from a variety of disciplines in addition to occupational therapy and physical therapy and has been a great success.

Part of what had attracted me to the job of chairing my department was the opportunity to instigate and facilitate change. Our immediate need was to prepare for the next major change in occupational therapy education. In the United States, a professional master's degree was being phased in and would soon be the only option for accredited occupational therapy programs. A professional master's degree was on the horizon in Canada but not yet in place. We took our first step toward the change by restructuring our undergraduate program to require two full years of arts and science content (rather than just one, as previously required) prior to entry, followed by two years and three months in OT, for what we called our "2+2+ program." This change established the twenty-four-month OT program format (but not the content), which was eventually what students would take after coming to OT with a four-year under-graduate degree. At that point, we would enhance the content of the OT curriculum, and our graduates would earn an MScOT degree.

It was also time to review our pedagogical approach. In our search for better methods, we explored problem-based learning (PBL), which had been successfully used with medical students at McMaster University since 1969 and was later adopted for their OT program.[7] At U of T, PBL was introduced for medical students in 1992 and seemed to be going well. Our review of the literature indicated positive student outcomes with PBL, and we decided to adopt it. Once implemented (after much preparation on our part, running workshops, writing cases, and train-ing tutors), it was apparent that students were engaged by the method; they enjoyed the small-group, case-based, investigative learning. Lec-turing, as we had known it, was radically reduced.

The final structural change needed to prepare for offering the mas-ter's degree was to reorient our fieldwork program to provide more community-based placements for our students. Health planners were predicting more work for health professionals in the community, and this was a welcome direction for us. In 1995, the Ontario government provided $1,000,000 to our OCUPRS group (Ontario Council of Univer-sity Programs in Rehabilitation Science) for clinical education projects in the community. I worked on one of these projects with Helene Polata-jko (who was then at the University of Western Ontario and who would succeed me as chair of our OT department). We oversaw the devel-opment of two types of community sites: one at agencies that would typically employ OTs but happened not to (such as a community health centre), and the other at sites where there had never been an OT, but we thought there should be (for example, in a homeless shelter). We had funds from our grant to pay supervisors at the new sites so that there were no costs to the agencies during the demonstration project. In many cases, the agencies went on to hire occupational therapists on an ongoing basis, providing just the type of development within the field that we had hoped for.[8]

While all of this preparation for implementing a master's program was occurring, I was dealing with a measure of criticism from some of our faculty and others in the clinical community for the change itself: Was it really necessary? Wasn't it just "creeping credentialism"? Change is particularly difficult for some, and I understood that many people disliked the process, not to mention all the extra work that was involved. However, within a year, I could not be blamed for the change. The Canadian Association of Occupational Therapists announced its projected new standard for accreditation: effective 2008, only those programs that led to a professional master's degree in occupational therapy would be accredited. There was no choice.

We were glad that we were ready. While U of T was not going to be the first OT program to move to a master's (that happened at the University of Western Ontario in 1998), we were certainly not going to be the last. After considerable work to raise the level of the content in the curriculum, we submitted our proposal in January 2000 to the Ontario School of Graduate Studies. Although I was then on sabbatical, and no longer chair, I was available to help shepherd the proposal through. Approval was granted a few months later and, after further changes were made by the new chair and her team, the master's degree program was phased in that fall.

There's no question that my "worker" role was heavy when I was a department chair. But it was manageable as long as there weren't too many other calls on my time, calls that, if family related, I would always honour. By the mid-90s, there were several family-related calls on my time: some good and some not so good.

A not-good call on my time occurred with Mike and May's car accident. When they were still in the hospital, it was just a matter of visiting (and worrying). Then I helped them settle back in at home and tried to make sure they had the services they needed. However, as time went on, May began to deteriorate cognitively and Mike physically: she left the kettle to boil dry on the stove, and he showed signs of chronic heart failure. May would call me in the middle of the night to say that they had called an ambulance because Mike had chest pain. I would dress, drive up north, and meet them at their local hospital within the hour. The chest pain would be tended to, and, after a few days, Mike would be discharged. One of these stays was particularly upsetting – for both Mike and me. The hospital called me to ask if I could come to calm him down. After being transferred from the ICU to the cardiac unit, Mike was confused and kept trying to pull out his intravenous line and other tubes until the nurses finally tied his hands to the bed. When I arrived, he pleaded with me to untie his hands. "I can't do that, Dad. If I do, you will pull out your tubes and they are needed to keep you alive." Mike glared at me and, in a strong and angry voice, said, "If you won't help me, then you are not my daughter anymore. You should leave." I felt ashamed of myself for not being able to figure out some other way to calm him down. I felt helpless as I slunk away.

When he returned home, I urged them to accept more help in their day-to-day living: Meals on Wheels, some homemaking help, a nurse to help with bathing, and someone who could check on their pills. I could get them to agree to more help whenever Mike was in hospital, but once he was back home the agreement fell apart. Containers with food from Meals-on-Wheels piled up in the fridge, unopened. They didn't think much of the homemaking help and sent the women off, and they decided a nurse wasn't needed at all. The neighbour who was to check on the pills daily went away for a holiday. They vetoed the idea of moving into a supported living environment and remained at home in ever-declining health. Their situation was a constant source of worry and a not insignificant call on my time.

One of the good family calls on my time occurred when our son, Tom, and his girlfriend Jacque decided to marry. In the year before the wedding, they had both taken leaves from their jobs and travelled the world, spending their last six months working in Cape Town, South Africa. We'd never been to South Africa so, of course, we had to visit. After stopping in Johannesburg (and Kruger National Park), and Pretoria, we went on to Cape Town to be with them. From there, the four of us travelled along the Garden Route to Grahamstown, where we all stood for a memorable Johnny Clegg concert. Marty and I went on to Fort Hare to visit the law school that Nelson Mandela had attended. A former student of Marty's was a faculty member and kindly showed us around.

The following day, we were in our hotel in Port Elizabeth, and watching TV as we packed up. There was Mandela making his first visit to London, complete with an audience with the queen. Seeing his life go full circle from his days as a law student at Fort Hare, to his lengthy imprisonment, and to this royal honour was especially moving.

Tom's wedding was in Atlanta, Georgia, the bride's hometown. New to this wedding business, and especially a Jewish wedding in the American South, we were careful to do as asked. We were told there would be a dinner for out-of-towners the night before the wedding at which we were to make a speech about our son, complete with slides. We dug into old photo albums for good pictures, prepared slides, and wrote an accompanying script. On the afternoon preceding the dinner, we stayed in our hotel room and dutifully ran through the slides. We'd brought our own carousel with us from home. Everything was fine.

That night, just after dinner, we were introduced, and started our little presentation. We clicked the projector to show the first slide. Nothing came on the screen. No slide. After checking the electrical connections and everything else we could think of, we finally checked the carousel. It was completely empty. It was not the carousel with our slides. That one was back in our hotel room, several miles from where the dinner was. All we had with us was our script and a major case of panic.

Marty remembered having had a similar experience at a lecture he was giving when the projector didn't work, and he had to verbally describe the slides that would have otherwise been shown. We decided to do the same but when we read our script, we *pretended* to show each missing slide. "Here you see Tom in his crib, or learning to ride a bike," etc. We must have been convincing, because many people asked us later whether we really did have slides!

Neither Mike nor May was well enough to attend our son's wedding. Just six months later, in June 1997, Mike had a heart attack and died. He was ninety-four.

The weather on the evening of the funeral was beautiful, a warm, early-summer evening with just a slight breeze. The shiva was at our house, and on that first night our rabbi came to lead the mourners' *kaddish*, the traditional prayer for the dead. Given the weather, he suggested we do the prayers outside on the deck overlooking the garden, the garden that my father loved to look at and had so often sat and admired. It was a touching ending to a life so well lived.

While Mike and May were deteriorating, Marty's mother, Mina, was starting to deteriorate as well. We had helped her move into a retirement home when she was eighty-nine and for a time, she did well. Before that move, she had been living successfully on her own for some twenty years following the death of Marty's father. She had lived alongside a somewhat autocratic husband, and it was interesting to see her become more self-reliant when she was on her own, working for several hours a week for the first time since her marriage all those years ago, socializing, and seeking out activities within the city. I had a good, if not close, relationship with Mina. She was a lovely woman, warm and kind, with an unabashed pride in her son Marty's accomplishments. By the late '90s, Mina's cognitive decline meant a move to a nursing home where she died in 2000 at the age of ninety-seven.

There was another good family call on my time. In the summer of 1999, our daughter Nancy was married in the garden at our home

Nancy and Brett's wedding in our backyard on Belsize, 1999

on Belsize Drive. An old friend of ours, Frank Iacobucci, then a judge of the Supreme Court of Canada, performed the ceremony. Traditional Jewish ritual mixed with ecumenical content appropriate for this "mixed" marriage (Brett was not Jewish) made for a beautiful service. The speeches were great and so was the food. A band played Klezmer music for dancing after the dinner and no neighbours complained.

By 1999, I had finished nine-and-a-half years in the role of "leader": three-and-a-half years as division director, five years as department chair, and two six-month stints in an acting position. I thought it was time to step down. The department threw a wonderful party for me at the Faculty Club. Guests included the well-known – and, by then, retired – professors in occupational therapy, Isobel Robinson and Thelma Cardwell. Work colleagues from my COTA (Community Occupational Therapy Associates) days came, as did many former students, colleagues in other departments, and some people from the central administration with whom Marty and I had become friends. My own family and friends turned out in full force. There were several touching speeches – from colleagues and students. The dean under whom I had served the longest, Arnie Aberman, who had a great sense of humour, noted how relentless I could be when I wanted something. That drew a laugh, for sure, but, in its way, I thought it was also a compliment.

With Isobel Robinson (right) and Thelma Cardwell (left) at the reception marking my stepping down as chair

I spoke too. After giving my thanks to everyone, and touting the future of occupational therapy, I closed my speech with comments on a fundraising effort we were launching that night. I spoke about the underutilized role of occupational therapy in oncology. I referenced my own life experience with my mother dying of leukemia when I was so young and how I thought an occupational therapist could have helped. An OT could have helped my mother to do what she wanted to do and needed to do before she died and could also have helped our family deal with our new reality as it unfolded. We sought donations that night for the Judith Friedland Fund for Occupational Therapy Research in Oncology (later extended to include palliative and end-of-life care). The money we raised was matched by the university, and a small but significant endowed fund soon became available.

To keep the festivities going a little longer, my colleague Sharon Friefeld hosted a delightful brunch just for the faculty and staff the next morning. I received some precious poems and other tokens along with a special gift from the whole group: a regular delivery of flowers to my home throughout the coming year.

I believe I got things done in my role as chair, much as I had done with the Home and School at Davisville years ago, and, again, I don't think I was particularly popular – at least not at the time. I preferred to weigh and measure issues as they arose, rather than look to precedents, and I wasn't keen on spending time on all kinds of policies and procedures. I expected a lot from our faculty, and I often took on tasks where others were less than enthusiastic. Not only was it expedient for me to do certain tasks myself, but it also made sense for me to do more: I had tenure and my children were grown, while others had more calls on their time. I also had a helpful husband, one who knew the ropes within the university and who could be counted on to pitch in at home as needed.

I think my most important achievement as chair was the faculty I was able to assemble. Existing faculty upgraded their qualifications, and almost everyone was at the doctoral level by the time I finished. Several new tenure-stream positions were filled under my watch, and I hired a number of people into part-time positions. Without exception, all of these individuals turned out to be excellent members of our department. Our research contributions were numerous and of high quality. We prepared reports of scholarly activity to share with other departments – as much for recording our achievements as letting others know about our work. Any concerns about our place in the university that had surfaced when I had first joined the faculty, when Dean Lowy met with the faculty of the Department of Rehabilitation Medicine to warn us of the need to produce more quality research to justify our presence at the university, were finally laid to rest.

I had agreed to stay on as acting chair through January 2000 until our new chair was in place, and then Marty and I were both on leave. We stayed in Toronto for the first few months so I could wind down, and Marty could keep working on his mega project, writing *The University of*

Toronto: A History. Then we left in March for a wonderful three weeks in Italy. We rented a house just outside Fiesole, an affluent suburb of Florence. It overlooked olive groves and vineyards where naturalized red tulips still lingered and wild garlic grew underfoot. Large pots of rosemary, so familiar in Europe, lined our front walk. I revelled in the surroundings, even doing a little sketching outside on the few sunny days of a cold but fresh March. Roberto, a local farmer, came by each week with fresh vegetables and chickens. We went into Fiesole regularly to shop and look around, and we took the bus into Florence from time to time. We met Vera, my old friend from university, and her husband, Giorgio, in Cinque Terre, and then Vera came back and stayed with us for a few days. During her visit we took in nearby sites, including the Villa I Tatti and the Villa Medici. Before we left for home, Marty and I visited Siena and Venice. It was an idyllic stay.

I returned from leave and settled in again as a faculty member. I still had four years to go before I had to officially retire, given that the province still had a policy of mandatory retirement at sixty-five. I had no idea then that I would choose to stick around for such a long time after that.

14 Post-Chair and Retirement: Not Ready to Stop

When I returned to the Department of Occupational Therapy as a regular faculty member, I tried to stay out of the new chair's way. Helene Polatajko was an experienced administrator and an excellent researcher. I would be available if she needed me but would otherwise keep my distance. It would be better for me and for her: I didn't want faculty members to worry about my feelings when, or if, things I'd established got upended; they needed to be free to make a new attachment.

In addition to teaching one course and providing some single lectures in other courses, I took on two major service roles within the department: I chaired the Post Professional Degree Committee and a committee to celebrate the seventy-fifth anniversary of the start, in 1926, of the occupational therapy diploma program at the university. I was heavily invested in the Post Professional Degree Committee. Our goal was to provide an advanced standing option so that therapists with a bachelor's degree – a BScOT – could upgrade to a master's degree. During our community consultations for the master's program that I had been championing, I saw how anxious clinicians were about their status, given that new grads would be starting practice with higher credentials than they had. I had reassured them that we would provide a means to upgrade for anyone who wished to do so. After all, we had offered a similar program to diploma grads for about two decades after the BScOT degree was introduced in the '70s; surely we could do that now for those with an undergraduate degree.

My committee's proposal was finally approved in 2004, but it was not fully implemented until more than a decade later. By then, many of the clinicians who had wanted to upgrade had found other routes to do so or had given up. I was disappointed that we had not been able to live up to my original pledge more quickly, but I appreciated that the department had many other priorities. Not only was I no longer in charge, but

I had chosen not to get involved with the day-to-day workings of the department. I could hardly complain.

Graduates of the first occupational therapy diploma course, 1928. Courtesy of University of Toronto Archives

I enjoyed organizing our seventy-fifth anniversary event. By that time I had become more interested in the history of OT at the university, and planning the event put me in touch with alumni from across the decades. I felt a new form of connection to my profession. We held our celebration in the magnificent Great Hall at Hart House on September 10th, 2001. The university's president, Robert Birgeneau, attended the dinner and so did the dean of the Faculty of Medicine, David Naylor. Representatives of the various professional associations were on hand to bring us greetings and there was a good turnout of alumni. The speeches were interesting, and everyone was taken by the memorabilia on display. Students were on hand to help out. One of them, dressed in a green uniform from the early '40s, complete with cap and veil, wandered around the room, eliciting many looks of recognition. After all, it was only in the '60s that the uniform was done away with. I myself had worn a derivation of that original as a student – albeit without a starched white collar and cuffs or veil.

By all accounts, the evening was a great success. But however special the evening was, it would be forever linked with the next morning and the horrors of 9/11. Such a juxtaposition of events: to be celebrating at night only to be utterly devastated in the morning. One guest, a former faculty member of ours who was then teaching at New York University, had come to Toronto just for the event. It took more than twenty-four frantic hours until she could contact her family, and it was several days before she could travel home. Of course, those troubles were but a minor inconvenience, given the thousands of deaths and the horrific trauma experienced by so many people. Nonetheless, it took all of us time to resume our usual activities and return to our previous lives.

In my now less hectic schedule, I welcomed the opportunity to serve as a member of the Faculty Council for the Faculty of Nursing. I was very comfortable interacting with this cognate discipline whose work was so complementary to OT. Having previously sat on some of their tenure and promotion committees, I had come to know many of their faculty. I particularly enjoyed interacting with Dean Dorothy Pringle. I admired Dot's engaging personality and her enthusiasm for taking on new challenges. We also shared our concerns over the plight of largely female faculties in general and our struggles to be housed appropriately.

Serving on health-related boards was a good way to gain some insight into the world where our graduates would work. While chair of my department, I had been appointed by the dean to serve on the West Park Hospital Board, and also to do what turned out to be a brief stint with the "Alliance" group during those confusing days when Women's College Hospital and Wellesley Central were considering a partnership.

I joined the Ontario Neurotrauma Foundation (ONF) board just two years after the organization began, and it was interesting to be part of its development, particularly in the way that consumers – people who had experienced neurotraumas – were involved. I was keen on the research the ONF supported, in part because my father had only narrowly escaped becoming quadriplegic as a result of his car accident. The ONF's offices were at Lyndhurst Hospital, where he had been treated, so that board was close to my heart.

Joining the board of COTA (Community Occupational Therapy and Associates) in 2004 gave me an opportunity to serve the agency where I had worked so happily as a clinician when I had first returned to work almost three decades earlier. The last board I sat on (in 2006–8) was JVS (Jewish Vocational Services). The agency, whose services were available to all people, regardless of religion, was run by the former executive director and co-founder of COTA, Karen Goldenberg, someone to whom I could never say "no." The work that JVS did in helping people find employment was so important, and so well-aligned with occupational therapy, that I was sure I would feel right at home.

But no matter which board it was, I never did feel comfortable. I never felt I was contributing. I think I made appropriate comments when information was presented by staff, but it seemed that few truly meaningful issues came forward for discussion. If board members asked probing questions, it seemed almost an affront and was construed by the administration as wanting to "micro-manage." Committee work within the boards was less frustrating but very time-consuming, with additional meetings and interactions with whichever institution's bureaucracy. As wonderful as each of the organizations was in their day-to-day operations – and they all were – I could not find a way to feel useful. And, of course, there is no pay for sitting on non-profit boards: it's not like sitting on a corporate board.

The main change in the use of my time was that I could spend more of it on research. I had just received new funding for a qualitative study on safety for senior drivers. Like much of my research, it was prompted by a personal experience – in this instance, the car accident my father had had at age eighty-nine.

I worked with Debbie Laliberte-Rudman, who had been my student several years before and was now a faculty member, as well as Mary Chipman, an epidemiologist and biostatistician. Two OT students (Amy Steen and Paula Sciortino) became part of our team while using the project to fulfill their research course requirements. We wanted to understand how, or if, people anticipated and dealt with the almost inevitable major change in their daily lives that would come when they stopped driving. To get a broad picture of the issue, we held focus groups with three different categories of drivers: pre-seniors (aged 55–64), seniors who were still driving, and seniors who had stopped driving of their own volition. We also held focus groups with family doctors to understand how they saw their role with respect to this issue, both in terms of requiring cessation and of prevention: Did they ask their older patients if they were still driving and if they were having any trouble?

Analyses of the focus group discussions underscored how difficult driving cessation was: hard for the driver, for the driver's partner, and for the rest of their family. For seniors, the change from coming and going on their own to depending on the goodwill of others for rides was upsetting. Public transportation was not always available, and most of our participants considered taxis an unacceptable extravagance, even though they knew that, in reality, taking the occasional cab was less expensive than maintaining and insuring a car. Discussions about driving cessation were hard for family doctors, who feared harming the doctor-patient relationship. It was clear that much had to change to make driving safer for seniors. However, people's fierce determination to never give up driving would be the hardest.

We had no difficulty publishing our papers from this study.[1] I presented our work at conferences, including two in St. Petersburg, Florida. I had taken Marty to a few of my conferences over the years, but this was one we especially appreciated as it gave us an excuse to have a holiday in the winter. Unlike me in the earlier years of our marriage, Marty seemed to manage "tagging along" without any trouble, always interested in the topics, and usually finding a way to sneak in to hear some presentations.

With my official retirement looming, I wanted to attend to some unfinished business that affected me personally. I wanted to become a full professor, even though I would have only a few years to enjoy that status. In 2001, I very carefully put together my promotions dossier. I knew it was hard to meet the standards for promotion to full professor at the university.[2] I took advantage of a section in the *Promotions Manual* that described research activity *and* creative professional activity as a category on which to go forward. That combination was perfect for me, reflecting, as it did, what my accomplishments had encompassed.

I submitted the dossier and anxiously waited for the Promotions Committee's decision. When it came, I was upset – and confused. I learned that they had looked at my creative professional activity *only* and completely ignored all of my research activity – my publications, grants, and presentations. It was very strange. Used to these hiccups in my career by now, I calmly wrote a letter to the committee, pointing out the section in the *Promotions Manual* that listed research activity *and* creative professional activity – combined – as one category for promotion. I reminded them of my research achievements and noted that these were to be assessed *alongside* my creative professional activity. Then I waited.

One evening in the spring of 2002, Marty and I were at a university function that was also attended by David Naylor, then dean of the Faculty of Medicine. After we greeted one another, and with a big smile on his face, he said, "Judy, I shouldn't be telling you this – but I just signed off on your promotion today." That was a relief.

Meanwhile, my research was beginning to move in a new direction. I had stumbled into historical research beginning in 1988 with the publication in the *American Journal of Occupational Therapy* (*AJOT*) of an article on the controversial topic of diversional activity, where I used historical material to make my case for its place in treatment.[3] A decade later, I published another article in *AJOT*, arguing that, as occupational therapy became incorporated into rehabilitation, the profession's core values had eroded.[4] To support my argument, I again relied on historical material. In between these two articles, and at the request of Professor Edward Shorter, the Hannah Chair in the History of Medicine at U of T, I had written a chapter on occupational therapy for his book *TPH: History and Memories of Toronto Psychiatric Hospital, 1925–1966.*[5] That was the hospital where I had so happily interned as a student and where I worked when we returned from Cambridge in 1961. I found writing that chapter fascinating: hunting for information in archives, interviewing people who had worked at TPH in the early days, identifying issues, creating a story. In 1994, I was invited to give a keynote address at Dalhousie's Spring Institute, hosted by their Occupational Therapy Department, and I talked about our discipline from an historical perspective. Other presentations on our history followed over the next few years, and in 2001 I co-authored an article on the beginnings of the profession (1926–39) with the two former heads of the program, Isobel Robinson and Thelma Cardwell.[6]

My commitment to historical research increased dramatically one day in 2002 as I was walking into a faculty meeting. I was absent-mindedly opening my mail when one letter made me stop in my tracks. The letter announced that I had been awarded the Muriel Driver Lecture Award. The award, which requires the honoree to present a major lecture, "recognizes a member of the Canadian Association of Occupational Therapists (CAOT) who has made an outstanding contribution to the profession and is considered the highest honour given by the Association." I was excited to read the news and immediately blurted it out to everyone at the faculty meeting. The honour was gratifying for me, and good for the department. Everyone shared in my excitement. However, one part of the letter gave me pause – the part where it said that I was expected to present my lecture on an historical topic.

I was being recognized in part for my work in the history of occupational therapy in Canada – a field that was wide open. There were books and articles on occupational therapy's history in the United States and the United Kingdom, but very little had been written about the history of OT in Canada. Now I had my work cut out for me. Over the following year, I visited archives, tracked down materials, and prepared slides.

The title of my lecture was "Why Crafts? Influences on the Early Development of Occupational Therapy in Canada, 1890–1930."[7] The first part of the title came from the perennial question asked by students and those practising occupational therapists who distanced themselves from the "old days" when crafts, then a part of daily life, were in greater use as therapy. I wanted both groups to understand *why* crafts had been

Giving the Muriel Driver Lecture, 2003

used, especially in psychiatric hospitals at the beginning of the previous century, but also in general hospitals during and just after the First World War. I wanted to show the mental health roots of the profession, with its emphasis on building confidence and raising morale.

I gave my lecture at the 2003 annual conference of the CAOT, held that year in Winnipeg. Although very anxious beforehand, I was relaxed when I gave the presentation. By this point in my career, I knew I could present well, and that confidence took over once I started. I finished the lecture and, to my great surprise, everyone clapped – *and* stood up. I was overwhelmed with this response from the 400 or so people in the audience. However, what I didn't realize until later was that, no matter who gave this prestigious lecture, or how good – or bad – it was, a standing ovation was *always* given!

The president of the CAOT gave me a large bouquet of long-stemmed red roses, a plaque, and an honorarium, and many pictures were taken. A small lunch was given in my honour, with guests of my choosing. Comments made after the lecture were gratifying, especially those that came in the form of "I had no idea that we had such a history!"

In the following year, I produced a video using the slides from the lecture and a voice over of the spoken text. I sent a copy to each of the occupational therapy education programs in Canada, hoping students would see it and gain a better sense of their identity.

I had learned so much while preparing my Muriel Driver Lecture that I decided to continue researching my profession's history. I didn't have a grand plan. I thought I would just chip away at areas that interested me. But to do even that, I needed some funding. I had already received three small grants from the Associated Medical Services Hannah History of Medicine Fund. The work I did with the support of those grants, including the Muriel Driver Lecture, helped position me to secure a larger grant from the Social Sciences and Humanities Research Council (SSHRC) in 2004 – ironically, in the year I was to officially retire. The SSHRC grant allowed me to do more work at various archives. I spent time at Library and Archives Canada in Ottawa, delving into materials from the First World War. I went to Chicago for material on early OTs in the United States including their involvement with Hull House, the legendary settlement house, and I went to Baltimore, where I pored over the archives of the American Occupational Therapy Association. A small grant from the British Council was enough for some time in England to pursue my interest in the Arts and Crafts movement and William Morris, the socialist, craftsman, and philosopher whom I and others saw as an important influence on occupational therapy.

Family life continued to weave its way through my day-to-day life. With both sets of parents gone, our focus was shifting to the grandchildren, who had begun to appear: Michael (who was named for my father) in 1998; David, in 2000; our first granddaughter, Tillie (named for my mother), in 2002; Daisy and Elliott, in 2004; Levi, in 2005; and the last two, Cecilia and Nate, in 2008. It was a busy time. The births of the grandchildren were wonderful events, though not without their dramas – with pregnancy risks discovered here and there – amnios and ultrasounds, miscarriages, early births, and dilemmas about circumcision for the boys born into a mixed marriage. I did not commit to regular babysitting times, as some good grandmas do, but I helped whenever asked and made it clear that I was always available in an emergency. One way or another, I had a lot of contact: I took some grandchildren to daycare and picked up others after school, took some to piano lessons, and others to hockey. I cuddled them, read to them, fed them, and played with them – and of course, I worried about them.

In the early grandparenting years, we provided sleepovers, especially for Tom's older two boys, who had come along first. We included "adventures" (usually hikes in local ravines, much as my father had done with our kids), and I made a special effort to cook meals that I knew they would like. As the grandchildren grow older, it is sometimes difficult to maintain close relationships, but we persevere and enjoy being a part of their young adult lives – hearing about school, friendships, sports activities, jobs, and travels.

I turned sixty-five in 2004, but I was by no means ready to fully retire. I had worked at the university for just twenty-two years – what with all my time at home, and my years of part-time work – whereas faculty typically retired after forty or so years. I wanted to remain in the working world, and so, I just kept on working. It would be odd to receive a pension cheque and not a paycheque, but my day-to-day life, my "occupations," wouldn't change that much. Of course, I could have found other things to do, but there seemed no good reason to stop doing what I found interesting.

I didn't want any sort of party for my official retirement because I had already been honoured when I'd stepped down as chair just a few years earlier. I also think I didn't want a fuss, as it would make me feel as though I *should* be separating from the school. However, there was a lovely dinner at Bonnie Kirsh's home with a clever and funny slide presentation. The brains behind the effort were my colleagues Barry Trentham, Debbie Hebert, and Jill Stier. Marty was the secret source of the slides of a younger me, which brought forth much laughter.

Then it was time for a break to mark this so-called retirement, and that meant travel to somewhere special. Although Marty and I had always planned and arranged our travel ourselves, and had only once taken a tour (in Russia in 1989, when it was hard to travel there on one's own), some destinations required help, especially as we got older, and Southeast Asia was one of those places. Tov Mason's travel company came highly recommended and did not disappoint. Tov had been a law student of Marty's but, after graduating, had decided to do what he loved most and went into the travel business. He organized our trip from Thailand to Myanmar, Cambodia, and Vietnam. We saw extraordinary sites day after day and enjoyed them at our own pace. Everything was perfect. After that, we relied on Tov whenever we wanted to do more complicated travels. He got us to Poland to visit Krakow and Auschwitz and also Czestochowa, where my grandparents had lived. He got us to our "family castles": Friedland Castle in the Czech Republic and Pless Castle in Poland (neither of which had even a remote connection with our families, despite having our surnames). He organized our trip to South America for the Amazon Delta, Machu Picchu, and Patagonia in 2007. We also took a trip to India to visit Rajasthan, Varanasi, Kerala, and Darjeeling – places we had missed on our first visit when we had gone on our own. He arranged our trip to the Baltics in 2015, which included visits to our fathers' birthplaces in Lithuania.

When we came back from Southeast Asia in 2004, I settled back into post-retirement "work." I took on some consulting jobs with a team with whom I had worked when they led the Ontario Ministry of Health's Rehabilitation Reform Initiative Reference Group. I also did a review of a program for CAMH (the Centre for Addiction and Mental Health). Later, in my capacity as the chair of the Research Ethics Policy and Advisory Committee at U of T, I provided a report and recommendations for the future of that committee to the vice president research. I thoroughly enjoyed this type of work. It allowed me to dig into issues and also connect with the individuals involved. I always wished I had been asked to do more of this sort of thing.

One project that carried over into my retirement was work on the Gender Issues Committee that Dean Naylor had established in 2002. He asked us to look at the question of career development in the Faculty of Medicine, given that there were concerns about the "under-represented gender" (aka women) there, as in the university generally. We carried out a survey of all salaried members of the faculty and found that unequal pay was but one of the many issues facing female academics in the Faculty of Medicine. Time-to-tenure was a major concern with younger women, knowing they had to work flat out – and possibly delay childbearing – to achieve tenure. For those who already had children, the juggling of family and career was difficult: supports from the university were few, and family stress was high. For women, there seemed no way out: family life impacts an academic career especially while the tenure clock is ticking, and an academic career threatens family life.[8] As the late Berkeley professor emerita Mary Ann Mason put it, "for men, having children is a career advantage; for women, it is a career killer."[9] This difficult problem remains today. Although the change from five years to six for time-to-tenure at U of T is seen by all as a step in the right direction, this change may have the effect of still favouring those without child-care responsibilities – be they men or women.

I was surprised to see from our survey results that only 17 per cent of faculty in the rehabilitation science sector, the majority of whom were women, had reported negotiating their starting salaries – and this some twenty years after I had been faced with that issue. At the same time, I was not surprised to see that junior faculty felt burdened with committee work and service, while senior faculty (typically with their positions secure and usually with lighter family responsibilities) appeared to have more time protected for research. We presented our report to a meeting of all chairs in the Faculty of Medicine in 2005, but it did not cause much of a stir. Like female faculty salaries, gender equity gaps of one sort or another continue to appear.

From 2000 to 2018, I was involved with research ethics. This area of work, which continued well into my retirement years, started innocently enough in 2000, when I became a member of the Health Sciences Research Ethics Board (REB) at the University of Toronto. It started out as just another "service" duty – my turn to do a required task. I would review research ethics protocols each month and attend a two-hour meeting with the committee to discuss and make decisions on whether to give ethics approval to the protocols.

A research ethics board must approve all research involving human participants: although some researchers see ethics review as a burden, they know it cannot be avoided. Major funding bodies will not release funds until ethics approval has been granted, and no reputable journal will publish research involving human participants without a statement indicating ethics board approval.

As a researcher myself, and as a supervisor of student research projects and graduate theses, I had come to believe that the ethics review process, though burdensome, almost always strengthened a research protocol by taking, as it does, the research participant's perspective. With this appreciation and respect for the role of ethics boards, I was happy to agree to serve on the board when asked. Being required to read a variety of research proposals was a form of continuing education, learning about different research methods and areas of inquiry. Six years later, I was pleased to be asked to take over as chair of the Health Sciences REB. The position gave me an opportunity to use the ethics knowledge accrued over my years as a member, as well as the group leadership skills I had honed through my clinical and administrative work. I worked hard to establish a collegial and convivial environment for our discussions. Two members of the board were "community members," and the other members were generally academics representing their own departments. The academics were often reluctant to join the board, seeing it as yet another unwanted call on their time. However, after a short period of time, they invariably remarked on how much they learned and how enjoyable the meetings were. I, in turn, enjoyed working with my board members. We learned from each other, problem solved together, came to a consensus, and, in the process, rendered good decisions.

I liked my role as chair. In addition to running the meetings and following up with researchers about what was needed to improve their protocols with respect to protection of participants, I had opportunities to meet with others about research ethics, both locally from Toronto's teaching hospitals and nationally at conferences. Just as I was nearing the end of my second (and final) three-year term chairing the U of T board, staff from Public Health Ontario (PHO), then a newly established provincial government agency, asked me to help them select members for their own ethics review board. While helping with this process, I learned that they were looking for someone with experience to chair the new board. It was 2012, and with the university job just about to end, it was perfect timing for me. I applied and was appointed.

The work was different from that at U of T because of PHO's mandate to review not only what might be called "capital R research" but *all* evidence-generating initiatives involving human participants, including program evaluation, enhanced surveillance, and quality improvement projects.[10] I found it interesting – and sometimes challenging – to consider ethics review within that wider framework, but I soon came to see its strengths. I worked with excellent colleagues at PHO, planning and developing the new board, recruiting and orienting new members, and establishing an appropriate culture with this new entity. The PHO Ethics Review Board had a broad membership, with representatives from different fields of public health and various geographic areas in the province as well as community members.

With all this time working on research ethics boards, I had questions about the ethics review process and wanted to do some research in the area. I had a perfect collaborator in Elizabeth Peter, a professor in the Faculty of Nursing, who succeeded me as chair of the U of T Health Sciences REB and later the PHO board. We are extremely compatible collaborators. We always follow the same order of business at our research meetings: we meet over lunch; we talk about our families, our own work, and whatever else is of interest or concern first; and then we get down to business and talk about our research project. The approach works well for us. We have successfully presented our work at conferences and published two studies so far.[11]

I continued with my historical research over the next few years, delving into whatever seemed of interest, with no long-term plan in mind.

I interviewed several alumnae from the class of 1928 – the first year of the diploma program. I did an oral history of Isobel Robinson, a major contributor to the profession since her graduation in 1939.[12] My student Hadassah Rais and I published an article on Helen LeVesconte, the head of occupational therapy from 1933 to 1967 and a great contributor to the profession.[13] One of my favourite projects was my work with Brenda Head, from Memorial University. In an article and a conference poster, we told the story of Jessie Luther and her work at the Grenfell Mission in St Anthony, Newfoundland.[14] Luther was an American occupational therapist whom Sir Wilfrid Grenfell brought out to the mission annually for many winters, beginning in the early 1900s, helping to build community life during the fishers' off-season. Luther's work connected many dots in the profession's early history: the settlement house movement (she had worked at Hull House in Chicago), the role of art (she was a graduate of the Rhode Island School of Design), the Arts and Crafts movement (she was a member of the Boston Society of Arts and Crafts), and the mental hygiene movement (she was the director of occupational therapy at the Butler Psychiatric Hospital in Providence Rhode Island).[15]

When I realized the connections between occupational therapy and educational reform in the late 1800s, I knew I had found a strong line of inquiry for going forward. Manual training was a major aspect of educational reform, and manual activities – generally in the form of crafts – became an integral part of occupational therapy in asylums around the same time. Learning about manual training in schools led me to Thomas Bessell Kidner and his important role in the development of the profession.

Kidner was brought from Bristol, England, to Canada in 1900 to organize manual training classes in schools; first in Nova Scotia, then in New Brunswick, and, in 1911, in Alberta. His reputation was such that during the First World War, he was appointed vocational secretary to the Military Hospitals Commission. From 1916 until the end of the war, he oversaw programs designed to help discharged soldiers, including those who had been injured, return to their former jobs, where possible, or be trained for new work. Among the programs he oversaw were those that included "ward aides," female volunteers who provided occupations for injured soldiers, usually in the form of crafts. They offered "bedside occupations" during the soldiers' lengthy convalescence, and, as the soldiers' health improved, they provided activities on the wards and in workshops, hoping to restore their spirit while helping them prepare for a return to work or for vocational rehabilitation.

By 1917, when the US government was planning to enter the war and knew it would soon be dealing with injured soldiers, it sent officials to see the work being done in Canadian hospitals.[16] Kidner was invited to be one of the seven founders of the (American) National Society for the Promotion of Occupational Therapy (NSPOT) that same year. He was seconded by the US government to help establish services for their injured soldiers in 1918; by 1919, he had moved permanently to the United States. In 1922, he was elected president of the American Occupational Therapy Association, a post he would hold for six years.

In Kidner, I had found a strong thread to take me through the profession's early history, and a way to stress Canada's important role in its development in the United States. I published one paper with my student Naomi Davids-Brumer about his career and his contributions to occupational therapy in Canada. A second paper, written with another student, Jennifer Silva, described Kidner's contributions to occupational therapy in the United States. I wrote a third and somewhat speculative paper on his involvement in the United Kingdom on my own.[17] I say speculative because I had difficulty finding records about his life in England and had little to go on aside from what I gleaned from relatives I found in the United Kingdom, the United States, and Canada. Meeting or just corresponding with these people made the project very real for me. And, because of my project, some family members were connecting for the first time in many years. In one instance, my inquiries brought a mother together with her estranged son. Connections between eighteenth- and nineteenth-century educational reform and early occupational therapy continue to interest me. Elizabeth Townsend, a colleague at Dalhousie University, and I published an article on this topic in 2016.[18]

By now I was thinking seriously about writing a book on the beginnings of occupational therapy in Canada. Assuming I could get it written and it was good enough, I considered who might publish it. I would not want to approach the University of Toronto Press, where Marty had already published several books and had been the chair of its Manuscript Review Committee for many years. That would be too awkward all around.[19] McGill-Queen's University Press (MQUP) had a history of medicine series, and I decided to give them a try. I did not discuss my plans with anyone in advance; rather I went ahead and submitted a proposal using the instructions on the press's website.

I sent off the proposal just before we left on a trip to South America in February 2007. In the excitement of the trip, I forgot about the proposal. Then, one day somewhere in Peru, as I was checking my email, I found a message from MQUP. It said, "As we are keenly interested in your manuscript, could you provide your written assurance that we have the right of first refusal to the work?" I was ecstatic.

This new project alone would have been enough to keep me busy. But that same year, we decided it was time to move from our home of thirty-nine years into a condo. Always wanting to anticipate events, so as to have more control, I thought it would be good to move at a time when we were healthy and able to enjoy the process, rather than be forced into it by altered circumstances. The occupational therapist in me wanted to make the adjustment to our new environment as easy as possible. The book would have to wait.

Marty was reluctant when we started our condo search. In similar situations, he sometimes preferred to leave well enough alone and resisted change. But he soon came around and became as excited about the move as I was. We developed criteria for the place we wanted. We needed a balcony so we could continue to do some gardening, and an indoor swimming pool for our own exercise and as an activity for visiting grandchildren. We needed to see nature, and we needed access to public transportation and grocery shopping nearby. We also wanted to replicate the feelings we had in our first apartment by having a spectacular view. It was a tall order.

Our search took time but eventually, we got the view (and everything else) on Queen's Quay in a heritage building that sits on the shore of Lake Ontario. Our condo faces southwest, and our view includes the lake, one of the islands, and part of the city. We see the ever-changing surface of the water: smooth and flat one day, choppy with whitecaps the next. In winter we see the lake freeze up in sections resembling giant jigsaw puzzle pieces. The lake glitters in the sun and looks ominous when the day is overcast. We see the CN Tower and the lights of downtown Toronto, and, on a clear night, we can see the lights of Hamilton, some fifty kilometres to the west. The sunsets are breathtaking, especially in the fall, when the sun is low on the horizon.

The day after the sale of the condo closed, a complete renovation began under the direction of our friend, Jerome Markson, the wonderful architect who had designed the renovations to our previous homes (once on Hillsdale and twice on Belsize) and to our cottage. Although all the work on the condo was not yet complete, it was good enough for us to move in at the end of October. It was a busy time for us, selecting materials, making decisions as we went along, dealing with the usual unanticipated costs in a reno. It was exciting to watch the new place take shape, and we were thrilled with how it all turned out.

As exciting as the condo move was, it was also stressful. Aside from the emotional aspect of leaving our home of almost four decades, the move meant that lots of details needed attending to – from simple things like setting up telephones and redirecting mail, to more complicated ones with the bank. To top things off, Marty had a new book coming out, his own memoirs, and that anxiety was also in the air.[20]

Just two weeks after we moved in, Marty was on the phone with someone at the bank and lost his temper. Because he was normally well-mannered and calm, I was surprised to see him so agitated. That night, he complained of some vague tightness in his chest and shoulders, a bit of a sore throat, and some stomach cramps. But no chest pain, no shortness of breath, no sweating or chills. The anxiety seemed understandable – the move, the fight with the bank, the new book coming out. The book launch was two days away.

I decided to check his symptoms with Dr Google and – sure enough – anxiety was listed as a symptom of a heart attack. That was enough to send us to Emerg in the early hours of the morning. The ECG revealed a minor infarct – and that was enough to send hospital staff scurrying. An angiogram was scheduled for later that day, and two stents were implanted.

Marty was admitted to the cardiology floor for what was to be a two- or three-day stay, to recover and be observed. Although the stents meant he was now in better condition than before, he had had a mild heart attack and undergone a procedure that warranted a hospital stay. The drama continued, however, as Marty tried to convince the cardiologist to allow him out of the hospital for the book launch for his memoir. It became clear that the event meant a great deal and that cancelling it – or holding it without him – would be complicated and upsetting. The doctor finally relented. He gave Marty an evening pass: to leave the hospital, attend the event, and return that same night.

With very mixed feelings, I brought his suit, tie, shirt, and shoes to the hospital in the afternoon. Marty changed from his hospital gown into his business attire, and off we went to the book launch, which was held at the Law School. No one other than the immediate family knew what had transpired the day before. Marty spoke about the book, as one would expect. Then his speech took a dramatic turn. He talked about not knowing what's around the corner in life and punctuated his words by holding up his arm and showing everyone his hospital identification bracelet. After their audible collective gasp subsided, he briefly told them the story of the past forty-eight hours. Then we took him back to the hospital!

Knowing that he officially has cardiovascular disease, and with a strong history of heart disease in his family, we are now much more alert to any possible symptoms. However, nothing else has changed, other than that we try to live a healthier life with better food choices and more exercise. So, a very good heart attack indeed.

Marty was fully recovered, and so we saw no reason not to celebrate the year of our fiftieth wedding anniversary with more travel. In May

2008, we visited Barcelona, and, after a stop in Paris, moved on to England and the South Downs for the opera at Glyndebourne. We knew in advance that the setting, with its perfect lawns and gardens, rolling hills and grazing sheep, would be bucolic, but we were surprised by just how beautiful it was. The sight of people in elegant dress strolling about or picnicking on the grounds, champagne in hand, was extraordinary. Indeed, the surroundings somewhat overwhelmed the opera performance itself. To top off this celebratory trip, we stayed at Gravetye Manor, a spectacular sixteenth-century estate in the Sussex countryside. Wandering through its historic gardens and hiking in the surrounding hills made for a perfect ending to the trip.

On June 19th, 2008, exactly fifty years after our wedding, we celebrated our anniversary with family and friends in the newly renovated condo. Although our space is not all that large, the open plan of the kitchen–dining–living room enabled us to have about eighty friends and family join us over the course of the evening. We felt so lucky to have had each other all this time and to have shared so many meaningful experiences. That night, a fireworks display just happened to take place on the lake, and it topped off our joyous occasion.

As part two of the celebration, our kids had planned a trip for the immediate family to Niagara Falls for the following weekend. We had seven grandchildren at that point, with the newest addition not quite four months old. There was more than the usual amount of tension in the air, and it soon became clear that there was serious trouble between the parents of that new baby, and by the time we had returned to Toronto, they had officially split up. Our daughter Jenny and her partner had been together for ten years. They had a four-year-old daughter, as well as an infant. It was a great shock and a very difficult time for everyone. It took many months for us all to find a new equilibrium. In the years since the split, the family unit has stayed strong, and relations between the parents (and their extended families) have become more than amicable.

One never knows what is around the corner.

15 From Some Darkness into Light: When the Margins Aren't Clear

In between moving, dealing with Marty's heart attack, celebrating our anniversary, and surviving a family upheaval, I was trying to work on my book. I visited archives, searched the literature, and interviewed people. Preparing for a speaking engagement at Homewood Health Centre in Guelph, Ontario, in 2008 helped move my research forward. It was the hospital's 125th anniversary and, as I learned about its history as the first privately owned psychiatric facility in Canada, I saw more evidence of the use of occupations in the early 1900s. In 1913, when a "Miss Scott" had been hired as director of occupations, the medical superintendent of Homewood, Dr A.T. Hobbs, proudly described the new program saying, "It fills in the spare time of patients, keeps them busy, at the same time turning their energies into useful work."[1] I knew that other Ontario institutions such as the London Asylum and Rockwood, in Kingston, were also providing patients with occupations, but this was the first evidence I had of a named individual being hired specifically for this purpose. (Sadly, I was never able to find detailed information about Miss Scott, despite many efforts.)

I kept working away on the book for the next year and a half, and, by the winter of 2010, I only had two more chapters to complete. But as it turned out, 2010 was not a good year for me.

It all started on a beautiful winter day in early March. Marty and I decided to go skating on the outdoor rink just a few hundred feet from where we live by Lake Ontario. The rink was closing the following day, and we knew it would be the last skate of the season. The ice was slushy. Signs warned skaters about the poor conditions, and some sections were already cordoned off. We read the signs, hesitated, and then laced up our skates. We didn't need the best of conditions; after all, as septuagenarians, we would not be speeding about.

It was a glorious day. Blue sky, brilliant sunshine, and no wind off the lake. The air was just cold enough to bring on the usual dripping nose.

We headed for the section of ice that looked most solid. After a round or two skating together, we separated, thinking it might be safer for each of us to skate around on our own. The slushy surface made for slow, jerky movements, and gliding was all but impossible. After only one turn around the rink, I decided I'd had enough. As I carefully skated over to the side of the rink, I also took a tissue from my pocket to wipe my dripping nose.

And then I was down. Both arms out behind me to break my fall. Excruciating pain, the right arm much worse than the left. Unable to use my hands to get up. I shouted for help and I'm sure I swore. Finally, a guard and Marty both appeared at my side. Never having broken a bone in my life, it was abundantly clear that I had done so now. This was what people meant when they said, "You know when you've broken something."

After a mercifully quick chat at triage in the nearest hospital's Emergency Department, I was given a shot of morphine and taken for X-rays. The technician asked, "Are you sure you've never broken your *left* arm before?" He thought that what he was seeing on the screen might be the result of an old fracture – not a new one. However, my negative reply meant that my less painful left arm was also broken. So that was that: two broken wrists (bilateral fractures of the distal radius of each arm). The ER physician injected a short-acting but heavy-duty anaesthetic (propofol, the drug that Michael Jackson died from when he took too much, reportedly to help him sleep). I came to with both fractures reduced and both arms in plaster casts. I went off with an allotment of too much oxycodone, and one of my daughters and my husband leading the way.

I managed to get seen by a hot-shot hand surgeon just a few weeks after my fall. He was low key, matter of fact, but compassionate, even though my case was likely the least complicated of all the injuries he would see that day. He careened around the room on a swivel stool, moving quickly from patient to patient, but still taking his time with each one – or at least making one feel that he was doing that, which, as all health care professionals know, is the big trick. Over the next month or two, I received excellent therapy in the department's hand clinic, where several of my former students worked. They were shocked to see me. I sensed some discomfort (how would I judge their skills?) and some embarrassment at the reversal of our relationship.

Those heavy plaster casts were clumsy and brought on a variety of unique challenges. One cold night soon after my fall, Marty and I ventured out to a concert. It was probably too soon for an outing and the stress left me feeling tired and agitated by the end of the concert. When we returned to our car, I started an argument about our route home and soon found myself in tears. When we reached our parking garage, and Marty went to help me out, I demanded to be left alone. "Just leave me be. I'll leave when I'm ready." Alas, the melodrama took a turn when I realized I could not even open the car door by myself. Fortunately, Marty hadn't listened to my Garbo-like demand and had remained nearby, and he opened the door for me. Once back in our suite, and still very distraught, I needed help to get my coat off. It was frustrating and somewhat humiliating to have my dramatic turn cut short by my dependence.

The plaster casts made me look like a prizefighter. People – even strangers – would greet me with disbelief and say things like "How does the other guy look?" Once the plaster casts were replaced with fibreglass ones, life became easier. I worked away at my hand exercises, and, although I continued to gain range of motion and muscle strength, there were still difficulties with my activities of daily living; dressing, bathing, preparing meals, and just moving about were problematic. On the subway, I worried about keeping my balance, and so I avoided travelling during rush hour.

Work on my book came to a standstill because of my inability to type. One of my occupational therapy colleagues suggested I try a voice-to-text program. I bought Dragon NaturallySpeaking, but no matter how hard I tried, I could not train the still-quite-new software to use only my words and not automatically substitute its own: the program readily inserted talk of "Rome and legions of armies marching on the enemy" in among my words about the beginnings of occupational therapy in Canada.

It was salutary for me to experience the discomforts of dependence. As a giver and supporter of others, I soon realized how difficult it was to need, ask for, and accept help. In my research into the psychosocial aspects of illness and injury, I had written about the over-valuing of independence in Western society and the importance of being able to accept help from others. But writing about it and actually doing it were two different things.

I was lucky with my fractures, my treatment, and my progress. By early June, just three months after my fall, I was almost back to normal and carrying out my usual activities. However, life has a way of intervening.

It all started with a phone call from my family doctor's receptionist late on a Friday afternoon. She asked me to come in for an appointment the following Monday. As luck would have it, my own doctor was away, and it was his replacement who had received the results of my routine mammogram. She wanted to break the news to me in person; hence, the request for me to come in. But there was no way I could go through the weekend without hearing more. I insisted on being told the news.

There was something suspicious in my mammogram; appointments for a biopsy and various scans had already been arranged. I doubt the word cancer was actually spoken. Fortunately, Marty was home with me when I heard the news. I sobbed briefly and then I felt completely enveloped by sadness. A level of despair quickly set in and, along with it, a sort of handing over of my fate. While Marty and I learned what we could about the disease, as fast we could, I had a sense of this knowledge being of little use. I knew I would have little control over what would happen.

I had the biopsy and the scans. I was told that my tumour was malignant but very tiny (not even palpable). Everyone (healthcare professionals, friends, and family) said I would be fine – a lumpectomy would do it. For sure.

Would that it was all so simple. The trouble started after the lumpectomy, with the return of the pathology results. My surgeon sat down opposite me in the examining room and looked me straight in the eye as he said, "The margins aren't clear." This news meant that all the cancerous tissue was not excised. It's always difficult to get good margins but, to make matters worse, my form of cancer – invasive lobular – does not respect boundaries. It likes to jump around. And there's no way of knowing if all of the cancerous tissue has been removed until the margins of the excised tissue are examined.

With the poor results from the lumpectomy in hand, my surgeon asked if I wanted to try for another lumpectomy or have a mastectomy. What to do? Having a mastectomy was a huge step but it would put a stop to the guessing. It would save a month or more of being in limbo waiting for a surgery date and pathology reports from a second lumpectomy. On the other hand, the biopsy of several sentinel nodes made at the time of the first lumpectomy did not show any spread of the disease. It was reasonable to think a second lumpectomy might just get what remained. Yet, it seemed wise to seek a second opinion.

There is no easy way to get a second opinion in the medical world. It's difficult to arrange, you insult your own doctor by asking for it, and, when you get the consult, the consulting physician is put in an awkward position. Favours from well-placed friends helped me get an appointment with the "star" oncology surgeon whom I had tried to see initially but who was out of town. It was an unpleasant experience. I stumbled through my explanation of why I was there. Marty – sporting his Companion of the Order of Canada pin just in case it might make the doctor feel more inclined to help – also tried to explain the dilemma, to no avail. We felt we were wasting the star's time. There were pros, there were cons; it was up to me, he said. I left as I had arrived, in a quandary.

Throughout this whole process, my various "medical connections" (at the university and among family and friends) stood me in good stead. I was pleasantly surprised to see how easily I could contact colleagues in the Faculty of Medicine to ask for advice. One physician, an expert in this field of research, had been a member of a committee I had chaired at the university, and I felt comfortable asking her opinion. That began a process of sharing my case with a worldwide consortium through email and receiving an array of opinions. However, as could have been predicted, it too ended with equivocal advice, including that of "watchful waiting," which, given my age (then seventy-one) and there being no evidence of spread or family history, also seemed worth considering. But not for long. "Watchful" was the operative word – and, for me, that translated into anxiety-filled waiting. I doubted I could do that.

I decided to proceed with a second lumpectomy. It too showed poor margins. Now I was faced with choosing between two extreme options: the already dismissed watchful waiting – in other words, doing nothing beyond regular monitoring – and the mastectomy. After much deliberation, and sensing that my surgeon thought the mastectomy was the right choice, I decided to go ahead with it. As it turned out, the pathology results revealed *several* tiny (invasive lobular) carcinomas and several indications of lobular carcinoma in situ. Mastectomy had been a good choice.

The lumpectomies had been day surgeries, and I had had quick and complete recoveries. For the mastectomy, I stayed in hospital overnight and then kept watch over drainage tubes for the following week. Still, it too was an easy recovery, at least physically. It was, of course, a major psychological adjustment. My breast was gone. I had a neat but vivid scar to always remind me that I had had cancer – and could have it again. And my body image was forever altered.

I knew I was getting off easy compared to others. Most everyone I knew who had had breast cancer had to have radiation and chemotherapy. Although mastectomy is traumatic and disfiguring, it can be a quick way out of treatment mode. I had no radiation and no chemo, just medication for five years – hard to complain about that.

My surgeries played out over the course of five months, and I soon become a regular in the breast cancer clinic in the Princess Margaret Hospital. It is nothing to be kept waiting more than an hour before being called into an examining room. A further wait occurs after you change into an always ill-fitting examining gown and sit in a room that is usually too cold. And then, once the doctor enters, you try to listen carefully to what you are being told and remember all the questions you wanted to ask. Everything then moves quickly, and your appointment is over. But cancer being what it is, and oncology surgeons doing what they do, one readily forgives the indignities of the process. On your way out, you book your next appointment. It becomes routine.

The scene in the waiting room never ceased to move me. Everyone is tense, of course. It's very quiet and there is an air of sadness in the room. Some patients keep busy reading a book or a magazine, doing a crossword puzzle, making phone calls, but many just sit and stare into space. Most have someone with them: husbands accompany wives, daughters are with their mothers, and friends come along too. Most everyone seems contemplative. A few appear more matter of fact, even blasé, and seemingly accepting of their plight; perhaps they've been in treatment for a long time. Some women have scarves covering up their newly bald heads. A few are in wheelchairs, indicating their debilitated state and signifying that they may be near the end of their journey. The young women are the saddest to see: their lives now marked with anxiety, difficult decision making, pain, and sorrow – possibly for as long as they live. The waits – in the waiting room, in the examining room, and at home waiting for test results – all seem interminable.

Clinic areas are named for the cancerous body part (breast, colon, brain, lung, and so on). Although a good organizing principle for the staff, it adds to the already dehumanizing effects of a cancer diagnosis. In the Breast Clinic, for example, it's enough that breasts and hair – so much of a woman's identity – can go when breast cancer comes. But some indignities could easily be avoided: robocalls, reminding patients of upcoming appointments, are a prime example. The voice of the robot is yet another way of underscoring that you have become somehow alien and live in a different world.

Prior to the mastectomy, I was sent for a consult with a plastic surgeon to discuss the options for reconstructive surgery. The decision had to be made in advance because, if I did want reconstruction, preparatory steps would be taken during the mastectomy. I decided against it. For one thing, it seemed almost unseemly to be creating a new breast just as I was losing the old one. Also, I felt pessimistic about the future and was quite certain that there would be an occurrence in the other breast sooner or later, so why bother. I also worried that, with a reconstructed breast, any remnants of my cancer, for example in the chest wall on that side, might not be as easily noticed. I knew there was a risk of infection with the procedure, and I was also not keen for what would have been the fourth round of surgery. I was tired of it all.

Most of my friends thought I was making a mistake in not having the reconstruction; interestingly, neither my daughters nor my husband were keen on me having the surgery. I guess they were all tired of it all too.

I have bouts of sadness for the missing breast, but I doubt a reconstructed breast would have helped me very much. It would not have had any sensation. It's a cosmetic procedure and practical; it looks better in clothing and makes a prosthesis unnecessary. I'm used to wearing the prosthesis now – and my family is used to dealing with it; indeed, on one occasion not long after the mastectomy, when one of my granddaughters was with me as I was dressing, she said that my mastectomy side looked more "normal" than the other side! It was before she entered puberty, so that visual seemed about right to her. Sometimes when I hug one of my grandchildren, they will ask if they're being held against the fake boob or the real one.

At some level, all the illnesses and injuries for me and for the members of my family are reminders of my mother – a sharp reminder that something awful can always happen. Once I had passed my thirty-eighth birthday, the age at which my mother died, I magically thought – now I am OK: I will not follow in my mother's footsteps. And, indeed, I was healthy over all the ensuing years. A little high blood pressure, and some other minor health issues, but nothing major. It was not until I was in my 70s that I began to pay back for that free ride.

I deal with medical crises (mine and others') calmly, but my anxiety is apparent to all. What is even more apparent is my anticipatory worry; I am always worrying about what might happen and thinking about what could be prevented. As I reread this last sentence, I am reminded of the research literature on coping with serious illness and the "Why me?" questions that are prompted by the feeling that one is being punished for having done something wrong.[2] Blaming oneself is also a theme with the death of a parent. Looking back over all the decades since my mother's death, I truly do not believe I ever felt "why me?" When injury and illness struck me, I just believed I was lucky to have been well for so long. However, my extreme concerns for prevention – so as not to feel responsible when something bad happens – may belie my words.

Somehow, I was able to finish my manuscript that summer. I told people that working on the book was good occupational therapy for me: my mind was diverted, and I did not dwell on negative thoughts. I was meaningfully engaged. From the publisher's perspective, there was no rush to finish, but I wanted the book to come out before the end of 2011. I had received publishing support from the Ontario Society of Occupational Therapists, which was celebrating its ninetieth anniversary that year, and I knew they wanted to have the book available by then. That organization had been the major force behind formalizing the profession at the end of the First World War, and I had highlighted their important role. It was a good fit for them to support the book.

My book, *Restoring the Spirit: The Beginnings of Occupational Therapy in Canada, 1890–1930*, was indeed published in 2011, and the official launch took place at the University of Toronto Faculty Club in October. The evening was hosted by my department chair and good friend Susan Rappolt, and included remarks from Susan and the then dean of the Faculty of Medicine, Dr Cathy Whiteside. It was a wonderful event. Family – including all eight grandchildren – were there, along with friends, faculty members, some former students, others from the university, and several research assistants who had worked with me on the book. Books were sold, and people lined up for me to sign their copy. People of all ages milled about, a drink or some food in one hand and my book in the other.

When it was my turn to speak, I referred to my *annus horribilis* – just like the queen had in 1992, when Windsor Castle burned, and divorce, separation, and scandal enveloped several of her children. In telling my audience about my skating misadventure, I held up my wrists and asked my grandchildren sitting on the floor just in front of me, "And how many wrists did I break?" And they all shouted "TWO!" That got a good laugh from my audience. Then I told my audience the saga of my breast cancer. The room turned quiet. Everyone has had someone in their lives, if not themselves, who has had cancer, and among my guests, the majority of whom were women, everyone has a breast cancer story. I told everyone how lucky I thought I was and how truly grateful I was for all the support I had received.

In the years that followed the book's publication, I gave presentations to almost all the occupational therapy hospital departments in Toronto. I tailored the content of each presentation to reflect the various settings; for example, I highlighted our work with injured soldiers and veterans when I spoke at Sunnybrook Hospital, described discrimination against Jewish health care professionals when I spoke at Baycrest, and stressed the psychiatric focus of all our work when I spoke at the Centre for Addiction and Mental Health. I did a talk for occupational therapists in the Alberta Health System – remotely – and

At my book launch with granddaughter Cecilia, 2011

told them about individuals from Alberta (Sir James Lougheed, Hilda Goodman) and western hospitals (Strathcona, North Battleford) that were so important in early OT history. I continue to give a lecture to first-year OT students at U of T each year, hoping to give them a solid grounding in where we came from and why. The students are a good audience and always seem amazed to learn about our beginnings.

I have also given talks to some groups that were not directly related to occupational therapy. One of the most interesting of these was a talk for men who volunteered with an organization known as DesignAbility. Primarily retired engineers and carpenters, they make one-off special equipment for people with disabilities. They were interested in how manual training became established in the schools in the early 1900s and how manual activities were used with injured soldiers from the First World War. For a presentation to a large group of U of T senior alumni in their Canadian Perspectives lecture series, I stressed the influence that the OT program at the university had on the profession, both nationally and internationally. I noted that all the occupational therapists in Canada were our graduates (except for those who had immigrated to Canada) until 1950, when the program at McGill began, followed, in 1954, with the first French-language program at l'Université de Montréal. Knowing that my audience on this occasion was composed of seniors, I slipped in some references to modern-day OT practice, stressing our work in seniors' driving safety. I was thrilled to be asked to give a talk at a meeting of the William Morris Society of Canada. In my presentation, "Through Mind and Hand to Health," I focused on the influence of the Arts and Crafts movement and of Morris himself on the profession of occupational therapy – a relationship that was unknown to most members of the society (and most occupational therapists).

My book brought me to the attention of others at U of T with an interest in medical history. Pier Bryden, a psychiatrist with a strong background in the area, met with me one day to talk about a group she was organizing. Before I knew it, I was helping her plan a conference and agreeing to speak at it. The Health History Partnership, as we called ourselves, has now run three medical history events.[3] It has been stimulating for me to work with a whole new set of people with whom I share an interest, and in a multidisciplinary group. I am now a member of the Toronto Medical Historical Club, founded at U of T in 1923.[4] When I attended their annual meeting for the first time, I felt terribly out of place. Almost all the members were physicians, and the few with whom I spoke left me, as the author of a book on the history of occupational therapy in Canada, feeling that I did not warrant a place at their table. In the years since, either I have become more confident, or the membership has broadened, or both. Now, when I attend meetings, I know a lot of people, I have interesting conversations, and I feel at home. I have even given a presentation on physicians' early involvement in our history.

I like attending events like these on my own, and I have stopped attending events of Marty's when I know my invitation is just a nicety. It's not that I mind being left to my own devices to socialize – I can make conversation with most anyone. But I have run out of patience for standing quietly by or chatting about nothing of importance, off to the side, not involved in the main event. I share historian Alison Prentice's description of her own changing role as a faculty wife, when she stated that her "tentative interest in the role changed to ambivalence – and ambivalence sometimes verged on hostility."[5] I still attend functions that involve colleagues of Marty's who, after all these years, are now friends of mine as well. And I certainly attend the many ceremonies where he is given an award or an honour.

When Marty was made an Officer of the Order of Canada in 1990, the pomp and ceremony – and just the fun of being at the governor general's residence at Rideau Hall – was exciting. Some of our children flew in to attend the investiture in the morning and watch Governor General Ramon Hnatyshyn present the award. It was a moving ceremony, and we were all very proud. In the evening, Marty and I attended the buffet dinner, which was relaxed and somewhat informal. Some twelve years later, Marty was elevated to the rank of Companion of the Order of Canada – the highest honour that can be awarded. Again, some of our children flew in for the ceremony, and we were even more proud than on the first occasion. There was a formal dinner that evening, and, this time, the whole event was more sophisticated than the earlier one had

Marty becomes a Companion of the Order of Canada

been. The invitation had expressly said "black tie," and I made a great effort to find just the right formal outfit – and a Canadian-made one at that. Unlike that first buffet dinner, where we all sat together, the awardees were separated from their guests. Marty sat with the governor general, Adrienne Clarkson, and the only other companion being honoured that night, the Canadian singer-songwriter Joni Mitchell. I sat together with all the other guests of the honorees and enviously looked over to Marty's table from time to time.

Interestingly, I have never invited Marty to attend any of my talks. They seemed to be part of *my* life, not *our* lives. However, the COVID-19 pandemic has had an effect even there: I gave a few virtual talks from home and, of course, Marty was in attendance.

16 Last Chapter

For some years after what should have been my retirement, I've been torn between keeping on with some form of work and stopping. So far, keeping on keeps on winning. There always seems to be something new that piques my interest, and, before I know it, I am giving it my attention.

Within my department, where I still have some office space, I try to earn my keep. I have reviewed student admissions packages, a task that helps keep me aware of changes in the profile of our student body. I teach one class a year (on the early history of OT in Canada) and am a "guest" in seminars when students are learning about aging or living with a chronic illness. I prepare award nominations from time to time – a task that must be done to help further the careers of others but is time-consuming. I have reviewed tenure and promotion dossiers and I mentor other faculty and a few clinicians in an unofficial capacity. And sometimes, I meddle.

In 2008, the rehab sector (which included OT, PT, Speech, and what was then known as the Graduate Department of Rehabilitation Science) was being encouraged to consider leaving the Faculty of Medicine to establish a free-standing school or faculty of rehabilitation. I wrote a letter to the committee in charge, arguing that, when occupational therapy's identity is tied too closely to rehabilitation and the goal of promoting a return to as normal a condition as possible, it risks losing its identity. "Occupations" become more a means to an end – a way to fix broken parts – than an end in themselves, rather like Professor Bott's mechanotherapy in the First World War.[1] Occupational therapy, in contrast, focuses more on helping people with those same injuries, illnesses, and diseases to get on with their lives – helping them to find ways to do what they want to do and need to do. We don't ignore the functions that have been compromised, but we work around them, and, in the process, we teach skills, raise morale, and build self-esteem. With a move to a free-standing school or faculty of rehabilitation, I feared our discipline's unique approach to health and well-being would be subsumed within the larger construct of "rehabilitation."

Trying to keep occupational therapy true to its roots has been a crusade of mine for decades. I had argued that, given our history, "rehabilitation" was not the best home for occupational therapy. I thought our alliance with rehabilitation had been borne of pressure from the medical establishment and our own concern with "fitting in."[2] In my view, our presence in the Faculty of Medicine served as a reminder to tomorrow's doctors of the larger health care agenda, where curing or restoring patients to their former selves was not always possible. Indeed, the value of occupational therapy is expressed rather poignantly (and succinctly) in the marketing of products like T-shirts that say "The doctor may save your life, but an occupational therapist helps you live it."

While biomedicine continues to dominate health care and medical education, there is a growing awareness that it does not have all the answers. A biopsychosocial approach has been promoted for years,[3] and it may soon have more prominence in medical education, where the social sciences and humanities are being seen by medical educators as essential and are becoming more integrated.[4]

The last major task I took on for the OT department was to help plan the hundredth anniversary of the first occupational therapy class at the University of Toronto. Being a subject dear to my heart, this was a labour of love. It was to be a year-long celebration, and we wanted it to raise our profile in

MOMENT IN TIME

FEB. 21, 1918

UNIVERSITY OF TORONTO ARCHIVES

CANADA'S FIRST OCCUPATIONAL THERAPY PROGRAM

As the First World War raged, the injured needed a way to rehabilitate and return to regular society. War aides would help soldiers regain strength in body, mind and spirit by teaching them new skills and ease them into regular, daily activities. But as the war came to an end and the number of injured soldiers increased, the Military Hospitals Commission knew it needed help. The University of Toronto stepped in and began running courses to train aides on this day 100 years ago (class pictured above). It was the catalyst into developing the first occupational therapy program in Canada. The program started as a six-week course with 21 women. In a year and a half, the classes expanded to a six-month course with more than 300 women who worked across the country. The Department of Soldier's Civil Re-establishment ran these courses until just after the war, until graduates of the U of T program went on to help establish the first occupational therapy program, which was the only one of its kind until 1950. The program is still at the university today and occupational therapy education now includes 14 graduate programs in universities across Canada. SHELBY BLACKLEY

"Moment in Time," *Globe and Mail*, February 21st, 2018. Courtesy of the *Globe and Mail*

the university and beyond. We began with a breakfast reception on February 21st, 2018, to commemorate one hundred years to the day of the start of that first class, which had been designed to educate women who were working with injured soldiers returning from the First World War. Over one hundred people attended the breakfast, including several provincial and federal members of Parliament, U of T officials, alumni, faculty, and students. I was happy to help develop an exhibit that took visitors through the early years of the past century with photos and artifacts. We were thrilled to have been able to convince the *Globe and Mail* to acknowledge the anniversary in their "Moment in Time" section on that same day.

I still have a few projects on the go, and I'm not sure when I'll actually stop, but, if I do, I may finally start doing some of the things I have said I would do in retirement: take an Italian language course, visit children in hospital who don't have any family nearby, or teach literacy skills to adults. I've had this list for years and have not yet acted on any of it. I could also go back to sewing and knitting and cooking and entertaining more often. I miss doing those creative activities that were such a large part of an earlier me. Now that there are no real excuses about lack of time, I do more exercise. I've even joined a ballet class for over 55s! That class, in which I am the oldest member, takes me back to my youth as I stand at the barre and let the pianist's music carry me along.

I have been attentive to friendships all my life. During the times when I was overloaded with work or studying hard or had heavy family calls on my time, I was aware of the friendships I was letting slide and hoped I'd be forgiven. I have kept a number of old friends – people I grew up with or knew from university; others who had young children when I did. There's something special about old friendships, people who have lived in the same time periods and environments and usually had similar life experiences. We use a sort of shorthand when we speak, not having to explain the context, as we know a lot about one another, our families, even our politics. We also know what to say and what not to say. Old friends connect you with your former self, reminding you of an earlier iteration of who you are, not a better or worse you – just another you.

I have made some enduring friendships in my various work situations: people from my days working clinically as an occupational therapist, teaching at U of T, and my work with research ethics boards. Some of these people are almost a generation younger than me, older than my own children, but not by much. Yet, it seems to work. These friendships are invigorating for me, and I think supportive for them – they are reciprocal in their way.

It's probably not surprising that, as I near the end of my life, I feel the need to tidy up. When I die, I don't want my kids to have to wade through all the stuff that I know I could have taken care of. They'll have enough trouble dealing with everything that was intentionally kept.

I think about all the things I've kept that were my mother's but were of no practical use. That bottle of watered-down cologne, the costume jewellery, some now paper-thin scarves, belts that are out of style or no longer fit, a small blue cardboard box with pennies from 1949, the year of her death. There are also memorabilia from my own past – things that I don't want to part with but that I also don't want others to deal with. There's a tug between hanging on to the personal objects to which I am attached and letting go.

Old age could be a time to stop spending so much time on my appearance – or it could be a time to fuss even more. I'm envious when we are dressing to go out somewhere together and Marty casually asks, "Should I wear a tie?" That's it! No other decisions to make. I have never incorporated that easygoing attitude into concern over my appearance. Now I spend time and money adapting to my advancing age, looking for higher necklines, lower heels, and so on. I still haven't figured out why most women – myself included – focus on their appearance so much. I don't believe it's just vanity, or women trying to attract men, or compete with other women. I believe it's mainly an aesthetic issue: these colours, that shape, this look, just to please our own eye.

What I want to do with my time as I near the end is inextricably tied to what *we* – Marty and I – want to do with *our* time. While we will both keep on working away on our own projects, neither of us will hesitate to stop in order to do other activities: to visit with family, to attend concerts and plays or movies, and most certainly to travel while our health still makes it possible.

Marty introduced me to travel when we were first married. Once we established some ground rules about how much risk-taking I was prepared for, and what I thought was an acceptable accommodation, we were in it together. Travelling has been a big part of our lives, and we are determined not to end it before we must. We travelled when we were first married, and then as a family when the children were young and missing school was not an issue. Once the children had flown the coop, and we had two good incomes, we set out again on our own. When the children were grown and spending time abroad themselves, we visited them – Jenny in Spain, Nancy in France and Israel, and Tom in South Africa.

We love what the experience of travel brings: to live at a different pace, appreciate new surroundings, be on neutral territory where we are discovering and learning together. We might book some activities in advance depending on the place, but our favourite activity is just wandering around and coming upon things.

We have started to talk about how we will have to curtail our travels – where we can go and how we can go. We're more cautious – making sure that there are decent medical services, or at least that we can make a quick exit to get to them. We realized this necessity when we went to Nunavut in the summer of 2016. It was a trip I had wanted to make for some time, having been interested in the works of art coming from the area and wanting to learn more about the land and the people liv-

With an Inuit carver, Pangnirtung, 2016

A boy on an ice floe, Cumberland Sound, near Pangnirtung, 2016

ing there. I also admit to having had a hankering to see the land of the midnight sun. We flew to Iqaluit on Baffin Island, and from there to Pangnirtung, a hamlet of some 1,400 people known for its carvings, tapestries, and prints. We saw the stunning beauty of the area, looking across Cumberland Sound to the fjord and the magnificent Auyuittuq National Park. Because our plane left Iqaluit late, we had to shorten the boat trip on the fjord we'd booked for our first day. That may have been just as well because, despite a bright summer sun, the air was piercingly cold as we bumped across the waves in an aluminum boat open to the elements, wearing every piece of clothing we had packed. We learned first-hand how the weather controls all plans in fly-in communities like Pangnirtung. Bad weather added extra days and great uncertainty to our trip, as it does for everyone who flies in to do work there or who needs to get out.

We were shocked to see for ourselves the extremely high cost of food and everyday necessities in

Pangnirtung, as well as the lack of jobs and the consequent poverty. Sadly, the work of the various craftspeople was not on display, as it was being catalogued for sale to the tourists who would soon be disembarking – in droves – from a large cruise ship. A real midnight sun eluded us, but we did have continuous dusk when day was done.

Visiting Pangnirtung got us close to the Arctic Circle but not within it. Nonetheless, we can now say that we have seen Canada, *almost* from coast to coast to coast. There's just one more bit of Canadiana on my list. I have long wanted to go to Haida Gwaii, but that will likely not happen – the travel years lost to COVID-19 will not be regained at our age.

In 2018, we took what will surely be our last exotic trip abroad. We went to Cairo and took a Nile cruise, complete with a fly-in visit to Abu Simbel. There was a Canadian travel advisory for Cairo that said to "avoid non-essential travel due to the unpredictable security situation," and there was advice to exercise a high degree of caution along the Upper Nile, from Luxor to Aswan, all on our itinerary. But Egypt had been high on Marty's list for a long time, and it was now or never. I tried to put my anxiety

Marty and I in Egypt, with the pyramids at Giza in the background, 2018

aside, packing it away for the duration of the trip, rather like holding my breath. And just a week after we left, a tourist bus ran over a roadside bomb, killing three people aboard and injuring many others. The incident occurred near the Pyramids at Giza close to the hotel where we stayed.

There is a place much closer to home that makes us feel we are far away. We get that feeling when we go to our cottage in Kearney, just west of Algonquin Park. We bought it in 1983, just after I started working at the university and when our kids were still teenagers. No one minded the lack of plumbing, electricity, or telephone, all of which gradually appeared over the years. In the summer, the lake that my father would have called "delectable" invites all swimmers, canoeists, sailors, kayakers, and paddle boarders. We can hike all over our land in the day and watch the sunset from our screened-in porch after dinner. In the winter, the snow lies heavily on the branches of the evergreens and sends out brief bursts of flurries when the wind blows. Patches of

Winter at the cottage

Hockey on the frozen lake

Our garden on the hill behind
the cottage

snow cling to the trunks of birches and maples, making them look like they belong in an early Lawren Harris painting. The scene is breathtaking, especially when the sky is blue and the sun is shining, or when snow falls silently from a night sky.

We used to go to the cottage several times during the winter, mainly to cross-country ski. Now it's just for the week, from Christmas through New Year's Eve, and even that will end soon, as the cottage is isolated and a large snowfall can prevent us from getting out under our own steam. As it is, Nancy and her family stay with us from Christmas until Jenny and her family come up for New Year's, between them providing the support we need. Yet we're not quite ready to give up that winter stay.

There's often a good enough freeze-up by Christmas that our son-in-law can clear a patch on the lake near the shore for skating. Marty and I still do a little cross-country skiing along the side of the frozen lake and in the forest higher up. But there's a sense of an ending: shortness of breath, a twisted ankle, an inadvertent crash into a tree. Do we keep on going?

In the summers, gardening is a preoccupation at the cottage. Although we take pains to plant a good show on the balcony of our condo in the city, it's the cottage that provides us with our only chance to really dig in. It's an aesthetic pleasure and a stress reducer, an activity that distracts from present-day worries and projects into a positive future – one where what we have planted will at least survive and will usually bloom.

My garden with sweet peas

We have three garden areas at the cottage: one is a raised bed that slopes upwards at the back of the cottage and has been partially reclaimed from the surrounding forest. Its lower section can be worked while standing, which makes it accessible for us. The beds are filled with perennials but Marty always adds nasturtium seeds to that garden and they *always* blossom. In the front garden, along the side of the cottage, I plant sweet pea seeds each year, even though they rarely bloom well – I plant too late or I'm not there enough to water. I plant the seeds near to near the cottage wall because I envision them climbing up it as they *once* did – about twenty years ago. I captured that profusion in a photo – thank goodness – or even I would not believe it happened. We're also slowly taming a third, rock-strewn area, where grass that won't grow elsewhere grows with impunity.

The spring brings tulips and daffs and a blanket of vinca. Several areas of wild roses start to bloom in early summer. Mainly rugosas, the roses make a wonderful show and smell divine. They don't mind the cold winter temperatures and are rarely bothered by insects. They not only thrive, but, along with the wild raspberries, they try to take over.

We do the cottage garden as we have done much of our life together. Marty does the broad strokes – including almost all the planting and transplanting. I do the finer details, including the weeding, pruning, and deadheading. And I do the worrying. I fret over plants that look sickly and I notice the weeds that are encroaching. I do the emotional labour, even with the garden! It's how we manage generally, how we have unconsciously divvied up the tasks in our lives. I anticipate and often argue for change; Marty initially resists change but (almost) always agrees. I do the mundane; he does the more dramatic.

A love of plants and flowers, if not gardening, has been passed on to our children, and they each have their own distinctive collections, indoors and out. We buy cut flowers during the year: tulips, alstroemeria, or maybe gladioli, depending on the season. If I'm feeling particularly happy – or sad – I'll have flowers on the dresser in the bedroom (anemones, or maybe freesias). If sweet peas are available, which they rarely are, they will sit on my night table right beside my bed, where I can smell their perfume. They were my mother's favourite flower and have been mine for as long as I can remember.

Marty and I talk about death. Usually, it's with humour, but it's a reference, nonetheless. We see a new building under construction and ask, "Will we be here to see it finished"? Or we talk about how each of us will manage when we are left on our own: I'll mention a housekeeping nicety that Marty will have to improve if he is living on his own ("You'll need to clean the countertops with soap, not just water"), while his comments to me center on the garbage and how I have no idea how often he takes it down the hall to the incinerator. We talk about where we want to be when we can no longer manage on our own: at home with help or in supported living of some form or other. Memory lapses send us down the worrisome path of whether dementia lies ahead; not remembering words, people's names, plots of movies just seen, is concerning should it get worse. For the moment, we laugh as we help each other find a missing word or name, solve a problem with our computers, and just carry on.

Having married at such a young age, it's hard to know how much of my life is about me, and how much is about us. Although I was confronted with this question as a young wife, when my own identity seemed determined by that role, when I think of "us" now, it is in a very different way. There's no struggle. It has become a different and very comfortable us.

In many ways, we are more content now than ever before. We are more caring and patient with one another. When we do argue and get angry, we are quick to make amends, not wanting there to be hard feelings during any of the time that's left. Seeing friends and family die with increasing frequency makes us more acutely aware that our days are indeed numbered, that life is finite, that there will be an end. It's hard not to see death looming.

We have secured our burial plots. We decided some time ago to be buried in Dawes Road Cemetery and found plots near those of my parents, grandparents, and some of my aunts and uncles; Marty also has some relatives there. We rather like the idea of being in this simple cemetery – simple, in comparison to Beth Tzedec Memorial Park, which is much grander and better-landscaped. Our double plot is right next to where members of the Shopsowitz family, owners of one of the first Jewish delicatessens in Toronto, are buried. We are assured, therefore, that, if there is some form of life after death, we will not go hungry.

I remain grateful for my Jewish upbringing. It gave me a sense of belonging when that feeling was threatened by my mother's death early on. With my grandparents being such observant Jews and seemingly such good people, it's not surprising that my parents continued to follow their ways, and that I did the same, albeit in a less strict manner. Carrying on the traditions that my grandparents had established seemed right; not doing so seemed wrong. In my younger years, I was not prepared to tempt fate, or interfere with what just might be God's will. I had learned that bad things could happen in life. I was not prepared to take chances – just in case.

For the most part, Jewish observances are a sort of glue that keeps families together. Celebrating Jewish holidays is almost always a comforting time. Friday night dinners, the Jewish New Year, and Chanuka are fun. We get together, we say a (very) few prayers, and we eat. Celebrating Passover each year is also good, but not quite as straightforward – at least not for me. Given that Passover occurs each year just days after the anniversary of my mother's death (according to the Jewish/lunar calendar), my family suggests that it is this connection that makes me irritable. I acknowledge that possibility, but I argue that it's also the hard work of preparing for a Seder dinner – setting the table with special dishes reserved for this holiday, providing all the symbolic foods, and cooking for twenty or more people – that makes me tired and irritable. It's a big job, even with all the help that I get from my family. But as our dinner unfolds, and everything is under control, I relax and enjoy myself. I look around at the family and feel a special joy in our connection with one another.

When I visit Israel, I also feel a connection and a sense of belonging. I don't worry about saying something aloud that might attract attention to my being Jewish, and I'm not wary of comments from others. I am conflicted about my feelings for the country: I don't want Israel to be occupiers; I don't want Israel to deny anyone their rights; but I do want there to be a place where Jews can feel safe. I know that I feel more secure as a Canadian Jew because of Israel's existence. Despite the real dangers, I feel safe in Israel. My attachment to Israel in no way diminishes my

Passover *Seder* in the condo

being Canadian. I am enormously proud to be Canadian. I cherish the values by which we live. I am awed by the beauty of our land and the diversity of our people. There is no conflict with my feelings for both places. I am tethered to Canada and connected to Israel.

While I am less observant now than years ago, many customs remain. I light a *yahrzeit* candle and try to attend synagogue on the anniversary of each of my parents' deaths to say *kaddish*, as a child is meant to do. We've been known to go to synagogue when we're worried about something, and also when something good has happened, suggesting, perhaps, there might be some vestigial belief in a higher power. Shabbat ritual at home is sporadic when we are on our own, but it has *always* been followed when grandchildren are with us. Indeed, we may be more concerned with continuing the observances than we are with the observances themselves.

I cherish my family more with each day. There is something unique about a time when all of us are together. It fills my heart and is the best gift I can ever be given. For many years now, I have asked my children to give me that as a combination birthday and Mother's Day present. I ask for a minimum of twenty-four hours with all sixteen of us together, once a year. It used to be easy to do when the grandchildren were young, and we could just all go to the cottage. But now the older grandchildren are spread out and it's not possible. So I take what I can get, whenever and wherever I can get it: Friday night dinners, Jewish holidays, and family birthdays bring most, if not all, of us together for short visits – at least it did before the pandemic began in 2020.

It's also important for us to spend time alone with each of our grandchildren, to know them as individuals. As each one has their bar/bat mitzvah, we take them on a holiday for a few days to a nearby city of their choice. So far there have been six trips: two to Washington, two to Chicago, one to New York, and one to Halifax. These trips have given us a chance to draw closer to our young adults, sharing experiences that are just for the three of us. There are two more grandchildren trips to come as soon as COVID-19 lets us travel safely.

Lighting the sabbath candles with granddaughter Tillie

There's another ritual with the grandchildren, one that they are more ambivalent about. We take each of them to a production by the Canadian Opera Company. Each child. Just once. We choose an opera that we think is likely to appeal to a newly minted teenager – *Traviata*, *Bohème*, *Tosca*, something dramatic. It's a night out with us, and they survive. One or two have even asked to go a second time!

I try to keep in touch with all the grandchildren in some way: by phone, text, email, and in person. I find myself trying to defend or protect whichever of those children appears to be struggling in some way. It's not that that child is a favourite (as others have suggested!), rather, it's that I want them to see me as an ally. The reason for the heightened relationship is never explicitly labelled – it just is.

As much as I want to be with my grandchildren, I want to be with my children even more. I feel extremely fortunate to have had children; to have created three human beings, cared for them, taught them, worried about them, respected them, fought and laughed with them – and always loved them. My children are an integral part of me. I am proud of them, and I am proud of myself for my role in their upbringing. I was enthralled by the childrearing process. Perhaps it helped that, as an occupational therapist, I knew about child development and was fascinated to watch and encourage them as they passed through different stages. I was never bored. I was happy to play make-believe, always ready to read a story, to watch TV shows with them, to help with homework, to laugh with them. Of course, I was frustrated at times, lost my patience, became angry. But I feel privileged to have been able to have the time to make a good home for my children, my husband, and myself. We all reaped the benefits. I feel a pang in my heart at the thought of separating from my children, and although I would like to talk with them about that time, the time when my life will end, I have avoided doing so, so far.

I continue to do some "emotional labour" with my family. Aside from the health-related issues that I am often asked for an opinion on, I try to be there for whoever needs me. When my children were teenagers, it often wasn't till they were saying goodnight that they shared something that was troubling them. One had to be ready to listen then, as one does now, whenever and wherever they want to talk. Although I *try* not to meddle, I don't always succeed. I don't always wait to be asked to talk about an apparent problem. As a parent, I think you are damned if you do, and damned if you don't. I prefer to be in the former position and take the flak if and when it comes.

After all this time, I know myself fairly well. I doubt that, as a person, I am any deeper or wiser for all my years, but I'm at peace with whoever I am. I am fortunate that there has been very little real despair in my life, and what there has been was short-lived. I have been depressed from time to time, but never in a deep, existential way. Events have taken their toll, for sure, but perhaps the experience of losing my mother so early in my life inoculated me. It prepared me for what life might bring and set me on a path of resilience.

I found the years at home fulfilling. They also prepared me, unknowingly, for the next stage of my life. When I volunteered at my children's school, I developed the leadership skills that had first surfaced when I was in high school. I developed my organizational skills while I ran a household, raised children, and supported my husband's career. As a "wife of," I honed my social skills and became adept at initiating and carrying on conversations with complete strangers. I was able to continue my formal education, which gave me something for myself and more academic standing. When I returned to work in my field, I added new skills. And when I became a faculty member, I developed a whole other part of me. I became a teacher, a researcher, and an administrator. Concerns about my own place in life faded as I saw my research grow, witnessed the success of our students, and took pride in the growing importance of my profession in people's lives. Taking it all together, I have been very lucky.

I believe I have had it all.

There has been a time for everything.

Notes

Prelude

1 There is a passage in the Jewish Daily Prayer Book, *Siddur Lev Shalem*, that speaks of "creating light and fashioning darkness." I suggest that when darkness comes to us, we can fashion that darkness, and create light. Ed Feld, ed., *Siddur Lev Shalem* (New York: The Rabbinical Assembly, 2016).

2 Natalie Zemon Davis, *Women on the Margins: Three Seventeenth-Century Lives* (Cambridge, MA: Harvard University Press, 1995).

3 Mikael Nordenmark, "Multiple Roles and Well-Being: A Longitudinal Test of the Role Stress Theory and the Role Expansion Theory," *Acta Sociologica* 47, no. 2 (2004): 124. See also Monika K. Sumra and Michael A. Schillaci, "Stress and the Multiple-Role Woman: Taking a Closer Look at the Superwoman," *PLoS One* 10, no. 3 (27 March 2015), doi:10.1371/journal .pone.0120952; the authors suggest that role quality be considered.

1 Tillie

1 For some of the many accolades that Vera Peters has received, see Susan Bélanger, "Vera Peters, Quiet Revolutionary," https://medicine.utoronto .ca/magazine/article/dr-m-vera-peters, and the page on Dr Peters on the Canadian Medical Hall of Fame site, M. Vera Peters, MD, Cancer, the Early Days – Health Care Pioneers, Women in Medicine, http://www.cdnmedhall .org/inductees/verapeters. My own memories of her interactions with our family have been added to the descriptions of this important woman.

2 The play, *Radical*, by Canadian oncologist and playwright Dr Charles Hayter, shows a rather different Dr Peters than the one I knew, more assertive and even aggressive in her work life. She was a dedicated scientist whose work on Hodgkin's disease first brought her to prominence. Later, when she set out her theories regarding conservative management for early-stage breast cancer, she had to overcome opposition from

surgeons, especially in the United States. A historical account of this major contribution is found in D.H. Cowan, "Vera Peters and the Conservative Management of Early-stage Breast Cancer," *Current Oncology* 17, no. 2 (2010) 50–4. Once a nearly forgotten Canadian hero, Vera Peters is now widely celebrated. In 2020, she was honoured as one of six Canadian medical groundbreakers, with a stamp issued by Canada Post.

3 Somewhere in the family's folklore is the suggestion that my grandmother may have tried to abort this pregnancy, presumably on the grounds that she would be the sixth child born within eight years to a newly immigrated family. Fortunately for me, there was no abortion.

4 This practice followed the description found in Job 2:13, "They sat *to* the ground," symbolizing being "brought low," emotionally, by the passing of a loved one. The practice is uncommon now, and so is the edict that "No one said a word to him, because they saw how great his suffering was." The opposite is practised today: visitors to a shiva purposely talk to the mourners about the deceased person as a way to support them in their grief.

5 John Bowlby, *Loss: Attachment and Loss*, vol. 3, *Sadness and Depression* (Middlesex: Penguin Books, 1980). Bowlby's work brought attention to the effects of the death of a mother and loss of the attachment figure in the first five years of a child's life (particularly in terms of depression and helplessness). He also noted the power of early attachment to influence resilience when there are strong environmental supports. For a less scholarly exploration of the topic, see Hope Edelman's work on a daughter's loss of her mother – at any age. Edelman's *Motherless Daughters: The Legacy of Loss* (Don Mills, ON: Addison-Wesley, 1994) was a welcome gift for me and many other girls and women, reassuring us that so many of our feelings were shared.

6 While the idea that resilience influences psychological outcomes is not new, there is still little understanding of how it comes about, other than through adversity. Research by Martin Seligman suggests it can be built. Martin Seligman, "Building Resilience," *Harvard Business Review*, April 2011, https://hbr.org/2011/04/building-resilience. For attempts to teach resiliency to first-year medical students, see Shayna Kulman-Lipsey and Yezarni Wynn, "Resiliency Can Be Learned," University of Toronto, Faculty of Medicine, *Dean's Report* 3 (2016–17).

2 Mike

1 M. Bakalczuk-Felin, ed., *Memorial Book of Rokiskis* (Rokiskis, LT: Jewishgen. Inc., 2017).

2 My brother taped a series of interviews with my father just after his eightieth birthday and periodically in the years that followed. He transcribed the tapes and printed them for family members as *Mike's*

Memories: The First Fifty Years (2017). Much of the information on Mike's early life comes from these interviews.

3 Gerald Tulchinsky, *Taking Root: The Origins of the Canadian Jewish Community* (Toronto: Lester Publishing, 1992), 160–1. Tulchinsky provides a description of the lives of Jews in small Canadian towns like Brantford – in comparison to larger cities like Toronto and Montreal, where an existing social structure provided a sense of belonging and protection. See also Louis Rosenberg, "Two Centuries of Jewish Life in Canada 1760–1960," *American Jewish Year Book* 62 (1961): 28–49, https://www.jstor.org/stable/23603227. The section titled "The Second Hundred Years, 1860–1960," covers a wide range of social and political issues, including immigration, population and occupational distribution, anti-Semitism, and discrimination.

4 Students could get an automatic "pass" if they worked on a farm during the war. The Soldiers of the Soil (SOS) initiative, run by the Canadian Food Board, encouraged adolescent boys to volunteer for farm service. "In exchange for their labour, SOS recruits received room and board, spending money, and – in the case of high school students – exemption from classes and final exams." "Farming and Food," Canadian War Museum website, https://www.warmuseum.ca/firstworldwar/history/life-at-home-during -the-war/the-war-economy/farming-and-food/.

3 The Jolofsky Family

1 When we were living in Cambridge, England, in 1980, my daughters, then aged nine and thirteen, wrote to Harry and asked him about his role in the Second World War. The details provided here come from his written response and from a speech given by his nephew, Dr Ronald Landsberg, at a dinner in Harry's honour. Some of the letters Harry sent home are cited in J.L. Granatstein, *Canada's Army: Waging War and Keeping the Peace* (Toronto: University of Toronto Press, 2011).

2 Joe Jolley was appointed director of the Civic Theatre Association in 1947 and was responsible for organizing courses based on the Stanislavski method. Anton Wagner, "Infinite Variety or a Canadian 'National' Theatre: Roly Young and the Toronto Civic Theatre Association, 1945–1949," *Theatre Research in Canada* 9, no. 2 (Fall 1988), https://journals.lib.unb.ca/index .php/tric/article/view/7335/8394.

3 Telephone and in-person interviews with Hinda's daughter Mari Silverman, December 2018 and January 2019.

4 "Displaced Persons Camps," Yad Vashem, n.d., https://www.yadvashem .org/articles/general/displaced-persons-camps.html.

5 Information from Max and Gittel Glicksman and, more recently, their children Harry Glicksman and Lisa Herschorn, and derived from the

Oral Testimony Collection: Sarah and Chaim Neuberger Holocaust Education Centre, recorded in 1993, Survivor Testimony Narrative Text created in 2009; 121 Glicksman, Max with Guta Glicksman. Additional notes from an interview by Misha Herschorn (grandson), *The Life of Greta Glicksman*, n.d.

6 Emails from Charles and Stephen Erlichman, 2022; see also the biographical information on Stephen on RiV, https://www.riacanada.ca/company -profile/stephen-erlichman/, and Charles on the Mayo Clinic site, https:// www.mayo.edu/research/faculty/erlichman-charles-m-d/bio-00086565.

7 Erlichman Lane, Seaton Village Lane Naming Project, https://www .kleinosky.com/domains/svlanes/2401.php.

8 Beth Tzedec, dedicated in 1955, was designed by Peter Dickinson Architects along with Harry B. Kohl, Isadore Markus, and Page and Steele, and renovated in 2017 by Hariri Pontarini. It is the largest synagogue in Canada and considered one of the largest synagogues in the world, with over 4,000 members.

4 Childhood and Adolescence

1 Hospital receipts and instructions found among family papers.

2 Adrienne Rich, *On Lies, Secrets and Silences* (New York: Norton, 1979), 24. See also Christine Overall, *A Feminist I: Reflections from Academia* (Peterborough, ON: Broadview Press, 1998).

3 I distinctly remember the fire. The studio was then at 780 Yonge, and although there are references to other fires (!), I cannot pin down the date for this fire.

4 Geraldine Sherman, "The Girls of Summer," *Toronto Life*, September 2001.

5 Jane Gaskell and John Willinsky, *Gender In/Forms Curriculum* (New York: Teachers College Press, 1995); Becky Francis, "The Gendered Subject: Students' Subject Preferences and Discussions of Gender and Subject Ability," *Oxford Review of Education* 26, no. 1 (March 2000): 35–48.

6 For a discussion of the charitable works of Canadian Jewish women, including the work of Hadassah organizations, see Gerald Tulchinsky, *Taking Root: The Origins of the Canadian Jewish Community* (Toronto: Lester, 1992), 197–8, 201–3.

7 I realized the personal impact of my summer at Boulderwood when I was working on *Restoring the Spirit*, my book on the early history of occupational therapy in Canada, and devoted the fourth chapter to the settlement house movement. Tracing its British, American, and Canadian roots showed me how much the philosophy of occupational therapy owed to the movement. See E.S. Maurice, *Octavia Hill: Early Ideals* (London: George Allen and Unwin, 1928); Jane Addams, *Twenty Years at Hull House* (New

York: Macmillan, 1951); and Cathy James, "Reforming Reform: Toronto's Settlement House Movement 1900–1920," *Canadian Historical Review* 82, no. 1 (2001): 55–90.

5 Daughter, Stepdaughter, Sister

1 Geoffrey Reaume, *Lyndhurst: Canada's First Rehabilitation Centre for People with Spinal Cord Injuries, 1945–1998* (Montreal and Kingston: McGill-Queen's University Press, 2007). Dr Jousse was highly regarded for his pioneering role in treating people with spinal cord injuries just after the Second World War. E.R. Botterrill, "Albin T. Jousse, Medallist of the International Medical Society of Paraplegia: A Profile," *Paraplegia* 26 (1988): 369–70.
2 Barry's admission to Toronto General might have had to do with Dr Peters and her ability to refer him to specialists who were at that hospital.
3 Barry Pless, *Barry's Bits* (Columbia, SC: WordPress, 2012), and *Ann Veronica: A Memoir* (Lexington, KY: WordPress, 2019).

6 Student/Wife/Worker

1 "Defenders Rally to Refute Varsity 'Trade School' Dig," *Mail and Empire*, 30 November 1929. Teasing about crafts seemed to be fair game. Marty used to tease me about getting an "A" in my (smocked) Apron and a "B" in my (woven) Basket, as if they were academic subjects.
2 Judith Friedland, *Restoring the Spirit: The Beginnings of Occupational Therapy in Canada, 1890–1930* (Montreal and Kingston: McGill-Queen's University Press, 2011).
3 Thelma Cardwell, in her inaugural address as the first occupational therapist to be president of the Canadian Association of Occupational Therapy, commented, "we are too diffident a group, both individually and collectively," and she went on to describe the behaviours needed to remedy the situation. Thelma Cardwell, "President's Address," *Canadian Journal of Occupational Therapy* 33, no. 4 (1966): 139–40. See also J.D. Maxwell and M.P. Maxwell, "Inner Fraternity and Outer Sorority," in *The Sociology of Work in Canada*, edited by Audrey Wipper (Ottawa: Carleton University Press, 1994), 330–58, and see Ruby Heap, "Training Women for a New 'Women's Profession': Physiotherapy Education at the University of Toronto, 1917–40," *History of Education Quarterly* 35, no. 2 (Summer 1995): 135–58, for a discussion of the early entrenchment of subordination of "a female-dominated occupation, subordinated to an allied but more powerful male profession" (137).
4 See David Coburn, Susan Rappolt, and Ivy Bourgeault, "Decline vs. Retention of Medical Power through Restratification: An Examination of the Ontario Case," *Sociology of Health and Illness* 19, no. 1 (1997): 1–22;

Ivy Bourgeault and Gillian Mulvale, "Collaborative Health Care Teams in Canada and the USA: Confronting the Structural Embeddedness of Medical Dominance," *Health Sociology Review* 15, no. 5 (December 2006).

5 The Toronto Psychiatric Hospital became the Clarke Institute of Psychiatry when it moved to new quarters in 1966. The Clarke was integrated into the Centre for Addiction and Mental Health (CAMH) in 1998.

6 The church was built in 1891 to house the Zion Congregational Church. It is considered an "architectural gem" and is designated as a historical site. "Toronto's Architectural Gems: Old Church at College and Elizabeth Streets," Historic Toronto, https://tayloronhistory.com/2013/08/24 /torontos-architectural-gemsold-church-at-college-and-elizabeth-streets/.

7 In 1951, Dr Barnet Berris became the first Jewish doctor to be granted a full-time faculty position within the Department of Medicine at the University of Toronto and appointed to the staff at Toronto General Hospital: Dr Barnet Berris, Wightman-Berris Academy, https:// wbacademy.utoronto.ca/about-us/dr-barnet-berris#:~:text=In%20 1951%2C%20Dr.,position%20he%20held%20until%201977.

8 University of Toronto Archives and Records (UTARMS), President Falconer correspondence, 20 October 1931, A1967–0007_131a_24.pdf. A reply from Falconer to Dunlop's query has not been located.

9 Excerpt from a lecture given by Dr J. Lockhart Robertson in Cambridge, "The Progress of Psychological Medicine since the Days of Dr. Caius," reprinted in the *Journal of Mental Science* and cited in David H. Clark, *The Story of a Mental Hospital: Fulbourn, 1858–1983* (London: Process Press, 1996), https://wellcomecollection.org/works/beqd92et.

10 More humane ways of treating people with mental illness also took hold in Ontario, for example, and could be seen in the late 1800s at Rockwood Asylum in Kingston, the Toronto Asylum, and the London Asylum.

11 An interesting example of this issue comes from the Homewood Sanatorium in Guelph, Ontario. As a private institution, it did not have patients do unpaid labour. But relatives and physicians recognized the need for patients to have something meaningful to do. It was also important that Homewood offer activities so that it could be competitive with private American institutions. In 1912, Dr Hobbs, Homewood's medical superintendent, hired Jessie Scott to establish their first craft room. Judith Friedland, *Restoring the Spirit: The Beginnings of Occupational Therapy in Canada, 1890–1930* (Montreal and Kingston: McGill-Queen's University Press, 2011), 79–82.

12 Maxwell Jones, "The Concept of a Therapeutic Community," *American Journal of Psychiatry* 112, no. 8 (1956): 647–50.

13 The car was, however, perfect for James Bond (007), who drove one in the movie *Dr No*, which came out in 1962.

14 Epidaurus had never shown opera prior to this performance. *Norma* had never been performed in Greece, and Callas had rarely performed in that country. She was at the height of her career, and the performance was highly anticipated. The opera was scheduled for three nights, but the first night was cancelled due to rain and could not be rescheduled. See Georgia Kondyli, "Callas: The Conflict about Epidaurus," *Hellenic Journal of Music, Education, and Culture* 3 (2012), www.hejmec.eu.

15 Arthur Jones and M.E. Miller, "Day Centre in Toronto for Psychiatric Patients," *Canadian Medical Association Journal* 83 (October 1960): 847.

16 Judith Friedland and Marge Murphy, "A Group Approach in Psychiatric Occupational Therapy," *Canadian Journal of Occupational Therapy* 32, no. 3 (1965): 109–17.

7 New Roles

1 It was not unusual for the wife of an academic to help her husband in such a concrete manner. See Alison Prentice, "Boosting Husbands and Building Community: The Work of Twentieth Century Faculty Wives," in *Historical Identities: The Professoriate in Canada*, edited by P. Stortz and E. Lisa Panayotidis (Toronto: University of Toronto Press, 2006), 274. See also Donica Belisle and Kiera Mitchell, "Mary Quayle Innis: Faculty Wives' Contributions and the Making of Academic Celebrity," *Canadian Historical Review* 99, no. 3 (Fall 2018): 456–86. My contributions certainly pale by comparison to those of Quayle Innis.

2 For a description of Mud Creek, see the Lost Rivers website, at http:// www.lostrivers.ca/content/DavisvilleR.html.

3 Sonia F. Epstein and Eva K. Rosenfeld, "Harvard Wives Tales," *Harvard Crimson*, 15 October 2018, https://www.thecrimson.com /article/2018/10/15/harvard-wives/; M. Armstrong, "Faculty Wives: Diverse Careers Co-exist with Teas, Children" *Harvard Crimson*, 13 November 1959, https://www.thecrimson.com/article/1959/11/13 /faculty-wives-diverse-careers-co-/.

4 The marriage took place on March 4th, 1971. We were living in Toronto, and I was still in bed on the morning of March 5th when Marty came upstairs with the *Globe and Mail* to show me the headline. The whole country was stunned by the news. Some thirty-seven years later, I had an occasion to meet Margaret Trudeau. She was invited to be our department's Thelma Cardwell lecturer to talk about her own experience of mental illness. I sat with her while she was waiting to speak and told her that I had been her "neighbour" in Ottawa when she was a newlywed. I was struck by how beautiful she still was – and I told her so.

5 Jane Errington, *Wives and Mothers, School Mistresses and Scullery Maids: Working Women in Upper Canada, 1790–1840* (Montreal and Kingston: McGill-Queen's University Press, 1995).

8 Multitasker

1 Donica Belisle and Kiera Mitchell, "Mary Quayle Innis: Faculty Wives' Contributions and the Making of Academic Celebrity," *Canadian Historical Review* 99, no. 3 (Fall 2018): 456–86; Alison Prentice, "Boosting Husbands and Building Community: The Work of Twentieth Century Faculty Wives," in *Historical Identities: The Professoriate in Canada*, edited by P. Stortz and E. Lisa Panayotidis (Toronto: University of Toronto Press, 2006).
2 On this issue, see Sarah Kaplan, "The Motherhood Penalty," *University of Toronto Magazine*, Autumn 2018. The issue of caring is approached differently by Gemma Hartley in *Fed Up: Emotional Labor, Women, and the Way Forward* (New York: HarperCollins, 2018). Hartley argues that men and women should embrace emotional labour as a valuable set of skills that everyone should develop.

9 Variations on a Theme

1 The street is one of twelve avenues leading to the Arc de Triomphe. It is named for the Battle of Friedland in which the French, under Napoleon Bonaparte, defeated the Russians.
2 Wm Robert Johnston, "Chronology of Terrorist Attacks in Israel, Part III: 1978–1985," http://www.johnstonsarchive.net/terrorism/terrisrael-3.html, updated 4 December 2017.
3 Leon Uris, *Exodus* (New York: Bantam Books, 1959), 494.
4 The Education Amendment Act, 1980, SO, c. 61, s. 63, https://digitalcommons.osgoode.yorku.ca/ontario_statutes/vol1980/iss1/63
5 Sandra (DF) Witelson, "Sex and the Single Hemisphere," *Science* 193, no. 4251 (July 1976): 425–7.

10 Academia

1 Jean O'Grady and Goldwin French, "Northrop Frye's Writings on Education," in *Collected Works of Northrop Frye*, vol. 7 (Toronto: University of Toronto Press, 2000), doi: 10.3138/9781442677913. See also Danielle Klein and Ethan Chiel, "Forty Years On," *Varsity*, https://thevarsity .ca/2013/03/17/forty-years-on/, for a brief history of women's efforts to be allowed into Hart House. John Boyko describes the visit by Senator John F. Kennedy in 1957 to take part in a debate with students, including

Stephen Lewis, and the (foiled) attempt by women to attend. Making matters worse, when Kennedy was met by demonstrators as he departed the building, he is quoted as saying, "I personally rather approve of keeping women out of these places . . . It's a pleasure to be in a country where women cannot mix everywhere," John Boyko, "The Day JFK Visited Toronto," 1 February 2016, https://johnboyko.com/2016/02/01/the-day -jfk-visited-toronto/.

2 Office of the Vice-Provost, Faculty and Academic Life, *Faculty Gender Equity Report 2015–16 and 2016–17* (September 2018), http://www.faculty .utoronto.ca/wp-content/uploads/2018/10/Faculty-Gender-Equity -Report-2015-16-and-2016-17.pdf.

3 Salary equity is a never-ending game of catch-up, as seen in the 2019 attempt at correcting the imbalance at U of T with an increase of 1.3 per cent to the salaries of tenure stream and tenured female faculty. See the provost's response to findings of the Advisory Group on Faculty Gender Pay Equity at the University of Toronto, 15 April 2019, https://www .provost.utoronto.ca/wp-content/uploads/sites/155/2019/04/Final -April-16-GPE-Admin-Response_AODA-Secure.pdf.

4 There continues to be a sense that it is not seemly for a woman to negotiate her salary. Linda Babcock, Sara Laschever, Michele Gelfand, and Deborah Small, "Nice Girls Don't Ask," *Harvard Business Review*, October 2003, https://hbr.org/2003/10/nice-girls-dont-ask. See also Hannah Riley Bowles, Linda Babcock, and Lei Lai, "Social Incentives for Gender Differences in the Propensity to Initiate Negotiations: Sometimes It Does Hurt to Ask," *Science Direct* 103, no. 1 (May 2007): 84–103, and Hanna Riley Bowles, "Why Women Don't Negotiate Their Job Offers" *Harvard Business Review*, 19 June 2014, https://hbr.org/2014/06/why-women-dont -negotiate-their-job-offers.

5 James Maxwell and Mary Maxwell, "Inner Fraternity and Outer Sorority," in *The Sociology of Work in Canada*, edited by Audrey Whipper (Ottawa: Carleton University Press, 1994), 330–58. See also Ruby Heap, "Training Women for a New 'Women's Profession': Physiotherapy Education at the University of Toronto, 1917–40," *History of Education Quarterly* 35, no. 2 (Summer 1995): 135–58, for an analysis of a similar situation in physiotherapy.

6 Judith Friedland, *Restoring the Spirit: The Beginnings of Occupational Therapy in Canada, 1890–1930* (Montreal and Kingston: McGill-Queen's University Press, 2011), 190. The paternalistic relationship continued, as did the ambivalence felt by occupational therapists both in academic and hospital settings.

7 On the ongoing discourse regarding the purpose of occupational therapy, see Barb Hooper and Wendy Wood, "Pragmatism and Structuralism in Occupational Therapy: The Long Conversation," *American Journal of Occupational Therapy* 56, no. 1 (2002): 40–50.

8 Mary Law, Barbara Cooper, Susan Strong, Debra Stewart, Patricia Rigby, and Lori Letts, "The Person-Environment-Occupation Model: A Transactive Approach to Occupational Performance," *Canadian Journal of Occupational Therapy* 63, no. 1 (2018): 9–23.

9 Mihaly Csikszentmihalyi, *Flow: The Psychology of Optimal Performance* (New York: Harper Collins, 1990), 71–93.

10 E.A. Bott, a psychologist, had run a course for masseuses (soon to be called physiotherapists) at Hart House during the First World War. Because he often used mechanical devices to help a soldier strengthen muscles while doing an activity, his mechanotherapy was often confused with occupational therapy. Bott championed this use of activities, saying, "the co-ordination of a partially paralysed arm, for instance, improves more rapidly by driving a nail, catching a ball . . . than simply having the lame joints flexed." See E.A. Bott, "Mechanotherapy," *American Journal of Orthopedic Surgery* 16, no. 7 (1918): 441–6. A confrontation occurred between Professor Haultain, who had developed the course in OT, and Dr Primrose, then dean of the Faculty of Medicine, when the latter suggested that it was Bott who had started the program in occupational therapy. See Friedland, *Restoring the Spirit*, 116–18.

11 Edward Jarvis, "Mechanical and Other Employments for Patients in the British Lunatic Asylums," *American Journal of Insanity* 19, no. 2 (1862): 129–45.

12 N. Ach, "On Volition," translated by T. Herz (1910), University of Konstanz, Cognitive Psychology website, https://www.cogpsych.uni -konstanz.de/pdf/Ach_1910_2006_OnVolition_book.pdf.

13 Hans Selye, "The Stress Concept," *Canadian Medical Association Journal* 115, no. 8 (1976): 718.

14 Aaron T. Beck, "Cognitive Therapy: Nature and Relation to Behavior Therapy," *Behavior Therapy* 1, no. 2 (1970): 184–200.

15 Friedland, *Restoring the Spirit*, 85–97. See also Judith Friedland, "Diversional Activity: Does It Deserve Its Bad Name?" *American Journal of Occupational Therapy* 42, no. 9 (1988): 603–8.

16 William Morris, "The Lesser Arts," in *William Morris on Art and Socialism*, edited by N. Kelvin (Mineola, NY: Dover Publications, 1999), 1–8.

17 Arts-based learning has become more prominent in the education of health care providers. See, for example, the Health, Arts and Humanities program at the University of Toronto. One occupational therapist who has never given up championing the wide-ranging benefits of art is Isabel Frysberg. See the Arts-Based Well-Being site, at https://www.artsbasedwellbeing .com, for her resources to support a program of arts-based well-being through an occupational therapy lens.

18 Although the imposter syndrome seems to apply to both genders, studies suggest that it plagues women. See Theresa Simpkin, "The Imposter

Phenomenon – and the Toll It Takes on Women in the Workplace,"
Independent, 23 November 2017, https://www.independent.co.uk/news
/business/analysis-and-features/the-impostor-phenomenon-and-the
-toll-it-takes-on-working-women-a8069826.html. Even faculty women at
Cambridge University suffer from the syndrome and fear being exposed
as not being good enough. See Jo Bostock, *The Meaning of Success: Insights
from Women at Cambridge* (Cambridge: Cambridge University Press, 2014).

19 The Lalonde Report of 1974 brought the ideas of health promotion to the
fore and begat a series of reports and commissions that led to a broadening
of the concept of *health* and solutions beyond the reach of medicine to
issues of social and economic disparities. Marc Lalonde, *A New Perspective
on the Health of Canadians* (Ottawa: Minister of Supply and Services,
1974). This perspective on health continues to evolve. Theodore Marmor,
Morris L. Barer, and Robert Evans, eds., *Why Are Some People Healthy
and Others Not?* (New York: Grutyer, 1994), and Michael Marmot and
Richard Wilkinson, eds., *The Social Determinants of Health* (Oxford: Oxford
University Press, 2005).

20 Steven Petranik, "Canada's Political Leaders Were Stunned by
the Suicide of ...," 19 October 1982, UPI, https://www.upi.com
/Archives/1982/10/19/Canadas-political-leaders-were-stunned
-by-the-suicide-of/3036403848000/.

21 After I graduated, John Kershner and I prepared a paper based on my
thesis. We tossed a coin to determine who would be first author and I won.
Judith Friedland and John Kershner, "Sex-linked Left-lateralized Central
Processor for Hierarchically-Structured Material? Evidence from Broca's
Aphasia," *Neuropsychologia* 24, no. 3 (1986): 411–15.

22 Sidney Cobb, "Social Support as a Moderator of Life Stress," *Psychosomatic
Medicine* 38, no. 5 (1976): 300–14.

23 T.H. Holmes and R.H. Rahe, "The Social Readjustment Rating Scale,"
Journal of Psychosomatic Research 11, no. 2 (1967): 213–18.

24 J. Friedland and M. McColl, "Social Support and Psychosocial Dysfunction
Following Stroke: Buffering Effects in a Community Sample," *Archives of
Physical Medicine and Rehabilitation* 68, no. 8 (August 1987): 475–80.

25 Benjamin Gottlieb, "Social Networks and Social Support: An Overview of
Research, Practice, and Policy Implications," *Health Education Quarterly* 12,
no. 1 (1985): 5–22.

26 J. Friedland and M. McColl, "Social Support Intervention after Stroke:
Results of a Randomized Trial," *Archives of Physical Medicine and
Rehabilitation* 73 (1992): 573–81. The intervention is described in detail
in J. Friedland and M. McColl, "Social Support for Stroke Survivors:
Development and Evaluation of an Intervention Program," *Physical and
Occupational Therapy in Geriatrics* 7 (1989): 55–69.

27 J. Friedland, R. Renwick, and M. McColl, "Coping and Social Support as Determinants of Quality of Life in HIV/AIDS," *AIDS Care* 8, no. 1 (1996): 15–32.

28 R. Renwick, T. Halpen, D. Rudman, and J. Friedland, "Description and Validation of a Measure of Received Support Specific to HIV," *Psychological Reports* 84 (1999): 663–73.

29 Doing graduate work in a cognate discipline such as education was common for occupational therapists, as there were still no programs for advanced degrees in our discipline anywhere in Canada. This situation was not an issue for me, as I welcomed the idea of learning in a different environment and gaining the perspective of a related discipline.

11 Difficult Times

1 Our experience was in 1986. See P. Robert Udall, "Bill 94 Threatens Quality of Ontario Medicine," *CMAJ* 134 (15 February 1986). Extra billing remains contentious in Canada. Over thirty years later, the issue was in the news in British Columbia: "Verdict in Cambie Surgery Centre Case: Public Health Care Wins!" Health Sciences Association, 10 September 2020, https://www.hsabc.org/news/verdict-cambie-surgery-centre-case-public-health-care-wins.

2 Jason Brown, Barbara J. Leader, and Cynthia S. Blum, "Hemiplegic Writing in Severe Aphasia," *Brain and Language* 19, no. 2 (1983): 204–15.

3 Anne Innis Dagg, *Smitten by Giraffe* (Montreal and Kingston: McGill-Queen's University Press, 2016), 41. Dagg is also the subject of the 2018 documentary *The Woman Who Loves Giraffes*, directed by Alison Reid, https://thewomanwholovesgiraffes.com/.

4 Judith Friedland, "Accessing Language in Agraphia: An Examination of Hemiplegic Writing," *Aphasiology* 4, no. 3 (1990): 241–57; Anton Leischner, "Reply to Friedland," *Aphasiology* 4, no. 3 (1990): 259–60.

5 Anton Leischner, "The Graphic Disconnection Syndrome" *European Archives of Psychiatry and Neurological Sciences* 234, no. 2 (1984): 125–36, doi: 10.1007/BF00381219.

12 Big Fish, Little Pond

1 On women and competition, see Sun Young Lee, Selin Kesebir, and Madan M. Pillutla, "Gender Differences in Response to Competition with Same-Gender Coworkers: A Relational Perspective," *Journal of Personality and Social Psychology* 110, no. 6 (2016): 869–86.

2 This observation is borne out by Cassandra Guarino and Victor M.H. Borden, "Faculty Service Loads and Gender: Are Women Taking Care of

the Academic Family?" *Research in Higher Education* 58, no. 6 (2017): 672.
Karen Pike sees this issue as a systemic problem requiring a cultural shift
that values service – a promising solution that will be hard to attain. Karen
Pyke, "Service and Gender Inequity among Faculty," *PS: Political Science
and Politics* 44, no. 1 (14 January 2011): 85–7.

3 On the challenges of negotiating, see Linda Babcock, Sara Laschever,
Michele Gelfand, and Deborah Small, "Nice Girls Don't Ask," *Harvard
Business Review*, October 2003, https://hbr.org/2003/10/nice-girls-dont
-ask, and Hannah Riley Bowles, "Why Women Don't Negotiate Their Job
Offers," *Harvard Business Review*, 19 June 2014, https://hbr.org/2014/06
/why-women-dont-negotiate-their-job-offers.

4 Dorothy E. Smith, *A Future for Women at the University of Toronto: The
Report of the Ad Hoc Committee on the Status of Women* (Toronto: Centre for
Women's Studies in Education, 1985).

5 "Equality in Employment: A Royal Commission Report – General
Summary" *Canadian Woman Studies / Les cahiers de la femme* 6, no. 4 (1984–5),
https://www.crrf-fcrr.ca/images/stories/Equality_in_Employment
.pdf. Justice Rosalie Silberman Abella, the commissioner, stated, "Most
provincial laws are limited to equal pay for equal work and are therefore
applicable only to men and women in the same or similar jobs in the same
firm."

6 Pay Equity Act, RSO 1990, c. P7, s. 4.

7 Canadian Association of University Teachers, *Underrepresented and
Underpaid: Diversity and Equity among Canada's Post-Secondary Education
Teachers* (April 2018), https://www.caut.ca/sites/default/files
/caut_equity_report_2018-04final.pdf

8 "U of T to Implement Salary Increase for More than 800 Women Faculty
Members," U of T News, 26 April 2019, https://www.utoronto.ca/news
/u-t-implement-salary-increase-more-800-women-faculty-members.

9 Melissa Moyser, "Women in Canada: A Gender-Based Statistical Report"
(2017) Statistics Canada, https://www150.statcan.gc.ca/n1/en
/catalogue/89-503-X.

10 UTARMS, Ursula Franklin Fonds, subseries 5, 2001. https://
discoverarchives.library.utoronto.ca/index.php/lawsuit.

11 The Sunshine List requires organizations that receive public funding from
the province to make public annually the names, positions, salaries, and
total taxable benefits of employees paid $100,000 or more in a calendar
year.

12 Acknowledging that women work in a different way, with different
activities, could be a start on righting this wrong. The idea that universities
over-demand and under-reward women's teaching and service is explored
by Ann Brower and Alex James, "Research Performance and Age Explain

Less than Half of the Gender Pay Gap in New Zealand Universities,"
PLoS One 15, no. 1 (January 2020). https://doi.org/10.1371/journal
.pone.0226392. See also Shelley M. Stark, "Research, Teaching and Service:
Why Shouldn't Women's Work Count?" *Journal of Higher Education* 67,
no. 1 (January–February 1996): 46–84.
13 Valuing of service activities needs to be translated into tangible
recognition. See Guarino and Borden, "Faculty Service Loads," 690; see
also Pyke, "Service and Gender Inequity."
14 Association of Schools Advancing Health Professions, http://www.asahp
.org/
15 An exception to this exercise of control over occupational therapy occurred
at the University of Illinois. This fact was brought home to me in a letter
to the editor by Nedra Gillette in the *American Journal of Occupational
Therapy*, following publication of my article "Occupational Therapy and
Rehabilitation: An Awkward Alliance," *American Journal of Occupational
Therapy* 52, no. 5 (1998): 373–80. See "Early OT Education at the University
of Illinois Not under Authority of PM&R," *American Journal of Occupational
Therapy* 52, no. 10 (1998): 930. See also Fred G. Donini-Lenhoff, "Coming
Together, Moving Apart: A History of the Term Allied Health in Education,
Accreditation, and Practice," *Journal of Allied Health* 37, no. 1 (2008):
45–52, and Glenn Gritzer and Arnold Arluke, "The Redivision of Labor,
1950–1980," in *The Making of Rehabilitation: A Political Economy of Medical
Specialization, 1890–1980* (Berkeley and Los Angeles: University of
California Press, 1985).
16 J.A. MacFarlane, "Occupational Therapy and Physiotherapy Combine at
the University of Toronto," *Canadian Journal of Occupational Therapy* 17, no.
3 (September 1950): 98–9.
17 Helen LeVesconte, "An Experiment in Pre-Industrial Work for Chronic
Women Patients," *Occupational Therapy and Rehabilitation* 13, no. 5
(1934): 323
18 Ruby Heap, "Training Women for a New 'Women's Profession':
Physiotherapy Education at the University of Toronto, 1917–40," *History
of Education Quarterly*, 35, no. 2 (Summer 1995): 137. Heap describes
the dilemma of being helped and hindered by male physicians. While
their patronage was needed to create a university-based course, it also
contributed to sex-segregation in the health sector, which would continue
for years to come.
19 See, for example, David Coburn, Susan Rappolt, and Ivy Bourgeault,
"Decline vs Retention of Medical Power through Restratification: An
Examination of the Ontario Case," *Sociology of Health and Illness* 19,
no. 1 (1997): 1–22; Ivy Bourgeault and Gillian Mulvale, "Collaborative
Health Care Teams in Canada and the USA: Confronting the Structural
Embeddedness of Medical Dominance," *Health Sociology Review* 15, no.

5 (December 2006): 481–95. Medical dominance went so far as to include accreditation of the U of T program in occupational therapy by the American Medical Association in 1935.

20 Rosalie Boyce, "Emerging from the Shadow of Medicine: Allied Health as a 'Profession Community' Subculture," *Health Sociology Review* 15, no. 5 (2006): 520–34. While self-management is an interesting idea, it does not address the issues of power and subservience.

21 See Elise Paradis and Cynthia Whitehead, "Louder Than Words: Power and Conflict in Interprofessional Education Articles, 1954–2013," *Medical Education* 49, no. 4 (20 March 2015), doi/10.1111/medu.12668, and Tavis Apramian, Emily Reynen, and Noam Berlin, "Interprofessional Education in Canadian Medical Schools," *Canadian Federation of Medical Students* (rev. ed., 2015), https://www.cfms.org/files/position-papers/2015%20CFMS%20Interprofessional%20Education.pdf.

22 Judith Friedland, "Being Our Own Sponsors," *Canadian Journal of Occupational Therapy* 80, no. 5 (2013): 269–72; Ruby Heap, "Training Women for a New 'Women's Profession': Physiotherapy Education at the University of Toronto, 1917–40," *History of Education Quarterly* 35, no. 2 (Summer 1995): 135–58.

23 Friedland, "Being Our Own Sponsors."

24 Machteld Huber et al., "How Should We Define Health?" *BMJ* 343 (2011): 1, doi: 10.1136/bmj. d4163. See also Adolph Meyer, "The Philosophy of Occupation Therapy," *Archives of Occupational Therapy* 1 (1922): 1–10, and G.L. Engel, "The Need for a New Medical Model: A Challenge for Biomedicine," *Science* 196 (1977): 129–36. While some of the work done by occupational therapists can be considered to lie within social services, the issue here is to broaden the medical model and not only accept, but embrace, the concept that social interventions are also good medicine.

25 Ayelet Kuper et al., "Well-Rounded Professionals," *Medical Education* 51 (2017): 158–73, online appendix, p. 13.

26 Bonnie Kirsh et al., "Experiences of University Students Who Are Living with Mental Health Problems: Interrelations between the Self, the Social, and the School," *Work: A Journal of Prevention, Assessment, and Rehabilitation* 53, no. 2 (2016): 325–35, doi: 10.3233/WOR-152153.

27 On the value of supportive, interpersonal relationships between teachers and students, see Christine Overall, *A Feminist I: Reflections from Academia* (Peterborough, ON: Broadview Press, 1998). Overall cites Mary Rose O'Reilly's philosophy that good teaching involves reweaving the spirit: see *The Peaceable Classroom* (Portsmouth, NH: Boynton/Cook Publishers, 1993), 46–7.

28 Universities Canada, Professional Programs Accreditation, https://www.univcan.ca/universities/quality-assurance/professional-programs-accreditation/.

29 Judith Friedland and Deirdre Dawson, "Function after Motor Vehicle Accidents: A Prospective Study of Mild Head Injury and Post Traumatic Stress," *Journal of Nervous and Mental Disease* 189 (2001): 426–34.

30 Carla Ruffolo, Judith Friedland, Deirdre Dawson, Angela Colantonio, and Peter Lindsay, "Mild Traumatic Brain Injury from Motor Vehicle Accidents: Factors Associated with Return to Work," *Archives of Physical Medicine and Rehabilitation* 80, no. 4 (1999): 392–8.

31 For whatever reason, female faculty apparently have more trouble saying "no" when asked to take on more service work. See Guarino and Borden, "Faculty Service Loads," 676, 690.

13 Little Fish, Big Pond

1 "Men overwhelmingly dominate the ranks of full and associate professors in Canada, and therefore have the highest-paid jobs in the country's professoriate – a fact that hasn't changed in more than four decades": Natalie Samson and Anqui Shen, "University Affairs: A History of Canada's Full-Time Faculty in Six Charts," *University Affairs*, 20 March 2018. In 2016, the number of full professors in Canada was 16,239, 72 per cent of whom were male. See also Andy Tagaki, "Data Reveals Extreme Gender Imbalances among Faculty," *Varsity*, 25 November 2018, for the administration's response to the data. One promising avenue for change comes from the idea that, while rates of participation for women in opt-in competitive environments (e.g., applying for promotion) are low, when participation includes everyone unless they opt out, women are more likely to remain involved. See Joyce C. He, Sonia Kang, and Nicola Lacetera, "Opt-Out Choice Framing Attenuates Gender Differences in the Decision to Compete in the Laboratory and in the Field," *Proceedings of the National Academy of Sciences* 118, no. 42 (October 2021), e2108337118, https://pubmed.ncbi.nlm.nih.gov/34635595/.

2 This idea is mentioned by Dagg, who recalls being told by the dean of science at the University of Waterloo that, among other reasons for not hiring women, was the rationale that "we all had husbands, mostly professors, so obviously we did not need the money." Anne Innis Dagg, *Smitten by Giraffe* (Montreal and Kingston: McGill-Queen's University Press, 2016), 42.

3 Hannah Rile Bowles, "Why Women Don't Negotiate Their Job Offers," *Harvard Business Review*, 19 June 2014), https://hbr.org/2014/06/why-women-dont-negotiate-their-job-offers.

4 In a podcast recorded by the *Harvard Business Review*, entitled "Women at Work: Make Yourself Heard" (30 January 2018), Deborah Tannen noted that the situation hasn't changed much since her landmark work "The

Power of Talk: Who Gets Heard and Why," *Harvard Business Review* 73, no. 5 (September–October 1995): 138–48.

5 Sheryl Sandburg and Adam Grant. "Speaking While Female," *New York Times*, 12 January 2015, https://www.nytimes.com/2015/01/11/opinion/sunday/speaking-while-female.html.

6 Tomas Dvorak and Shayna Toubman, "Are Women More Generous than Men? Evidence from Alumni Donations," *Eastern Economic Journal* 39, no. 1 (October 2013): 121–31.

7 Penny Salvatori, "Implementing a Problem-Based Learning Curriculum in Occupational Therapy: A Conceptual Model," *Australian Occupational Therapy Journal* 47, no. 3 (2000): 119–33.

8 Judith Friedland, Helene Polatajko, and Marie Gage, "Expanding the Boundaries of Occupational Therapy Practice through Student Fieldwork Experiences: Description of a Provincially-Funded Community Development Project," *Canadian Journal of Occupational Therapy* 68, no. 5 (2001): 301–9.

14 Post-Chair and Retirement

1 See Deborah L. Rudman, Judith Friedland, Mary Chipman, and Paola Sciortino, "Holding On and Letting Go: The Perspectives of Pre-Seniors and Seniors on Driving Self-Regulation in Later Life," *Canadian Journal on Aging* 25, no. 1 (2006): 65–76; Judith Friedland, Deborah L. Rudman, Mary Chipman, and Amy Steen, "Reluctant Regulators: Family Physicians' Perspectives on Monitoring Their Patients' Driving," *Topics in Geriatric Rehabilitation* 22, no. 1 (2006): 53–60; Judith Friedland and Deborah L. Rudman, "From Confrontation to Collaboration: Making a Place for Dialogue on Seniors' Driving," *Topics in Geriatric Rehabilitation* 12, no. 1 (2009): 12–23.

2 University of Toronto, *Facts and Figures, 2006* shows that just over 25 per cent of those at the rank of full professor were female. It is likely that, in the Faculty of Medicine at that time, the percentage would have been even lower. https://www.utoronto.ca/sites/default/files/Facts_Figures_20061283.pdf (link has expired).

3 Judith Friedland, "Diversional Activity: Does It Deserve Its Bad Name?" *American Journal of Occupational Therapy* 42, no. 9 (1988): 603–8.

4 Judith Friedland, "Occupational Therapy and Rehabilitation: An Awkward Alliance," *American Journal of Occupational Therapy* 52, no. 5 (1998): 373–80.

5 Judith Friedland, "Occupational Therapy," in *TPH: History and Memories of the Toronto Psychiatric Hospital, 1925–1966*, edited by Edward Shorter (Toronto: Wall and Emerson, 1996), 259–70.

6 Judith Friedland, Isobel Robinson, and Thelma Cardwell, "In the Beginning: CAOT from 1926–1939," *Occupational Therapy Now*, January/February (2001): 15–18.

7 Judith Friedland, "Why Crafts? Influences on the Development of Occupational Therapy in Canada, 1890–1930," *Canadian Journal of Occupational Therapy* 70, no. 4 (2003): 204–13.

8 Sandra Donnelly, Whitney Berta, Joyce Nyhof-Young, and Judith Friedland, "Career Development Survey for Faculty of Medicine, University of Toronto" (2005), http://www.facmed.utoronto.ca/userfiles /page_attachments/Library/13/GIC_Report_APR_FINAL_2005_2396591. pdf. Many of these same issues remain today: see Sarah Kaplan, "The Motherhood Penalty," *University of Toronto Magazine*, Autumn 2018, 65–7.

9 Mary Ann Mason, "In the Ivory Tower, Men Only," *Slate*, 17 June 2013, https://slate.com/human-interest/2013/06/female-academics-pay- a-heavy-baby-penalty.html. Mason makes clear how helpful women have been in their husbands' careers, while the reverse is not the same, especially for women in academia. Nicholas Wolfinger describes how so many female scientists change course when they encounter the difficulties of having children while trying to make tenure. "For Female Scientists, There's No Good Time to Have Children," *Atlantic*, 29 July 2013.

10 Ontario Agency for Health Protection and Promotion, A Framework for the Ethical Conduct of Public Health Initiatives (Toronto: Queen's Printer, 2021), https://www.publichealthontario.ca/-/media/documents /framework-ethical-conduct.pdf?la=en.

11 Elizabeth Peter and Judith Friedland, "Recognizing Risk and Vulnerability in Research Ethics: Imagining the 'What Ifs?'" *Journal of Empirical Research on Human Research Ethics* 12, no. 2 (2017): 107–16, doi: 10.1177/1556264617696920; Judith Friedland and Elizabeth Peter, "Recognizing the Role of Research Assistants in the Protection of Participants in Vulnerable Circumstances," *Journal of Empirical Research on Human Research Ethics*, 30 August 2019, 1–10, doi/10.1177/1556264619872366.

12 Oral History, Isobel Robinson, UTARMS, deposited 2006.

13 Judith Friedland and Hadassah Rais, "Helen Primrose LeVesconte: Clinician, Educator, Visionary," *Canadian Journal of Occupational Therapy* 72, no. 3 (2005): 131–41.

14 Brenda Head and Judith Friedland, "Jessie Luther," *Occupational Therapy Now* 8 (2006): 10.

15 Ronald Rompkey, ed., *Jessie Luther at the Grenfell Mission* (Montreal and Kingston: McGill-Queen's University Press, 2001).

16 Judith Friedland, *Restoring the Spirit: The Beginnings of Occupational Therapy in Canada, 1890–1930* (Montreal and Kingston: McGill-Queen's University Press, 2011), 95–6.

17 Judith Friedland and Naomi Davids-Brumer, "From Education to Occupation: The Story of Thomas Bessell Kidner," *Canadian Journal of Occupational Therapy* 74, no. 9 (2007): 37–47; Judith Friedland and Jennifer Silva, "Evolving Identities: TB Kidner and Occupational Therapy in the US," *American Journal of Occupational Therapy*, 62, no. 3 (2008): 349–60; Judith Friedland, "Thomas Bessell Kidner and the Development of Occupational Therapy in the United Kingdom: Establishing the Links," *British Journal of Occupational Therapy* 70, no. 2 (2007): 292–300.

18 Elizabeth Townsend and Judith Friedland, "Nineteenth and 20th Century Educational Reforms Arising in Europe, the United Kingdom and the Americas: Inspiration for Occupational Science?" *Journal of Occupational Science* 23, no. 4, on-line version, September 2016, doi: 10.1080/14427591.2016.1232184.

19 Indeed, I had a similar problem when it came time to publish this book. Fortunately, I got over my concern.

20 His memoir was entitled *My Life in Crime and Other Academic Pursuits* (Toronto: University of Toronto Press, 2008).

15 Darkness into Light

1 Judith Friedland, *Restoring the Spirit: The Beginnings of Occupational Therapy in Canada, 1890–1930* (Montreal and Kingston: McGill-Queen's University Press, 2011), 80.

2 Beatrice Wright, *Physical Disability: A Psychological Approach* (New York: Harper and Row, 1960), 258; see also Harold Kushner, *When Bad Things Happen to Good People* (New York: Schocken Books, 1981).

3 Taking Toronto's Healthcare History (2012), The Public's Health (2015), and "(IM)MATERIAL CULTURE: Health History Collections in a Digital Era" (2017). For details on these conferences, see "U of T's Health History Partnership," http://health-humanities.com/u-of-ts-health-history -partnership/.

4 Norman Gwyn, "A Short History of the Toronto Medical Historical Club," *Canadian Medical Association Journal* 52, no. 2 (1947): 218–20.

5 Alison Prentice, "Boosting Husbands and Building Community: The Work of Twentieth Century Faculty Wives," in *Historical Identities: The Professoriate in Canada*, edited by P. Stortz and E. Lisa Panayotidis (Toronto: University of Toronto Press, 2006), 274. See also Anne Innis Dagg, *Smitten by Giraffe* (Montreal and Kingston: McGill-Queen's University Press, 2016), who does not discuss her involvement in her husband's career, despite accompanying him for his graduate work and on sabbaticals. Nor does she mention his involvement with their four children. Her mother, Mary Quayle Innis, was

a great support to her husband, Harold Innis, professor of economic history at U of T: Donica Belisle and Kiera Mitchell, "Mary Quayle Innis: Faculty Wives' Contributions and the Making of Academic Celebrity," *Canadian Historical Review* 99, no. 3 (Fall 2018): 456–86. She was also a mother of four and a prolific writer, among her many other extraordinary accomplishments.

16 Last Chapter

1 Barb Hooper and Wendy Wood, "Pragmatism and Structuralism in Occupational Therapy: The Long Conversation," *American Journal of Occupational Therapy* 56, no. 1 (2002): 40–50.
2 Judith Friedland, "Occupational Therapy and Rehabilitation: An Awkward Alliance," *American Journal of Occupational Therapy* 52, no. 5 (1998): 373–80.
3 G.L. Engel. "The Need for a New Medical Model: A Challenge for Biomedicine," *Science* 196 (1977): 129–36.
4 Ayelet Kuper et al., "Well-Rounded Professionals," *Medical Education* 51 (2017): 158–73.

Index

Abella, Justice Rosalie (Rosie), 144, 221n5
Aberman, Dean Arnold (Arnie), 148, 158, 166
accessibility and accommodations, 119, 149–51, 158
accreditation, 150, 163, 223n5
Ach, Narziss, 123
Ad Hoc Committee on the Status of Women (U of T), 144
Addenbrooke's Hospital, 111. *See also* practicums
agraphia, 134–5, 142
Alberta Health System, 192–3
allied health professionals, 146–8
alumni, 160–1, 167, 170, 193, 198
Antonis family, 14, 38–9, 110

ballet, lessons, 36–7, 198
bar and bat mitzvahs, 102–3
Baycrest Hospital, 192
Beck, Aaron T., 123
Beth Tzedec, 31, 52, 204, 212n8
Bill 94, Ontario (Health Care Accessibility Act, 1986), 133
Birgeneau, Robert, 170
boards, service on, 171, 178–9
Bowlby, John, 12, 210n5

Brantford, 13, 15–16, 211n4
Brantford Collegiate Institute, 15–16, 211n4. *See also* Pless, Mike
breast cancer: news of, 187–8; decision-making, 188–91; waiting, 189–90; diversion from dwelling on, 191
Brentwood Towers, 61
Brown, Dr Jason, 135–6, 140
Brown School Stroke Group, 100–2
Bryden, Dr Pier, 193
building business, 16–17

Callas, Maria, 72, 215n14
Cambridge, England, ix, 68–71, 73, 75–8, 85–7, 110–13
Canadian Association of Occupational Therapists (CAOT), 147, 150, 174–5
Cardwell, Thelma, 114, 160, 166, 173, 213n3
careers: JF's expectations, x, xi, 115, 128, 134; Barry's, 57; Marty's, 68; disappointments, 137–8; 143; challenging outcomes, 138, 173; female academics with children, 177
caregiving, 54, 91, 101, 131–2, 155, 164. *See also* illnesses; injuries

Cedarvale, 33–4, 42
Centre for Addiction and Mental Health (CAMH), 177, 192
charity work, 23, 40, 43
Chipman, Mary, 172
Clements, Margaret, 36
coat(s): JF's new coat, 7; samples arrive, 17; modelling, 21; lab coats, 63; coat falls, 80; political buttons on, 133; unable to take coat off, 187. *See also* Pless, Mike
committee work (examples): accommodations of persons with disabilities, 151; degree completion programs, 151; Leyerle, 151; admissions, 151, 177–8; accommodation, resource and advisory group, 158; clinical sector, 159; gender issues, 159; principals, deans, directors, and chairs (PDD&C), 159–60; anniversary, 75th, 169; post-professional degree, 169; faculty council (nursing) 170; Ethics Review Board (Public Health Ontario), 179; Research Ethics Policy and Advisory Committee, 177; Research Ethics Board (U of T), 178–9; anniversary, 100th, 197
Community Occupational Therapy Associates (COTA), 97–103, 113, 166, 171
condo move, 182
Conway, Jill Ker, 82–3
cottage, 18–19, 201–3
crafts, 64–5, 69, 74, 81, 122–3, 174–5, 180, 193, 201
creativity, 123, 218n17
Csikszentmihalyi, Mihaly, 122

Dagg, Anne Innis, 137, 220n3, 224n2, 227n5
Daniels, Stan and Alene, 73

Davids-Brumer, Naomi, 181
Dawes Road Cemetery, 204
Day Centre, Toronto Psychiatric Hospital, 74–5
Department of Occupational Therapy, 155, 157
Department of Rehabilitation Medicine, 125, 155
DesignAbility, 193
developing programs and structures: degree upgrade, 151; departmental status, 152–3, 156–7; Graduate Department of Rehabilitation Sciences (GDRS), 161; "2+2+," 162; problem-based learning (PBL), 162; community-based fieldwork, 162–3; MScOT, 163; advanced standing/post-professional degree, 169
Dirks, Dean John, 148
doctoral studies, 124, 128–9, 134–6, 139
dogs: Skipper (Dee), 139, 140; Tippy, 22, 33–4, 81
Dvinsk (Daugavpils), 13

Ehrlich, Dr Bob and Ruth, 68, 80, 90
emotional labour, 97, 207, 216n2 (chp. 8)
Erlichman, Madzia (Mattel), Aaron, Charles, and Stephen, 30
Errington, Jane, 91
ethics, research, 178–9
expectations/aspirations: JF, x, 35, 40, 114–15, 128; Jolofsky girls, 27; Dagg, 137

female faculty salaries, 120, 217n3
female faculty service load, 145–6, 152
female faculty teaching and supervision differences, 146
female faculty underrepresentation, 120, 157, 177, 224n1, 225n2

feminism, 35, 82–3, 87–9, 91, 112, 120, 177
Feuerstein Clinic, 108. *See also* practicums
fieldwork: networking with providers of, 150; increasing community-based, 162–3
Fiesole, Italy, 168
Forest Hill, 38, 42
Franklin, Ursula, 145
Friedan, Betty, 82
Friedland, Jenny, 81, 129–34
Friedland, Martin (Marty): first meetings, 39, 45; boss, 45–6; at Glencedar, 56; Dean, Faculty of Law, 91–4; support, 128; Order of Canada, 194
Friedland, Mina, 165
Friedland, Nancy, 87, 90, 91, 93
Friedland, Tom, 79–81, 87, 106, 108, 131–3, 164
Friefeld, Sharon, 167
friendships, ix, 5, 7–8, 12, 41, 62, 66–8, 71–3, 78, 81, 192, 198
Front de libération du Québec (FLQ), 90
Frye, Northrop, 120
Fulbourn Hospital, England, 68–71, 76

garden parties: Buckingham Palace, 73–4; Belsize, 92
Garden Route, South Africa, 164
gardens: Glencedar, 35; Hillsdale, 81; Belsize, 83–4; Glyndebourne, 184; Gravetye Manor, 184; cottage, 202–4
Gateway Hotel, Gravenhurst, Ontario, 39
gendered education, aspirations, and work, 35, 40, 51, 144
Glencedar Road, #174: location, 33–4; playing, 34–5; flowers, 35; worms, 42; sale of, 50

Glicksman, Guta (Gittel), Max, Harry, Lisa, and Lenny, 29–30, 211–12n5
Goldenberg, Karen, 171
Gottlieb, Benjamin, 127
Gould, Glenn, 125–6
Graduate Department of Rehabilitation Sciences (GDRS) (Rehabilitation Sciences Institute), 129, 161
grandchildren, Friedland, 175–6, 207
grandchildren, Jolofsky, 28
"grandchildren test" for driving, 155
grandparents (Bubie and Zadie) Jolofsky, 6, 8, 11, 23–5, 28–31, 33, 56, 177, 204–5. *See also* Jolofsky
Grange Avenue, 23, 31–3
Grenfell Mission, 180

Hart House, 62, 120, 148, 170, 216n1, 218n10
Havdalah, 24
Hayter, Charles, 209n2
Head, Brenda, 180
Health History Partnership, 193
Heap, Ruby, 147, 222n18
Hebert, Debbie, 176
"hemiplegic writing," 135
Hewitt, Foster, 8
Hillman, Betty and Joe, 8
Hillsdale, 78, 181–2
HIV/AIDS, 127; women with, 127–8; SSIPWA (Social Support Inventory for People with AIDS/HIV), 128
Hobbs, Dr A.T., 185
hockey, 8, 9
Home and School Association (Davisville), x, 87, 94–5
Homewood Health Centre, 15, 214n11
Hospital for Sick Children/ SickKids, 65

Huggins, Rosemary, 71
"huts," physical and occupational
    therapy, 65

Iacobucci, Frank, 166
illnesses: Tillie, 5–12; Nancy, 90–1;
    Marty, 183; me, 187–91
imposter syndrome, 125, 136,
    218n18
injuries: Tom, 80–1; Jenny, 130–4;
    Mike, 153–4; JF, 186–7
Innis, Mary Quayle, 227n5
International Neuropsychology
    Society Conference, 136
Israel, 9, 24, 43, 72–3, 106–10, 205–6

Jarvis, Edward, 123
Jewish family life, 7–9, 14, 20, 23–4,
    32, 34, 56, 61–2, 103–4, 165–6, 175,
    205–6
Jolley, Rayna, 28
Jolofsky boys: Harry (Jolley), 25–7,
    211n1; Joe (Jolley), 27
Jolofsky girls: Tillie (Pless), 5–12,
    27, 33, 36, 38–9, 167, 191; Sarah
    (Garfield), 11, 27, 39; Eva (Geller),
    27; Ida (Benstein), 27–8; Emma
    (Landsberg), 27–8, 52
Jolofsky, Bubie (grandmother), 8–9,
    23–5, 32, 210n3
Jolofsky, Zaidie (grandfather), 9,
    23–4, 29–30, 31–3
Jousse, Dr Albin, 51, 82, 213n1
Judith Friedland Fund, 167

Kensington Market, 31–2
Kershner, John, 114, 219n21
Kidner, Thomas Bessell, 180–1
Kirsh, Bonnie, 151, 176
Kitchener, Ontario, 49–50, 52, 80
Kronick, Joseph (Joe), 45

Laskin, Justice Bora, 88
Laskin, Peggy, 88–9
Latvia, 13
Leischner, Dr Anton, 140
LeVesconte, Helen, 146–7, 180
Lewis, Joan, 158
Lithuania, 13, 110, 177
London, England, 14–15, 68, 71, 73,
    111, 164
London, Ontario, 50, 185, 214n10
Lowy, Dean Fred, 125, 167
Luther, Jessie, 180
Lyndhurst Centre/Lodge, 154, 171

male physicians, role of, 121, 146,
    222n18
Maple Leaf Gardens, 55
Markson, Jerome, 78, 88, 182
Mason, Mary Ann, 177
Maudsley Hospital, 68
Maxwell, James and Mary, 121
McCaul Street Synagogue, 6,
    23–4, 31
McColl, MaryAnn, 126, 142
McGill-Queen's University Press
    (MQUP), 181
McMurrich, Kathleen, 63
"meddling," 196–7. See also
    occupational therapy
Mehitza, 24
Micha, 108. See also practicums
Milner, Mickey, 138
Moment in Time, 197
Mount Sinai Hospital, 66
Muriel Driver Lecture, 174–5
Murphy, Marge, 74

Naylor, David, 148, 170, 173, 177
negotiating salaries, 120, 144, 157, 178
Neilson Chocolate Factory, 33
Netanya, Israel, 106–7, 109–10

occupational therapy: within rehabilitation, 147–8, 152, 173, 196–7. *See also* "meddling"

occupational therapy in Canada: early history, 181, 192. See also *Restoring the Spirit*

occupational therapy in the schools, 96, 113–14

Ontario Council of University Programs in Rehabilitation Science (OCUPRS) grant, 162. *See also* fieldwork

Ontario Institute for Studies in Education (OISE), 97, 108, 129, 138

Ontario Society of Occupational Therapists (OSOT), 191–2

opera, 28, 55, 72, 184, 207, 215n14

Orthodox ritual, 8, 23–5, 210n4

Ottawa, 88–91, 215n4

Passover, 9–11, 205

patriarchy, 121, 147

pay equity, xi, 144–5

Pay Equity Act, 156

Person-Environment-Occupation Model, 122

Peter, Elizabeth, 179

Peters, Vera, 5, 79, 209n1, 209n2

physical and occupational therapy (P&OT), 50–1, 62–8, 82, 96–7

piano, 36

Pless, Barry, 8, 14, 20, 28, 32–3, 40, 44, 54–7, 130, 132, 155

Pless, grandfather, 14, 15

Pless, Mike (Michael Abraham): salesman, 16–17; building business, 16–17; coat samples, 17; swimmer, 18; friends, 18–19; the van, 21; car accident, 54, 153–4; death, 165

Pless, Naomi (Bubie), 13–15, 32, 110

Pless, Tillie: life, 5–12; friends, ix, 7–8, 34; in hospital, 7; death, 7–8; shiva, 8–9; belongings, 10; Florida, 11–12; camp visit, 39

Polatajko, Helene, 162, 169

Pollock, Jack, 75

practicums for Master's degree, 108, 111

Princess Margaret Hospital, 189

Pringle, Dean Dorothy/Dot, 171

Public Health Ontario, 179

racial slurs and discrimination: dentistry, 25; at tea, 56; Toronto General Hospital, 66–7; Faculty of Medicine, University of Toronto, 67, 214n7, 214n8; P&OT class of '60 meeting, 67; OT professors' meeting, 150; in Brantford, 211n3

Rais, Hadassah, 180

Rappolt, Susan, 192

Reitapple, Percy, 7, 16

Renwick, Rebecca, 127

research: Broca's Aphasia, 114, 219n21; visit from Dean Lowy, 125; social support and stroke, 125–8; HIV/AIDS and women, 127; social support and HIV/AIDS, 127–8; agraphia, 134–6; function after motor-vehicle accidents, 151–2; seniors driving, 155, 171–2; community-based fieldwork, 162–3; occupational therapy at Toronto Psychiatric Hospital, 173; *Restoring the Spirit*, 173, 181, 185, 187, 191–3; Muriel Driver Lecture, 174–5; gender issues, 177–8; research ethics, 178–9; Helen LeVesconte, 180; Jessie Luther, 180; Thomas Kidner, 180–1

resignation, 138
Restoring the Spirit: first thoughts, 181, 185; first hiatus, 187; second hiatus, 188–9; book launch, 192
restructuring occupational therapy program, 151, 162–3
Robarts, John, 126
Robinson, Isobel, 166, 173, 180
Rockcliffe, Ottawa, 89–90
Roger Ascham School for Physically Disabled Children, 111. *See also* practicums
Rokiskis, Lithuania, 13–14
roles, family: wife and mother, x, xi; mothering, 52, 124, 128; stay-at-home mom, 81–2, 87; faculty wife, 87–9; living husband's life, 89, 194, 215n1, 226n9, 227–8n5; dean's wife, 92–4, 226n9
roles, work: choosing roles, 82, 94, 128, 151; maintaining roles, 124; service roles, 169
Royal Victoria Hospital, Montreal, 130–1
royalty, 73–4, 111–12
Rudman (Laliberte), Debbie, 172
Rusholme Drive, 33

sabbaticals, x, 84; 1960–1, 68–71; 1963, 76–8; 1968–9, 84–7; 1979–80, 103–13; 1991, 143; 2000, 163
salaries for women: billing for time, 100; negotiating salaries, 120; Franklin, Ursula, et al., settlement, 145; inequities, 145, 160; wage gaps, 145; married women, 158. *See also* Sunshine List
Sanmuganathan, Sam and Nirmala, 85–6
Schaffer, Robin, 138, 140
Sciortino, Paula, 172
second-class status, x, 65, 119, 121, 146, 148

Seder, Passover, 9, 111, 205
Selye, Hans, 123
Shema, 34
Shorter, Edward (Ned), 173
Siegel, Linda, 136
Silva, Jennifer, 181
Silver, Harvey, 36
Silver Slipper, 20
Silverman, Hinda (Helen), Carl, and Mari, 28–9
skating, 84, 89, 185, 186, 202
smoking, 34, 62, 77, 79
social support: following stroke, 125–7; as clinical intervention, 74–5, 99–101; after diagnosis of HIV/AIDS, 127; as research intervention, 127; assessments of, 128 (SSISS, SSIPWA, SSIPAD)
sorority, 42–3
Spadina Avenue, 17, 29, 30, 52
speaking up, 159, 224n4
Sri Lanka (Ceylon), 85–6
St Elizabeth's Centre, 111. *See also* practicums
Stanley Cup playoffs, 9
Steen, Amy, 172
stepmothers: Sally, 48–50, 52–3, 78; May, 54, 111, 153–5, 163
Stern, Bill, 44
Stier, Jill, 176
stroke: survivors, 100–1; psychosocial factors, 101, 125–6; Broca's Aphasia, 114; interest in, 125–6; stressful life events, 126; depression, 126; social support, 126–7; coping methods, 127; agraphia, 134
stroke research, 114, 125–6, 134–6, 139, 140, 142
student life (JF's): JR Wilcox, 35–6; Vaughan Road Collegiate Institute, 40; University of Toronto Physical and Occupational

Therapy, 50, 62–8; BA, 50–1, 82, 88,
97; graduate work (OISE) MEd,
97; MA, 97, 108, 111, 114; PhD,
128–9, 134–6, 139–40
student mental health, 149–50
summer camps: B'nai Brith, 38;
Kawagama, 40; Boulderwood,
43–4, 51, 212n7; Wahanowin, 44–5;
White Pine, 45–6; Woodeden, 50–1
Sunnybrook Hospital, 132, 140,
153–4, 192
Sunshine List, 221
Sures, Carol, 71

teaching: grade 2, 36; swimming,
44–6; Seneca College, 114; U of T/
OT, 115, 120–2, 123–5
tenure and promotion, 119, 137–8;
tenure and associate professor,
148–9; full professor, 172–3
Toronto General Hospital,
discrimination, 66–7, 214n7
Toronto General Hospital, Private
Patients Pavilion, 5
Toronto Medical History Club,
193–4
Toronto Psychiatric Hospital, 63,
65–6, 74–5, 173
Toronto Speech and Stroke Centre,
135
Townsend, Elizabeth, 173, 181

travels, 46, 57, 71–3, 78, 85–6, 89,
104–6, 108, 110, 113, 144, 164, 168,
176–7, 183–4, 199, 200, 201
Trentham, Barry, 176
Trudeau, Pierre and Margaret, 89,
215n4

University Settlement House, 43
upgrading: faculty to doctoral level,
149; bachelor's to master's degree
for graduates, 181

Varsity, The (newspaper), 64, 216n1
Vaughan Road Collegiate Institute,
40–1
Verrier, Molly, 152, 159, 161
Volkoff, Boris, 36
volunteering, x, 50–1, 81, 94–6, 108, 171

Weinstein, Phil and Di, 73
Whiteside, Catharine (Cathy), 148, 192
wife, ix, x, 57, 87, 92–4, 109, 113, 194,
208, 158, 215n1
Wijewardane, Sena, Janaki, and
Nishi, 85–6
Wilcox, John R., 35, 36
William Morris Society of Canada, 193
women and competition, 142, 224n1
wrist fractures, 186–7

Zemon-Davis, Natalie, x, 83

Milton Keynes UK
Ingram Content Group UK Ltd.
UKHW012351190424
441406UK00007B/588